24.00

D0796589

RELIGIOUS ADVOCACY
AND AMERICAN HISTORY

Religious Advocacy and American History

Edited by

Bruce Kuklick and D. G. Hart

WILLIAM B. EERDMANS PUBLISHING COMPANY
GRAND RAPIDS, MICHIGAN / CAMBRIDGE, U.K.

02 01 00 99 98 97   7 6 5 4 3 2 1

Library of Congress Cataloging-in-Publication Data

Religious advocacy and the writing of American history /
  edited by Bruce Kuklick and D. G. Hart.
      p.   cm.
  Based on a conference held at Wheaton College in the spring of 1994.
  Includes bibliographical references.
  ISBN 0-8028-4260-7 (pbk.)
    1. United States — Historiography — Congresses. 2. United States —
  Church History — Historiography — Congresses. 3. United States —
  History — Textbooks — Congresses. 4. Textbook bias — United States —
  Congresses. I. Kuklick, Bruce, 1941- . II. Hart, D. G. (Darryl G.)
  E175.R45 1997
  973'.072 — dc21   96-40840
                                                  CIP

Contents

Foreword vii
    HARRY S. STOUT

Introduction x
    BRUCE KUKLICK AND D. G. HART

Section One: Christian Faith and Historical Knowledge

Christian Advocacy and the Rules of the Academic Game 3
    GEORGE M. MARSDEN

Traditional Christianity and the Possibility
of Historical Knowledge 28
    MARK A. NOLL

On Critical History 54
    BRUCE KUKLICK

Advocacy and Academe 65
    MURRAY G. MURPHEY

CONTENTS

Section Two: Advocacy and the Politics of the Academy

*Marxism, Christianity, and Bias in the Study
of Southern Slave Society*   83
  EUGENE D. GENOVESE

Advocacy and the Writing of American Women's History   96
  ELIZABETH FOX-GENOVESE

*In Search of the Fourth "R": The Treatment of Religion
in American History Textbooks and Survey Courses*   112
  PAUL BOYER

What's So Special about the University, Anyway?   137
  D. G. HART

Section Three: Advocacy in the Writing of Religious History

*Understanding the Past, Using the Past: Reflections on Two
Approaches to History*   159
  GRANT WACKER

*A Transcendentalist's Aristotle: Nonevangelical Reflections on
Conviction and the Writing of History*   179
  CATHERINE L. ALBANESE

Seldon's Choice: Variations on a Theme by Asimov   190
  PAUL A. CARTER

One Historian's Sundays   209
  LESLIE WOODCOCK TENTLER

Afterword   221
  LEO P. RIBUFFO

Foreword

IT IS NO secret that religion has largely been ignored in our nation's textbooks and history courses. Only now are we beginning to appreciate the consequences of this neglect. While religion continues to be a central defining point of American culture, the nation's opinion leaders in politics and press remain appallingly ignorant about it. This ignorance is not merely a question of information shortage. If the problem were simply information, we could easily build it into schools and curriculum to "correct" the gaps. Unfortunately, the problem lies on the deepest levels of presuppositions. "Secularization" — a conviction that the profane increasingly dominates modern culture and does so rightly — continues to guide much American public life, not only among the nation's opinion leaders but even among a general public whose personal spiritual commitment remains high, especially by comparison with other Western societies. This assumption says, in effect, "Religion is on the way out, so don't waste time on it. Concentrate on the environment, or energy, or international affairs and political history, but not religion."

Many academics suspect religion for both personal and intellectual reasons, and some openly dislike it. Personally, religion is often identified with repressive upbringings and closed-minded attitudes that are hostile to the life of the mind. Professionally, religion was long equated with such features of American life as laissez-faire capitalism, imperialism, racism, sexism, and violence, which religion not only often rationalized but sometimes created. In this view, religion is something that might best disappear from American life because it both caused and reinforced these forces. Thus, religion is relegated to the periphery or simply ignored in a process that would itself speed "secularization."

Events of the past two decades suggest that this view is both false and dangerous. Practically, we realize as never before that religion represents a major animating force in world affairs. The once-touted "End of Religion" is dead itself. We face religious agendas on all sides, domestic as well as international. Why is this? How and why do those powerful religious impulses emerge? These questions require historical perspective. In fact, they necessarily engage a whole other set of questions. What historical patterns typified religion's interaction with American society and history? Were these patterns consistent from decade to decade and century to century or did they change substantially from the colonial era to the nineteenth century and then to the twentieth? How much difference do these patterns themselves make in understanding either the past or the present?

In the past decade, many of these questions have begun to be addressed by a new generation of American religious historians trained in history and religion departments at research universities around the country. But other problems still remain. If religion per se has been ignored until recently, even more have questions of personal religious commitment and the writing of American history. To a large extent this neglect also reflects secularization theory and the presumed "privatization" of religion in "modern" societies generally. Just as one would not discuss one's sex life or marriage as "context" for one's history writing, neither did one discuss one's religious commitment. Now, under the force of debates surrounding multiculturalism, the canon, and semiotics, both of these prohibitions are being lifted. Scholars can, and do, talk about sexual preference and their approaches to the past. And, as this volume makes clear, scholars can, and do, talk about personal religious belief and historical scholarship.

Most of the contributions to this volume grew from a conference held at Wheaton College in the spring of 1994. Unlike many conferences in which the participants are "preaching to the converted," the conference — and this ensuing volume of essays — is notable for the strong differences of opinion that it registers. There is no single point of view represented in these essays. Nevertheless there is a common perception, namely, that the relationship of religious commitment to scholarship is a subject worthy of serious discussion in the academy. No longer can it be left on the sidelines of polite academic discourse. It has emerged front and center as an epistemological and practical issue of pressing concern.

The essays contained in this volume can be viewed as a series of debates around three central questions. First is the issue of the place of religion in American higher education. Taking George Marsden's widely read and controversial book *The Soul of the American University* as its point of departure, these essays (including one by Professor Marsden) debate the modern university's exclusion of religious perspectives from the academy. A second grouping of essays frame debates over questions surrounding the degree to which religion is denied admission to the liberal culture of the modern academy. This debate, too, has a recent focus in Stephen L. Carter's much discussed *The Culture of Disbelief*. Finally, a section on "Advocacy and the Writing of Religious History" addresses the more personal question of religious belief and the teaching of religious history.

One scholarly reader, even one as insightful as this, will not settle the issue of religious advocacy in the modern academy. But hopefully it will elevate it to the status it deserves as an object worthy of debate and central to an understanding of the main themes of American history.

HARRY S. STOUT
Yale University

Introduction

IT HAS been over thirty years since the appearance of Henry May's 1964 *American Historical Review* article, "The Recovery of American Religious History." In that essay May observed the achievements of the previous three decades of scholarship, years in which Puritanism, Edwardsian Calvinism, revivalism, liberalism, modernism, and the Social Gospel had been "brought down out of the attic and put back in the historical front parlor." Even historians who had no intrinsic interest in religion, May added, were willing to acknowledge that religion constituted the "mode" and "language" in which most Americans before the twentieth century had thought about human nature and destiny.[1]

With the hindsight of three decades, what May considered a recovery now appears no more than a trickle of scholarship on American religious history. And while religious history appears to be a healthy venture capable of sustaining continued growth, it is usually relegated to the periphery in the professional study of history. Some of the evidence for this generalization is only anecdotal. For instance, while some history departments have begun to include courses in religious history, the experience of one graduate student at Indiana University is far more typical. She writes that the department admitted her to do church history in the late medieval and early modern periods. But because no one in the department now offers courses in scholasticism or Reforma-

---

1. "The Recovery of American Religious History," reprinted in Henry F. May, *Ideas, Faiths and Feelings: Essays on American Intellectual and Religious History, 1952-1982* (New York: Oxford University Press, 1983), 67-86, quotations from 67.

tion history, the chair asked her to transfer to the religious studies department or philosophy department where scholars study such things. To conclude, as this woman does, that Indiana's history department manifests "blatant discrimination" against Christian and traditional religions may show insufficient nuance. But her experience does raise the question of why the history department offers courses on medieval sexuality and medieval women's spirituality but won't hire faculty to teach courses on Aquinas and Calvin.[2]

Confirmation of a certain bias against religion within the historical profession also comes from sources easier to document. For instance, Carl N. Degler opined during his 1980 presidential address before the Organization of American Historians that some subjects, particularly the history of religion, "have fallen into disfavor among historians or been forgotten entirely."[3] While Degler later admitted that he had been looking primarily at studies of the Social Gospel and consequently had missed much of the literature in religious history, his comments were fairly representative of the perceptions of mainstream American historians. Anthologies devoted to the general themes and periods of the history of the United States, such as *The Promise of American History*[4] and *The New American History*,[5] virtually ignore religion as a field of American history. Studies of academic history also have given little consideration to the growth of American religious history.[6] These omissions make plausible the conclusion that Degler's reflections, even though written only halfway into the most productive period of religious history, were not unusual.

Degler's comments have recently been confirmed by historians who study American religion but who believe the profession is largely indifferent to it. Garry Wills insists that historians and political commentators neglect religion, so much so that in reading most texts one

2. Letter of Emily Nedell, *First Things*, April 1994, 3-4.
3. Carl N. Degler, "Remaking American History," *Journal of American History* 67 (1980): 13.
4. Ed. Stanley I. Kutler and Stanley N. Katz (Baltimore: Johns Hopkins University Press, 1982).
5. Ed. Eric Foner (Philadelphia: Temple University Press, 1990).
6. See, for instance, the otherwise fine books, John Higham, *History: Professional Scholarship in America* (1965; reprint, Baltimore: Johns Hopkins University Press, 1980); and Peter Novick, *That Noble Dream: The "Objectivity Question" and the American Historical Profession* (Cambridge: Cambridge University Press, 1988).

"could hardly guess . . . that nothing has been more stable in our history, nothing less budgeable, than religious belief and practice."[7] Leslie Woodcock Tentler concurs with Wills. She has written that the study of American Catholicism, despite a twenty-year period of "unprecedented fruitfulness," has had only a limited effect on the larger historical enterprise, even on historians whose principal interest is the industrial working class.[8] Meanwhile, Leo Ribuffo, no fan of "born again" Christianity but also no slouch in the field of twentieth-century history, doubts whether "the history of American religion will receive a welcome into the historiographical mainstream."[9] In the same way that historians of the United States have slighted political conservatism, so, too, Ribuffo notes that the history of American religion has generated a good deal of valuable literature only to remain marginal within the historical profession.[10]

Indeed, history departments at the leading universities are reluctant to offer courses or hire faculty dedicated to the study of religious history to the same degree that they provide instruction in intellectual, political, economic, or cultural history. Despite the desire on the part of many departmental chairs and faculty to be more inclusive and representative in their research and instruction, the results of these desires have rarely extended to religious history, nor have they caught up with public opinion surveys which continue to document the religiosity of the American people. Thus, even though the history of American religion has thrived within the last generation and despite the increased attention religion receives in debates about public policy, it is still segregated for the most part as a separate field within religious studies. Courses in American religious history are usually offered in religion departments, and university presses usually list books on the

7. *Under God: Religion and American Politics* (New York: Simon & Schuster 1990), 6-7.

8. "On the Margins: The State of American Catholic History," *American Quarterly* 45 (1993): 104-27, quotation from 104.

9. "God and Contemporary Politics," *Journal of American History* 79 (1993): 1532.

10. Leo P. Ribuffo, "Why Is There So Much Conservatism in the United States and Why Do So Few Historians Know Anything about It?" *American Historical Review* 99 (1994): 438-49. For a fairly recent indication of the growth of the history of American religion, see Martin E. Marty, "American Religious History in the Eighties: A Decade of Achievement," *Church History* 62 (1993): 335-77.

subject in a separate section on religion. To use Henry May's image, the historical study of religion may be impressive compared to that of a previous generation, but it has yet to find a seat in the front parlor of the historical profession.

Some discount the notion of bias against religious belief among historians. Jon Butler, for instance, thinks such arguments are basically foolish. He contends that historians are increasingly turning to religion to account for a broad range of phenomena. Evangelicalism especially has become the fashionable way for explaining everything from the American family to post–New Deal electoral conservatism. The "evangelical thesis," according to Butler, has been embraced on such a wide scale that "no other interpretive matrix compares with it" and in the process the once formidable Lockean-liberal perspective of an older generation of historians has been reduced to an "interpretive ashheap."[11] Though engaging in hyperbole, Butler does appear to be supported by the numerous studies which university presses and academic journals continue to produce. Religion — specifically, evangelical Christianity — has been fairly well integrated in accounts of the colonial, revolutionary, and antebellum periods. Yet in more recent periods of American history, religion has not been included in a larger interpretive framework.

Whether or not religion has been sufficiently integrated into the writing and teaching of American history, religion is a subject that provokes strong responses both from its supporters and from its despisers, thus raising the question of bias and advocacy. Indeed, an important factor in accounting for historians' reluctance to study religion comes from Henry May's observation about the recovery of religious history. He noted that most of what was considered mainstream religious history earlier in this century was being done in seminaries and divinity schools, a perception that still rings true to this day, though the rise and growth of religion departments must also be taken into account. Despite the increasing sophistication of religious history and despite the growing attention that religion is receiving from scholars in history departments, religion continues to carry the stigma of proselytism,

11. "Born-Again America? A Critique of the New 'Evangelical Thesis' in Recent American Historiography," paper delivered at the annual meeting of the American Historical Association, December 1992, 6.

sectarianism, and absurdity, traits which the academy has sedulously tried to avoid.[12]

Indeed, if the mainstream academy has a predisposition against religion, it may stem from the prejudice which fueled the field of religious studies. Religion departments did not become conspicuous in American universities until the 1940s and 1950s, when the cultural crisis surrounding America's opposition to fascism and communism prompted administrators and faculty to see the value of religion in higher education. Many of the prominent departments of religious studies were founded during these decades as part of a larger revival of interest in values, the humanities, and general education. Despite the civic or national purposes which lay behind the study of religion, religious studies was an overwhelmingly mainline Protestant endeavor. The faculty at most religion departments had been trained at Protestant divinity schools or seminaries, the curriculum resembled the standard division of courses in Protestant theological education, and the rationale for studying religion overwhelmingly conformed to the establishment aims of the denominations that comprised the National Council of Churches.[13]

Yet by the 1960s, the very time when Henry May noticed the recovery of American religious history, the foundations upon which the academic study of religion had been built came in for serious renegotiation. Just as Bible reading and prayer in public schools became objectionable, so faculty and administrators at many colleges and universities began to grow aware of the Protestant outlook in departments of religious studies. Professors of religion, accordingly, shifted from civic and spiritual reasons for studying religion to ones designed to be more academically responsible. In fact, the issue of indoctrination or advocating a particular religious tradition now became the *bête noire* of the religious studies establishment. It was one thing for professors to teach *about* a

12. For changes within the field which challenge this perception, see David W. Lotz, "A Changing Historiography: From Church History to Religious History," in *Altered Landscapes: Christianity in America, 1935-1985,* ed. David W. Lotz (Grand Rapids: Eerdmans, 1989), chap. 18.

13. On the rise of religious studies, see D. G. Hart, "American Learning and the Problem of Religious Studies," in *The Secularization of the Academy,* ed. George M. Marsden and Bradley J. Longfield (New York: Oxford University Press, 1992), 195-233.

specific religious belief or practice; it was another altogether to teach a particular doctrine or ritual. Representative of the transformation of the study of religion was the change of name for the professional academic organization of religion professors. In 1964 the National Association of Biblical Instructors was reconstituted as the American Academy of Religion, a shift that reflected an effort to include non-Christian religions in departments of religious studies, as well as an attempt to make the field more intellectually rigorous.[14] Nevertheless, despite changes in the discipline, the suspicion that religious motives lurked behind the academic study of religion has persisted. Thus, the bias against religion in the academy is understandable to the extent that the arguments for religion departments sprang more often from religious than academic criteria.

Recent changes within the historical profession as well as the university more generally have made it possible to address candidly questions of bias and advocacy. The rise of social history in the 1960s and 1970s challenged the seemingly elitist bias of a field long dominated by political and intellectual history, and encouraged the profession to be more aware of presuppositions that color not only a scholar's interpretation but also the very selection of a subject for study. At the same time intellectual historians took a "linguistic turn" that called into question many of the Enlightenment assumptions governing the history of ideas. Peter Novick's provocative book *That Noble Dream* summarized well many of these and other developments that have forced historians to recognize the importance of perspective and bias in shaping research, writing, and teaching.[15]

Contributing to the reexaminiation of perspective and partiality in the academy are current debates in higher education about multiculturalism, the canon, and hermeneutics. Thanks to the growing recognition that America consists of numerous cultures and that standard university education has been highly selective — some prefer to call it hegemonic — many scholars are calling for more and better treatment of marginal, dispossessed, and minority groups throughout the curriculum, written and taught from a perspective other than that of powerful white

14. Ibid.

15. For a good discussion of Novick, see James T. Kloppenberg, "Objectivity and Historicism: A Century of American Historical Writing," *American Historical Review* 94 (1989): 1011-30.

men. For instance, the American Council of Learned Societies, along with fifteen other professional academic associations primarily from the humanities, sponsored a conference to address these changes and tensions within higher education. "The Role of Advocacy in the Classroom" was designed to address questions of bias and objectivity in the academy, from classroom instruction to methodological considerations in various disciplines. This conference is just one of many indications that long-held assumptions within the university and various academic disciplines about the goal of academic study as well as the methods scholars employ are undergoing close scrutiny, if not sharp revision.

The aim of this book, *Religious Advocacy and American History*, is to explore the general question of bias and objectivity in the academy through the lens of the role of religious beliefs in the study of American history. With a few exceptions, the essays collected here stem from a consultation sponsored by the Institute for the Study of American Evangelicals at Wheaton College in the Spring of 1994. The individual scholars who prepared papers for this meeting were asked to respond to two questions: (1) How do personal convictions (religious, political, and so on) influence your historical work? (2) More generally, what place should personal convictions have in academic work and higher learning? Responses to these questions took a variety of forms and revealed that the subject of religion in the writing of academic history has several dimensions.

At the most general level the question of religious advocacy involves important theoretical considerations — particularly the widespread contention that modern understandings of historical processes are in principle unfriendly to the historical claims of traditional Christianity. Van Harvey put these matters sharply in his landmark book *The Historian and the Believer*, where he pinpointed the larger implications of doing history in a modern sense for traditionally Christian subjects. "It is not just that the 'results' produced by New Testament criticism are often inconsistent with important traditional Christian beliefs," Harvey argues; rather, it is "that critical historians must necessarily regard it as an intolerable surrender of their autonomous critical judgment to permit religious faith to tip the balance in ascertaining what is to count as historical fact."[16] On the other hand, there is the counterargument

16. This summary of the book, *The Historian and the Believer: The Morality of*

which Mark Noll develops in the pages that follow that Augustinian Christianity provides *"the best* foundation for restoring confidence in the human ability to know the past reliably," and should also, "even by the reasoning of relativistic theories of knowledge," be regarded "as true."[17]

In the first section of the book, "Christian Faith and Historical Knowledge," we devote four essays to the epistemological considerations involved in the place of religion in the academy. George Marsden, whose recently published *The Soul of the American University*[18] has touched off lively discussions about the place of religion in American higher education, makes a case for including religious perspectives in the academy largely by arguing for the inadequacy of claims for the value-neutral character of science. For Marsden the contemporary academy has inconsistently tolerated various ideological commitments that lack scientific justification. He believes it possible for Christian academics to play by the rules of the academy but also urges that religious perspectives make an important difference and contribution in professional scholarship. Rather than pointing out the deficiency of scientific knowledge, Mark Noll contends that Christian faith is not only valuable but necessary for doing history because the Christian religion provides the only adequate foundation for knowing the past. From the other side come essays by Bruce Kuklick and Murray Murphey, who in effect defend the modern university's exclusion of religious belief or perspective. They claim that the academy abandoned Christianity not merely for social or cultural reasons but because scholars were not convinced by the truth claims of the Bible and Christian dogma. Furthermore, for Kuklick and Murphey the falsity of religion is a valid reason — despite the claims of postmodernists or the historicist attacks upon science by believers — for keeping religious belief and perspective out of the academy.

Historical Knowledge and Christian Belief (New York: Macmillan, 1966), comes from Harvey himself in "The Intellectual Marginality of American Theology," in *Religion and Twentieth-Century Intellectual Life*, ed. Michael J. Lacey (Cambridge: Cambridge University Press, 1989), 187.

17. Noll, "Traditional Christianity and the Possibility of Historical Knowledge," *Christian Scholar's Review* 19 (1990): 394.

18. *The Soul of the American University: From Protestant Establishment to Established Disbelief* (New York: Oxford University Press, 1994).

Related to the epistemological questions surrounding religion and science is the issue of the secularist bias of the academy, raised implicitly by Stephen L. Carter in *The Culture of Disbelief* and explicitly by Marsden in his recent book.[19] Does the dominant liberal culture of the academy, as Carter argues, impose a common rhetoric that refuses to accept the notion that rational, public-spirited people can take religion seriously? Or as Marsden has argued, is there a bias in the hiring and admission procedures of universities against scholars and students with traces of religious conviction on their applications? The second section, "Advocacy and the Politics of the Academy," explores the ideological bias of the university and related concerns. The first two essays by Eugene Genovese and Elizabeth Fox-Genovese take up the contested terrains of Marxist and feminist history respectively. Both examine the assumptions inherent in these interpretive frameworks that make scholars who are part of these historiographical traditions vulnerable to the charge of practicing unscientific history. And both Fox-Genevose and Genovese uncover the presuppositions about religion among feminist and Marxist historians, presuppositions which may help to explain the more general hostility toward belief in the academy. The next essay by Paul Boyer picks up the question of the exclusion of religion from a different angle, namely the treatment of belief and religious motivations in survey courses and textbooks on United States history. While the author concurs with Fox-Genovese and Genovese that religion too often receives scant attention or is readily reduced to politics, Boyer also considers the more understandable reasons (e.g., public pressures, the nature of textbook writing) which cause historians to miss religion. The last essay in this section by D. G. Hart argues that the structures and nature of academic life should make believers wary of finding a home in the university. Rather than faulting the university for espousing certain biases and, in turn, calling upon faculty and administrators to be more open to religious perspectives and believing scholarship, Hart questions whether the very structures that sustain the university and the scholarship it produces are worthwhile and wholesome for Christian communities of faith.

19. Stephen L. Carter, *The Culture of Disbelief: How American Law and Politics Trivialize Religious Devotion* (New York: Basic Books, 1993).

The last section of the book, "Advocacy and the Writing of Religious History," contains four essays that concern the place of values and perspective on teaching and scholarship in the field of religious history. These papers raise some of the most personal dimensions of the book. The first two chapters, those by Grant Wacker and Catherine L. Albanese, though coming from somewhat different directions, address the place of a historian's convictions in research, writing, and teaching. Wacker sets out well the tension between the empathy and critical distance historians are supposed to have in their work, while Albanese unpacks the biases contained in the very notion of advocacy and offers alternative models for writing history. The third essay by Paul A. Carter moves from the more abstract and theoretical discussions of Wacker and Albanese to a personal narrative of one historian's experience in writing religious history for a seemingly unreligious audience. Along the way Carter reflects upon the place of his convictions in his scholarship and teaching and the ambivalence within the historical profession regarding the subject of religion. Leslie Woodcock Tentler, in the final chapter of the book, extends the personal reflections of Carter to discuss her own experience as a believing historian, how her beliefs have influenced her research and writing, and how her work has been received within the profession. In the end, Tentler argues not only that religious convictions may enhance the writing of history, but also that the secular bias of the academy is hindering a better understanding of American history and society.

Since this book is about advocacy, a word may need to be said about the bias of this project, specifically whether the preponderance of evangelical historians included in the pages that follow constitutes a hidden agenda. Some might suspect that the purpose of this book, since it originated from a conference sponsored by the Institute for the Study of American Evangelicals, is to provide a forum for special pleading by evangelical historians who feel left out of the historiographical mainstream. In other words, is this book really a sneaky way of moving evangelical Christianity back into the American academy through the back door of religious history? Whatever the appearances of this project and whatever self-deceit lurks in the souls of the project's designers, the simple purpose of this book is to bring together as many interesting and interested scholars as space will allow for a candid discussion of bias and objectivity in the academy and where religion fits in those considerations.

It must also be admitted at the outset that these papers in no way exhaust the topic of religious advocacy and the writing of history. Nor do we think this book is the final word on the subject of bias and objectivity in the American academy more generally. In fact, the original design for the conference and book was to include not just students of religion but also historians of race, class, and gender. But the constraints of space and funding have forced a narrower focus. Nevertheless, our purpose is not to give the upper hand to religion but rather to treat it as one among the many interests and values that factor in the production of scholarship. And our hope is that the discussion of these issues in the following pages will spur ongoing discussions about methodological and epistemological issues within the academy and put religious beliefs closer to the center of those discussions.

BRUCE KUKLICK AND D. G. HART

Christian Faith and Historical Knowledge

Christian Advocacy and the Rules of the Academic Game[1]

GEORGE M. MARSDEN

MODERN American academia was constructed in the late nineteenth century with great reverence for the scientific method. While enthusiasm for empirical science was nothing new for academics whose grandfathers had celebrated Baconianism, the new universities defined science in a new and more limited way. Only that which dealt with strictly natural causes would count. Theology, once queen of the sciences, was demoted to be their pawn. The broader category of religion could still be revered as part of the ongoing human quest for higher truths and moral ideals which might be explored by speculative philosophy, literature, or the arts as a complement to scientific knowledge. Increasingly, however, what gave most disciplines prestige was their emphasis on empirical inquiry into purely natural causes.

The gradual redefinition of the role of religion in the mainstream academy had to do with a variety of factors, practical and political as well as intellectual. Advocates of the new exclusively naturalistic definitions of science could point to their immense successes in the natural sciences and to the increased levels of professionalism and rigor they had fostered in other fields. At the same time many academic reformers

---

1. Substantial portions of this chapter appear in modified form in George .M. Marsden, *The Outrageous Idea of Christian Scholarship* (New York: Oxford University Press, 1996). I am grateful to the editors of this volume for permission to adapt the essay to that work.

3

were understandably eager to free academia from its long-standing dependence on the churches and their clergy. Furthermore, appeals to theological claims — such as that certain historical developments were manifestations of God's special providence — were ruled out of bounds as unscientific, as inhibiting free inquiry, and as divisive. If twentieth-century American higher education were to serve the public fairly, it could not continue to privilege Protestant Christian teachings which might be offensive to agnostics, nominal Protestants, Catholics, and (eventually) Jews.

By the mid-twentieth century the basic rules of the academic game were fairly well fixed. Religion could be welcomed as an extracurricular activity and perhaps even promoted in new religion departments, so long as the religion was an ecumenical, ethical, and scientifically respectable search for higher values. The other disciplines of mainstream academia would be defined as strictly secular. In those, reference to religious concerns or perspectives, especially those arriving from more traditional Christianity, would be considered unprofessional, unscientific, and simply in bad taste.

Since the 1950s the prevailing rules for academia have changed regarding many other subjects. Then it was still plausible to speak as though academia should be free from "outside" political influences and to regard Democratic and Republican commitments as based on a scientifically neutral liberal consensus. Now it is widely held that all scholarship is to some degree political and that interpretive traditions reflect the interests of competing communities. Few scholars, especially in interpretive disciplines such as history, will invoke the term "objective" anymore, except perhaps when talking about limited technical investigations. The political counterpart has been the rise of multiculturalism, which has challenged the old liberal heterosexist male WASP hegemony and promoted countervailing agendas that now have been given equal standing in the mainstream academic community.

In this more open academic setting it seems reasonable to reopen the question of how religious perspectives ought to be treated in mainstream academia. Religious outlooks have for so long been foreign to most leading scholarship that there is no danger of reintroducing a dominant outlook that would inhibit free inquiry. Religious communities today are too diverse to wield concerted influence, so that their voices would be adding to diversity, not inhibiting it. Multiculturalism, it would seem, ought to take into account cultures whose primary basis is religious as well as those who are united most by ethnicity, race, gender, or sexual orientation. Moreover, the original intellectual reasons for excluding religious perspectives seem much weakened. While the mainstream academy still usually requires scholars to follow empirical scientific and rational methods where appropriate, much of the most sophisticated scholarship accepted in the academy today recognizes that empirical research takes place within controlling frameworks of commitments and beliefs that cannot themselves be established on value-free scientific grounds. Hence there seems little basis to silence scholars concerning the religious basis of their deepest commitments, while commitments based on other affiliations are acknowledged as legitimate schools of thought.

Responses to my earlier versions of this seemingly modest proposal have included some strong negative reactions. These have been of two broad types. The first is what I would call "the political response." These arguments come from persons who view traditional religions as oppressive and are threatened by the possibility of the reintroduction of a strong conservative Christian presence in the academy. Many feminists, gay, lesbian, and Marxist scholars have political interests of this sort. So do ex-fundamentalists, a few African American revisionists, some Jewish scholars, and a smattering of others who have (sometimes justifiable) fears of resurgent Christian cultural imperialism. I cannot, of course, accurately generalize about all these groups, but my own characterization of what I hear from them is that they are advocates of multiculturalism who are not so much interested in arguments as in the political implications of what is being proposed. So they may identify my own position as essentially political. They may, for instance, characterize me as a neo-conservative, thus ignoring my repeated critiques of Christian establishments, either past or future.[2] I am not calling for the reestablishment of Christian hegemony in the mainstream academy, only that various Christian and other religious perspectives be evaluated on the same grounds as other academic outlooks.

2. Randall Balmer expressed a number of such political concerns in his "Response to George Marsden" presented at the forum on "Academic Freedom and Committed Scholarship: The 1992 ASCH Presidential Address Revisited," American Society of Church History meetings, January 8, 1994.

While I think it is important to discuss the practical political implications of such a policy, the prior question, it seems to me, is simply whether or not it is fair, given the other principles that currently govern the academy. So in this essay I want to address those who have more directly engaged the arguments I have advanced as to why the academy, if it is to be consistent with its own principles, ought to be more open to religious perspectives.[3]

This second set of criticisms can be characterized as "the liberal response." The proponents of this outlook take seriously that I have cited the wide acceptance of multiculturalism and of critiques of older demands for objectivity as reasons for reconsidering attitudes toward religious perspectives. They are uneasy about the more extreme expressions of these trends and therefore worry that, if we allow religious perspectives an equal place in the mainstream academy, we may further undercut some of the legitimate achievements of the liberal academy. Granting my point that so-called Enlightenment standards of objectivity are unrealistic for most interpretative work, they point out that nonetheless (or perhaps, all the more) we should value scientific methods of study and scholarly detachment.[4]

As a matter of fact, I share those concerns. The problem as I see it in the contemporary academy is how to balance the advocacy implicit in all scholarship with academic standards of evaluation that are scientific in the sense of being accessible to people coming from many

3. Stephen L. Carter, *The Culture of Disbelief: How American Law and Politics Trivialize Religious Devotion* (New York: Basic Books, 1993), offers some helpful principles in this regard.

It is indeed difficult to know exactly how to draw a line that allows religious groups — especially large religious groups — their due place in public life without allowing them to establish an undue dominance that is unfair to other legitimate political groups. This problem, however, is by no means unique to religious groups. Nor does resolving the problem by silencing a group on the grounds that it might gain undue influence seem consistent with the American tradition. One factor often forgotten is that most religious groups are not monoliths. Christians, for instance, are divided into countless denominations and even are divided within denominations. So like other political factions they will cancel each other out on many issues.

4. Thomas G. Alexander, R. Scott Appleby, and Amanda Porterfield, with varying degrees of sympathy, each raised versions of this point in their responses presented at the January 8, 1994, session of the American Society of Church History. Many people have also raised similar questions from the floor in various lectures and discussions of this topic.

different ideological camps. So my argument is not that multicultural-ism and postmodernism have triumphed in the academy and hence "anything goes." Rather, I am saying that multicultural and postmodern critiques of older so-called Enlightenment ideals do raise legitimate doubts about the policies of the older liberal academic establishment which effectively marginalized traditionalist religious viewpoints, such as those of Catholics or confessional Protestants. Such religious view-points, I am saying, ought to be granted a fully legitimate place in the mainstream academy so long as they prove themselves academically worthy in the same way that other points of view do, or ought to do. In other words, I do believe that the academy can have some widely accepted rules for judgments of academic merit. I see no good reason, however, why one of those rules should be, in effect, that all explicit reference to religious viewpoints should be marginalized.

The Value of the Liberal Pragmatic Academy

One recent critic of my proposals defended the liberal pragmatist tradi-tion and cited a very helpful passage from William James to make her point. In "What Pragmatism Means," James describes pragmatic dis-course as "like a corridor in a hotel. Innumerable chambers open out of it. In one you may find a man writing an atheistic volume; in the next someone on his knees praying for faith and strength; in the third a chemist investigating a body's properties. In a fourth a system of idealistic metaphysics is being excogitated; in a fifth the impossibility of metaphysics is being shown. But they all own the corridor, and all must pass through it if they want a practicable way of getting into or out of their respective rooms."[5]

If fact, I find this image quite congenial. Essentially my position is that in a pluralistic society we have little choice but to be pragmatists in public life. I am not then, as some might suppose, challenging prag-matic liberalism as the modus operandi for the contemporary academy. Rather I am affirming it for that limited role, but arguing that there is no adequate pragmatic basis for marginalizing all religious viewpoints

5. Quoted by Amanda Porterfield from William James, *Pragmatism and the Meaning of Truth* (Cambridge: Harvard University Press, 1978), 32.

a priori. There is no basic reason why the intellectual implications of particular religious beliefs may not be explicitly brought into public discourse. I would be happy, in fact, if someone like William James were in charge of setting the rules for these corridors, as I think he would have appreciated this point.

What I am wary of, however, is having the spiritual descendants of John Dewey in charge. The tendency of twentieth-century liberal culture has been to absolutize the pragmatic method. The absolute, that value than which there is none higher, is that which promotes civil discourse. Virtues such as tolerance, openness, dialogue, agnosticism, mutuality, equal opportunity, scientific method, truth-seeking, charity, and love of beauty might be on a list of "the top ten" commandments. John Dewey recognized the potential religious functions of such a liberal polity and even attempted to promote it as "a common faith."[6] So absolutized, liberal pragmatism has little tolerance for traditionalist religions that challenge the pragmatic absolutes.

If, however, pragmatic liberalism is recognized not as an absolute, but simply as a relatively good method for dealing peacefully with diverse peoples, then people for whom the public domain is not ultimate can readily support it as they should support any relative good.

Christians and Scientific Scholarship

The objection is often heard from liberal critics, however, that persons working from religious perspectives inevitably will violate the essential canons of scientific investigation of the mainstream academy. Clearly, however, this is not the case regarding vast amounts of largely technical scholarship. In the corridors of that pragmatic academy there is fairly large agreement on basic standards of evidence and argument. These are the generally accepted standards and they are generally accepted because they work. They separate good arguments from bad and on many topics they can establish a sort of "public knowledge" that persons from many ideological sub-communities can agree on and which

6. See, for instance, Dewey's list of "goods" in his *A Common Faith* (New Haven: Yale University Press, 1934), 51.

are not simply matters of opinion. It is a matter of fact that the New York Yankees won the World Series in 1950 (even though this author and the editors of this volume wish it otherwise). There is no reason why persons of conventional religious convictions might not be thoroughly expert at employing the scientific academic conventions that lead to establishing such widely attested beliefs.[7] The issue here is not essentially different from that of whether a conventional Christian might not be an excellent private detective, as G. K. Chesterton and Father Brown were among the first to illustrate.

The fact is that explicitly Christian convictions do not very often have substantial impact on the technique used in academic detective work, which makes up the bulk of the technical scientific side of academic inquiry. Christians, just as much as other scholars, must for instance employ the requisite degree of detachment in order to weigh evidence judiciously. And even though they may be passionately motivated to do the best job of truth-seeking, they must be duly dispassionate in order to think clearly and to present their results effectively without tendentiousness.

It might be objected, however, that if Christian scholarship involves anything that makes it distinctive beyond such technical knowledge, it is inherently unscientific just in those respects. In those respects that would make it distinctively Christian, it must depend on claims of revelation and miracles that are not scientifically verifiable. Such Christian claims, it is said, fail to meet the rules for discourse within the corridors of the mainstream academy since they are not fully testable before a diverse jury of one's peers. As one critic puts it, "What we question is the claim that faith assertions are in the same category as assertions bolstered by logic and evidence."[8]

This objection deserves serious consideration, in part because it is so widespread. On the one hand, the implication that all religious claims

---

7. I realize, of course, that there are lots of hard cases in which people using scientific procedures have legitimate difference over what constitutes "the facts," as Michael Polanyi and Thomas Kuhn pointed out. Also, "fact" is never entirely independent from the interpretive systems in which we view them. Nonetheless, in judging many topics there remain many common standards on which almost everyone can agree for all practical purposes.

8. Robert Primack, letter to the editor, *The Chronicle of Higher Education*, 25 May 1994, B5.

lack support from logic or evidence is obviously not true.[9] On the other hand, in a pluralistic setting it does not make sense for religious people to argue on the authority of special or private revelations that many other people do not accept. Christian scholars should take special revelation into account in their own thinking and may appeal to it as evidence when addressing audiences who share their views. However, in mainstream academic work, it does not advance one's case to argue on the authority of a revelation that many of one's audience regard as bogus. It would be like introducing such revelations to settle a point in a civil court.

Scholarship That Is Shaped by Background Religious Commitments

That being granted, there is another category of scholarship that relates revelatory or miraculous claims to one's research that should not be objectionable. One's worldview may be fundamentally shaped by beliefs that ultimately rest on scientifically unverifiable theological or moral claims. For instance, one might believe that all warfare is wrong because it violates a command of Jesus. Or one might think that Jesus' commands dictate that one should take a stand for racial justice or care for the poor. Others might hold that God's revelation shows that humans are naturally corrupt and that one should be suspicious of utopian hopes that presume a general improvement in human behavior. Still others may believe, on the contrary, that revelation shows that there is hope for a general improvement in human behavior.

Any of these viewpoints might be introduced into the mainstream academy for religious reasons, but defended with arguments and evi-

---

9. One variation of this argument, for instance, excludes religious beliefs by definition. For instance, one professor of philosophy is reported as arguing

> that any personal beliefs — religious or otherwise — that are discussed in the classroom have to be supported by evidence, and that evidence should meet the standards of the profession. But faith is, by definition, a belief in that for which there is no proof: once a belief can be supported by independent, scientific evidence, it loses its religious nature. . . . when considering any theory, "the evidence has to carry the day, not the fact that it is Christian."

Bernard Rosen, as his views are reported by Jeff Grabmeier, "Christian Professors, Public University," *Ohio State Quest* (Summer 1994): 15-16.

10

dence that are publicly accessible. The approach would be equivalent to Catholic natural law arguments. Pragmatists themselves would not have to believe in the principle of a God-given natural law in order to accept arguments based on widely held beliefs. So having a religious *source* for one's views does not automatically exclude one's views from acceptance in the academy, so long as one argues for them on other, more widely accessible grounds.

In practice, however, the academy does not work on such a consistently rational basis. Consider, for instance, someone whose religious beliefs lead her to maintain that abortion is a kind of murder, that homosexual relationships are sinful, or that the United States is God's chosen nation. Whatever the source of such beliefs, there is going to be strong resistance to relating them to one's scholarship in the mainstream academy. Sometimes the reason given for such resistance will be that people should not let their religious prejudices intrude into their scholarship. That argument, however, is a red herring since it is not consistently applied. Indeed, there is no way that it could be applied without excluding too much. No one, for instance, is going to rule out of bounds for the mainstream academy the views of a pious liberal Episcopalian psychologist who holds that homosexual relationships may be important to human fulfillment, even though that view may have ultimately a religious origin.[10] On the other hand, the views of an equally competent but very conservative Episcopalian psychologist who argued that homosexual relationships are likely to be destructive would be much more likely to be dismissed as illicitly religious in origin.[11]

10. Another example is that a Jew whose scholarship on the Middle East may be driven by a belief that God has a special place in the history of the nation of Israel is not likely to be excluded from the mainstream academy.

11. This is not to say that political concerns might not be legitimate grounds for excluding some religiously based views from the mainstream. If, for instance, one believes that God has ordained a hierarchy of races and racial separatism, those beliefs will be excluded both by law and by an overwhelming consensus. Such rules keep changing, however, and so raise some hard questions so far as religious belief is concerned. What of Muslim, Mormon, or fundamentalist views of women? Or Catholic views of homosexuality? Are they in the same class as racist views? On the other hand, is excluding these views a kind of religious prejudice? Regardless of how these issues are decided, however, the important thing to notice is that certain religiously based views are not being excluded because they are religiously based, but because of their political implications.

One should also notice that the operative rules in the pragmatic academy do not exclude all background beliefs[12] that are not empirically verifiable.[13] Any such rule would, of course, exclude far too many beliefs. For instance, widely held moral beliefs such as that humans should have equal rights regardless of race or gender, that it is wrong to murder infants, or that one should be especially concerned for the poor have no more empirical basis than does belief in a triune God.

Nor is the actual rule of the academy that no one may bring into her scholarship background beliefs that she will not give up, no matter what the evidence. Once again one can think of too many examples of persons and groups who would be excluded from the academy if there were such a rule. In principle, the academy should be a place where one is open to reconsidering his views in the light of the evidence for contrary interpretations. In practice there are many beliefs, such as the moral beliefs just mentioned, that are not going to be given up no matter what the contrary evidence.

For understanding what might be a reasonable set of rules for the

12. I am using this term as roughly equivalent, I think, to what Nicholas Wolterstorff calls "control beliefs," in *Reason within the Bounds of Religion* (Grand Rapids: William B. Eerdmans, 1976).

13. In fact, a good case can be made that in modern intellectual life the rules of rationality have often been too stringently drawn, in part just in order to eliminate religiously based claims which had been given an unduly privileged place in earlier academic establishments. In retrospect, one can see that in the claims of the old logical positivism of the mid-twentieth century which said that all language about God was, strictly speaking, nonsense. Or one can see it today in popular modern conceptions of rationality, still heard in arguments of many academics, that "I cannot accept anything for which there is no scientific evidence."

For instance, in correspondence with me on this point, Laurence Veysey presents an endorsement of this view as excluding religious and other ideologically driven views from the highest learning. He writes: "The method of science is one that grounds all knowledge in publicly available evidence, in replicable experiments. It also offers a tentative conception of truth which is at odds with an ideological view. Truth must be hard-won. Generalizations of all kinds are properly hard-earned. There are no purely intuitive short-cuts. One must always expect that a given conclusion is subject to overthrow by superior evidence at a later time. It seems to me that this scientific method and attitude did properly lie near the heart of rising academic endeavor of high quality at the end of the nineteenth century. Of course there are some academic fields, such as literature, which cannot be assimilated to a scientific model, but they have remained peculiarly faddish, possibly as a result." Letter to the author, November 20, 1989, quoted with Veysey's permission.

diverse mainstream academy, I think it is helpful to step back and to try to picture how belief systems actually operate. For this purpose I like the image of a web of belief that some philosophers use.[14] We can think of our belief systems as like a web, not every part of which is directly connected to every other. Some of these beliefs are peripheral to the system and may be readily discarded or modified if they can be shown to be inconsistent with other, more central beliefs. In every web there are some beliefs that are so deeply lodged and deeply entwined with everything else that in practice they are nonnegotiable. Belief in things like one's own personal identity over the years would be among these nonnegotiables. Certain moral commitments are held almost as firmly. Basic religious commitments may also be deeply entwined beneath many of our other beliefs. Occasionally people may give up a belief that is fairly deeply entrenched. Religious conversions or deconversions involve such transformations. Nonetheless, everyone has some deeply held beliefs that he will never give up.

The process that leads to this dogmatism in all human belief systems, I would add, is not purely rational. Rather, our rationality is always in the service of our social relationships. Some of our most firmly held beliefs are determined largely by the communities with which we affiliate. Family, peers, national cultures, racial or ethnic subcultures, and academic or vocational cultures all have basic traditions of belief that may create in us allegiances to beliefs that we will not give up without changing our basic identities. Of course, people do occasionally change their basic identities as they give up primary allegiance to one community and accept that of another. When they do so, however, it is seldom simply rationality that plays the decisive role. One can see the importance of this personal factor even within academia itself. Typically, we first adopt some of our beliefs because they were held by an admired teacher or because our peers hold such views. Then we look for reasons to assure ourselves that these beliefs are rational.

In academic communities, nonetheless, formal allegiance to certain rules of rationality is essential to membership in the community, and such allegiance can also play a role in leading academics to alter their other allegiances. Most academics affirm certain minimal stan-

14. I think this comes from Willard Quine. I was introduced to it by Nicholas Wolterstorff.

dards of rules of evidence and rationality, and these might force one to modify one's religious beliefs, outweighing one's personal allegiance to a religious community. Or such rules of evidence and rationality might rule out for us serious consideration of some beliefs regardless of the personal attractiveness of those who hold those beliefs. That being granted, we must recognize that for academics, as for other people, loyalties to communities of belief are determined by far more than sheer rationality.

It seems to follow, then, that there is nothing peculiar per se about religious beliefs that should eliminate them as a class from being legitimate background beliefs that would determine the most basic allegiances that we bring to the academy. As background beliefs, these are not beliefs that we would normally introduce into the pragmatic academy as the evidence for our views. For that we would look for other beliefs that are widely held by persons in differing ideological camps. Or we might appeal to some internal inconsistencies in the belief systems of others. In any case, we would be working on some ad hoc common ground of discourse.

It is, of course, fair game in academia to smoke out and to attack the background views that account for a fellow academic's dogmatism. If I can show that a colleague's controversial opinions are grounded on a blind allegiance to racism, Marxism, liberalism, humanism, anything French and obscure, or a religious dogma, I may have reason to be suspicious of such views.

Nonetheless, in cases of allegiance to ideologies such as those just mentioned, the love of one's basic commitments is not necessarily blind. On the one hand, each of these views rests on foundations that are ultimately mysterious, rather than scientific. So do liberal pragmatic views. On the other hand, there are versions of each of these viewpoints that are carefully reasoned and weighed against other sources of knowledge and which can be shown to rest on no shakier ground than do some of the most widely accepted views in the academy. If representatives of such views, including religiously based views, are willing to play by the other rules of the academy, there seems to be no reason why their views should be discredited just because those views involve some background dogmatism.

If the main point of this line of argument, then, is to say that religious beliefs might legitimately serve as important background

14

beliefs for tamed academics in the mainstream academy, it might be asked what the fuss is about. Such modestly held beliefs do already form the background for the work of many academics. There is little evidence of prejudice against scholars who happen to have such religious views. Quite a few critics of my views have reacted by making this point. My accusation of prejudice against religious scholars, they say, is vastly overstated. It is, they may even suggest, a disingenuous attempt to get in on the current fad of victimization.

Making Christian Views Explicit

My central question, however, is: Should religious scholars be virtually required to keep their religious views hidden? Should religious views be put in a special category of "personal beliefs" that only the self-indulgent would reveal in public? Should a Christian scholar be forced to pose as something else, usually as a liberal humanist, to be accepted in the academy? If religious beliefs are relevant to understanding one's other beliefs, why not openly reflect on that considerable dimension in one's intellectual makeup? Should mention of this religious background be out of bounds in teaching? Or would religious perspectives be more fairly treated if they were treated the way Marxist, feminist, liberal, neo-conservative, gay advocacy, and other such viewpoints that influence scholarship are? One would be free to mention them or not, as appropriate to the occasion. In other words, there ought not only to be the inevitable covert influences of religious perspectives on scholarship, there ought also to be identifiably religious schools of thought in the academy, just as there are other schools of thought.

This point, then, is not that Christians are victimized in the academy, do not get the best jobs, and so forth. There are some well-documented cases of such personal discrimination, but there are many counterinstances as well. The present argument has to do with a more subtle and pervasive suppression of explicit Christian *perspectives* in the mainstream academy. Political scientist John C. Green puts it well in a comment to the *New York Times* that, while claims of prejudice against scholars who are religious are often overstated, "if a professor proposed to study something from a Catholic or Protestant point of view, it would be treated like proposing to study something from a Martian point of view."[15] Another distinguished professor is quoted by *The Chronicle of Higher Education* as stating that the idea of relating religious faith to professional scholarship is "loony."[16] That is precisely the sort of prejudice I wish to address. Younger scholars who are Christian quickly learn that influential professors hold such attitudes toward open religious expression and that to be accepted they should keep quiet about their faith. So rather than attempting to reflect on the relationship between religious faith and their other beliefs, they learn to hide their religious beliefs in professional settings. Such self-censorship by its very nature proceeds quietly, but the attitudes it fosters are pervasive.

It is essential to reiterate that the alternative being proposed is that there be room for explicit Christian points of view (just as there are explicit Marxist or feminist views) for those who will play by the other rules proper to the diverse academy. Most often when people rule out religious perspectives they miss this latter qualification. They assume that the proposal involves opening the academy to all sorts of additional ideological dogmatism and preaching that would cut off intellectual exchange rather than promote it. That is a danger with any strongly held position and it is always a struggle to keep some partisans within the realm of fair discourse and argument. Recognizing that, I am simply proposing that the same rules apply to all. No matter what commitments one brings into one's academic work, one would have to argue for one's scholarly interpretations on the same sorts of publicly accessible grounds that are widely accepted in the academy. I have already argued this point with respect to background beliefs. I am now proposing only the addition of granting that scholars are not transgressing the integrity of public intellectual life if they occasionally identify or reflect upon the religious sources of their views. In most cases I would think that would be helpful to others in the academy in aiding them in understanding the roots of one's position. Feminists have often made a similar point: that our personal perspectives are relevant to our scholarship, and that it is deceptive for the academy to continue the old Enlightenment-based custom of posing as though one is a purely neutral observer.

15. Peter A. Steinfels, "Scholar Calls Colleges Biased against Religion," *New York Times*, 26 November 1993, A14.

16. Bruce Kuklick, as quoted by Carolyn J. Mooney, "Devout Professors on the Offensive," *Chronicle of Higher Education*, 4 May 1994, A18.

Furthermore, even though religious people should honor the rule that they cannot offer their special revelations as the public evidence for their views, they can still reflect on the implications of such revelations within the bounds of the mainstream academy by talking about them conditionally.[17] That is, it is perfectly legitimate to ask an academic question in the form of "if this religious teaching were true, how would it change the way we look at the subject at hand?" For instance, if one asked what difference it would make if it were true, as most of the major religions claim, that the universe is a product of an intelligence, it would have a major bearing on many topics. Most of the mainstream academy typically operates only on the basis of the opposite conditional statement. It operates on the basis of the conditional "if we assume there is no creator god, what sense can we make out of reality?"

For religious people, as for other committed scholars working within the mainstream academy, one of the rules is that they must not be simply proselytizing. Since proselytizing is so central to many religious movements, and since issues of church and state are involved in many academic settings, this issue is one to which religious scholars should be especially sensitive. It is, of course, impossible to avoid trying to persuade others of the merits of one's own views. Christians can and should explain and defend their own viewpoints and attempt to persuade others of their superiority, just as advocates of feminist or Marxist or liberal democratic views often do. But in the pluralistic academy that should be done in a framework of mutual respect and give-and-take that involves some willingness to listen as well as to speak. These rules of scholarly exchange are not always respected in the current academy; but they nevertheless present an ideal toward which the pragmatic academy should continue to aim. Otherwise the pluralistic academy will be reduced to a sort of Hyde Park where every evangelist has his own soapbox.

The rule that religious scholars should follow here is, I think, some version of the Golden Rule. How would we want scholars of other strongly ideological convictions to act in the mainstream academy? Traditional Christians, for instance, might ask how they would want Mormon scholars to act, or Marxist scholars, or feminist scholars. Nor should they argue that just because some other groups violate the rules for civil discourse, Christians should as well.

17. I am grateful to my colleague Alvin Plantinga for this point.

It is, I think, the analogy of religious scholarship to feminist, Marxist, African American, or gay advocacy scholarship that leads many liberals to be wary of opening the doors to religious perspectives. They assume that what we are talking about is all sorts of additional brands of tendentious scholarship. That is, of course, a danger; but I can only repeat that it is not what I am proposing. I do not favor tendentious scholarship whether it comes from religious scholars, advocates of multiculturalism, or from liberals. All these groups are prone to tendentiousness, but in none of them is it necessary to their scholarship.

My own view is that scholarship that is simply tendentious is in the long run self-defeating in the pluralistic academy. Usually it has an impact in the short-run, enlisting second-rate thinkers who substitute formulae for original thought. They can gain considerable political power. Nonetheless, I think in the long run they are intellectually self-defeating. Their views become drearily predictable, and other scholars cease taking them seriously. Nonetheless, even if some scholarship in the academy is inevitably tendentious, it is better that the sources of the tendentiousness be identified so that they can be the more easily discounted. The convention of insisting that all scholars and teachers pose as disinterested observers is more misleading than a general rule of frank identification of one's biases.

My ideal for Christian scholarship is one that looks not only for the bearing of one's Christian convictions on one's academic thought, but also reflects some Christian attitudes that shape the tone of one's scholarship. Not only should Christian commitments lead one toward scholarly rigor and integrity, they should also lead one toward fairness and even charity toward those with whom one differs. Scholarship of such quality will ultimately have the greatest impact in the academy, and the greatest chance of being accepted.

That leads, however, to the other frequent objection to the idea of explicit Christian scholarship. This objection is the opposite of that which claims explicit Christian scholarship would be necessarily tendentious. If Christian scholarship is ideally so generous in tone and rigorous in quality, and does not base its claims in the mainstream academy on appeals to authority, but uses methods and rules of evidence common to other scholarship, what difference could Christian perspectives possibly make?

What Difference Does It Make?

This is not the occasion to attempt a comprehensive answer to that question, which many have written on elsewhere[18] However, let me just summarize a few basic points.

By far the biggest difference that religious perspectives make is in the choices of the topics we study and the choices of the questions we ask about those topics. People with religious beliefs are going to have priorities that differ from those who lack them. This is not to say that occasionally a nonreligious scholar, such as a Perry Miller, may not take religious subjects seriously.[19] In general, however, religious people may have more interest in religious matters and will value more highly understanding the nuances of matters such as theology or forms of piety.

David Hollinger in a comment on some of my earlier reflections on this topic asks "whether Christianity is generating a number of exciting new research programs, as feminism has proved able to do."[20]

18. Many examples of Christian scholarship can be found in *Christian Scholar's Review* as well in many of the books reviewed in its pages. More specialized Christian journals include *Faith and Philosophy, Fides et Historia, Journal of the American Scientific Affiliation,* and *Christianity and Literature.* I have reflected on this question more fully in *The Outrageous Idea of Christian Scholarship* and have also provided other examples there.

19. Some people have objected that if some belief that many Christians hold is held also by many non-Christians, then it is not a good example of how Christian belief may shape scholarship. So if I say that Christians may be more sensitive to certain issues regarding piety or theology in their historical writing (just as I think women are more likely to be sensitive to woman's concerns, etc.), they counter that other people could be just as sensitive. That is technically true. Occasionally a scholar may be so good at sympathizing with another mind-set that she may write with the sensitivities of an insider. That is, however, also pretty rare. Ex-Christians may, of course, have many of the same sensitivities as Christians; but that surely is not an evidence that Christianity does not have an impact on one's sensitivities.

20. David A. Hollinger, "From Protestant Culture to Religious Pluralism," Paper presented to Wingspread Conference on the History of American Protestantism, October 1993, 33. It is astonishing how many scholars are not even aware of reputable Christian scholarship. Philosopher Benard Rosen, cited above for his views on evidence, is reported as saying that "Unlike Marxists and feminists, Christians don't have established journals or a scholarly community that examines history or sociology or other fields." Rosen, as summarized by Grabmeier, "Christian Professors," *Ohio State Quest* (Summer 1994): 15-16.

The answer to that question, I think, is clearly "yes it is." In Hollinger's own field, American history, for instance, I think it would generally be acknowledged that there are a number of innovative works that grow out of the Christian interests of their authors. I think, for instance, of Charles Hambrick-Stowe's *The Practice of Piety*, a wonderfully crafted and highly acclaimed account of Puritan piety. A Christian who regards piety as important for its own sake is much more likely to ask and answer the questions that Hambrick-Stowe does than would a person of no religious belief. Daniel Walker Howe's *The Political Culture of the American Whigs* and Nathan Hatch's *Democratization of American Religion* are other cases in point. None of these authors explicitly mentions that he is writing from a point of view of Christian interests or perspectives, but each brings the creative insights and sympathies of an insider. What Hollinger's comment illustrates, I think, is not the lack of some innovative Christian scholarship, but rather the inhibitions against identifying it as such.

Beyond bringing into the open the fact that there already *is* some Christian scholarship and thus raising consciousness about that enterprise and encouraging discussions about its implications, there are other areas where Christianity may legitimately have an impact on scholarship in the mainstream academy. The nature of what such an impact might be is best seen by considering what has happened in the field of philosophy in the past twenty-five years. Philosophy is the principal discipline that has become an exception to the rule of allowing no explicit place for Christian perspectives in the mainstream academy.[21] During the past twenty-five years an identifiable group of Christian scholars have had a considerable impact on that field. Philosophers discuss explicitly subjects such as the rationality of belief in God, revelation as a source of belief, or the viability of relying on religiously based moral principles.[22] It is ironic that in the field where there is by

21. Theology, of course, is another exception, but it has become a peripheral discipline, although it has some vestigial mainstream locations.

22. Alvin Plantinga and Nicholas Wolterstorff, eds., *Faith and Rationality: Reason and Belief in God* (Notre Dame, Ind.: University of Notre Dame Press, 1983), contains examples with which I am most familiar. Since that time there has been a great deal of such discussion, especially among the members of the Society of Christian Philosophers, many of whom are prominent in the American Philosophical Association as well. For an introductory overview of how some leading philosophers

far the most academic rigor in dealing with these issues, there has been considerable recognition that religious beliefs are inherently no less rational than are many other things that academics believe; yet academics in other fields will declare dogmatically that holding Christian beliefs is not intellectually responsible.

An interesting question is why such openness is found almost solely in philosophy among mainstream academic disciplines and why philosophers have so little impact on other disciplines. Philosophers are, of course, more open to talking about first principles and their implications and are professionally more inclined to discuss issues without immediate regard to their political implications. Moreover, questions about God, revelation, and religiously based morality are so integral to the history of the field that even in the positivist era such questions had continued to be discussed, at least in a historical context. Nevertheless, the fragmentation of our academic disciplines has meant that philosophers' recent discussions of these issues have not yet had much impact on other fields. I am hoping, however, that that will happen as word gets out that there are no decisive intellectual reasons to dismiss discussion of such topics in the mainstream academy.

What would be the implications of such opening of the mainstream academy to explicit talk about the meaning of religious perspectives for other disciplines?

First, there are many areas where religious perspectives would not have much appreciable impact. As I said earlier, in the technical aspects of disciplines, or in disciplines that are largely technical, religious and nonreligious people carry out most of their tasks in similar ways. Noting this commonality, many scholars will argue that since there is no Christian or Muslim mathematics, there is no Jewish view of photosynthesis, and so forth, therefore religion is irrelevant to real scholarship. Such arguments, however, are patently specious. Religious perspectives simply have more appreciable impact on some disciplines and some aspects of disciplines than on others. So there may not be a Christian mathematics, but there certainly could be a Christian view of

---

reconcile their faith and their learning see Kelly James Clark, ed., *Philosophers Who Believe: The Spiritual Journeys of Eleven Leading Thinkers* (Downers Grove: InterVarsity Press, 1993); also Thomas Morris, *God and the Philosophers* (New York: Oxford University Press, 1994).

justice in economic development for third world nations. Scholars in the humanities and the social sciences constantly make moral judgments. Such judgments are often shaped, in turn, by religious views. And, while such judgments may function largely as background beliefs, there seems to be no good reason why the sources of such views should be kept entirely out of sight in the mainstream academy.

Other larger issues might have some explicit impact on scholarship. A generation ago Reinhold Niebuhr showed how Christian views of original sin might be relevant to understanding the world. Or H. Richard Niebuhr and other neo-orthodox scholars showed how all human commitments may be seen as religious and tending toward idolatry. Since the neo-orthodox era, however, such discussions have gone out of style except among some theologians and among a minority of scholars in explicitly religious fields.

One of the most significant differences that one's background beliefs are likely to make on general scholarship has to do with the belief that God has created all that is. Although Christians may differ regarding the means of creation, they all confess that God is the ultimate creator. That affirmation, in turn, can have some important implications regarding the larger frameworks that shape modern scholarship. Modern scholarship is largely based on the premise that purely naturalistic evolutionary models provide the only legitimate ways to understand reality, including human reality. If, however, we believe that ultimately moral laws, for instance, are not only the products of social evolution but also have a relationship to moral principles created by God, it will change some of our fundamental scholarly assumptions. Similarly, in the current debates over epistemology that are so central to many disciplines, it could make a tremendous difference if one were convinced that both our minds and reality are created by God.[23]

---

23. Alvin Plantinga, "When Faith and Reason Clash: Evolution and the Bible," *Christian Scholar's Review* 21 (September 1991): 8-32, points out that belief in the existence of God could make some major differences in assessing the probability of the truth of some mega-theories in the sciences. See also the comments of other Christian scholars and Plantinga's rejoinders, ibid., 73-109. In my view Plantinga's logic would get a far better hearing if he did not illustrate it from the politically embattled and emotionally charged field of biological evolution. His argument is much more likely to be widely compelling when he illustrates it simply with refer-

In addition to influencing the subjects one chooses to study and the questions one asks, Christian beliefs are likely to have a major impact on the types of interpretive theories one is inclined to accept. Christians, of course, differ widely among themselves about many of their beliefs; yet it is nonetheless undeniable that strong religious faith will dispose believers toward some points of view that are current in the academy and rule out others. A conservative Catholic writing about the history of the family will be inclined toward a different set of interpretive traditions than will a secular scholar who is dedicated to sexual freedom and believes all moral systems are relative. Or a pacifist Mennonite scholar will write about the Vietnam War differently than will a secular neo-conservative. In each case the religious perspective will be making a huge identifiable difference in interpretation.[24]

The image that I like to use to explain how such underlying assumptions about the nature of reality may affect some of the most basic premises in our scholarship, but not necessarily change our technical scholarship, is the image of a gestalt picture. Let's say we have a picture that viewed one way is a duck and another way is a rabbit. According to this analogy, scholars might be deeply divided into two contending ideological camps, the duck school and the rabbit school. Yet on technical questions they can agree. They can measure the distances between the lines or the ratio between black and white in the picture. So in fields such as mathematics or physics, or in historical analyses of the order in which the lines that make up the picture were drawn, there would not be great difference between the schools. Yet on larger issues the two camps might differ sharply. What are ears for one is a bill for the other. Their research programs would differ accordingly. They would be asking differing questions about various parts of the

---

ence to the origins of the universe. Contemporary speculations on the origins of the universe are driven to great lengths to find the best explanation of how the universe can be self-generating or without beginning without resorting to the hypothesis of a creator, which is ruled out of bounds *a priori*. Persons who believed in a creator still might be interested in looking for the best physical explanation, but would be likely to invest the current best hypothesis with far less certainty than is typically given it by persons who exclude from consideration a God in any traditional sense.

24. Once again, the fact that non-Christian scholars may be inclined to some of the same interpretations as are Christian scholars is obviously no evidence that Christianity is not a major influence in the scholarship.

picture. On such issues there may be no common ground. But there should be room for the two schools to identify the source of their differences and hence to explain their differences to each other.[25]

So with religious and secular scholarship. There ought to be room in the mainstream academy for the discussion of the implications of such monumental differences, as, for instance, whether humans are best understood as the creatures of a wise deity, or simply the products of "the same forces that ripen corn and rust iron," as Carl Becker put it.[26] As far as I can see, however, such discussions are rare. Only the party that assumes that humans are the product of chance processes gets a hearing. As I have emphasized, the diverse academy needs a set of rules appropriate to itself, but I do not see why one of those rules should be that discussions of the implications of religious faith for scholarship should be virtually ruled out.

Christian Schizophrenia?

Finally, there is an objection to all this that may be raised by strongly religious people. Have I not conceded too much, they may say, in order to get a hearing in the mainstream academy for occasional discussions of the implications of such broad frames of reference? Am I not saying, in effect, that one has to water down one's religious faith and witness so that it will be acceptable to the diverse pragmatic academy? Does that not make a religious person schizophrenic, advocating and perhaps proselytizing for a life-changing worldview in one part of his life, but playing by rules that are not consistently Christian the rest of the time? Am I not saying in effect that on one day a week we say, "Choose you this day whom you will serve," and on the other six we serve the rules of the pragmatic academy?

Here I think the answer is that the very nature of human life every

---

25. One might argue that a third school of thought sees that the picture can properly be seen both ways — and that this school is simply the right one and represents what would become the consensus of the liberal academy. If, however, something crucial rested on one side or the other of the issue, then it is likely that the academy would be polarized as well.

26. Carl Becker, *The Heavenly City of the Eighteenth-Century Philosophers* (New Haven: Yale University Press, 1932), 14.

day is that we routinely move from one field of activity to another, each with its own set of rules. Such adaptability to the subordinate communities in which a Christian may operate is fully consistent with Christian commitment. It is the principle, I think, behind the saying of Jesus that "We should render unto Caesar the things that are Caesar's." It is also the fundamental principle of Augustine's *City of God*, which posits that, although our primary allegiance is to the City of God, we also have subordinate and limited allegiances to the civilizations of the world, which necessarily run on sub-Christian principles. We may live in the world as "resident aliens," as some of my friends say, but as resident aliens we should obey the laws of the land of our sojourn to the extent that it does not conflict with our higher allegiances.

I think it is helpful to view these adaptations to the rules of various institutions of the larger society as analogous to games that religious people may play. Christians, for instance, often spend hours playing by the rules of basketball. Literally applying the ethics of Jesus, passing the ball equally to your opponents as much as to your teammates, would ruin the game. Or try playing Monopoly with someone who does not want to gain at the expense of her neighbor. In fact, in the game situation the best way to show love to your opponent is to play fairly by the competitive rules of the game. So when religious people play by the rules of the various games of society — the rules of law, the pragmatic rules of the United States Constitution, the rules of the market, or the rules of mainstream academia — they are not necessarily violating Christian principles by temporarily accommodating themselves to those rules. At the same time, there are limits of one's allegiances to such rules. Christians can refuse to play some of the games of society and refuse to accept some of the prevailing rules of other games. Nonetheless, there are many social conventions to which Christians can give limited allegiance. When engaged in such activities, the situation of the religious believer may be analogous to that of a doctor who is playing softball. So long as she is in the softball game, she tries not to break its rules. If, however, she sees a car accident on a nearby street, she will stop running the bases and go to help. The rules of doctoring pre-empt baseball rules.

So with religious people in the academy. They play by the academy's rules to the extent that they do not conflict directly with their Christian commitments. As I said earlier, many of the pragmatic rules for getting along with our diverse neighbors and even with our enemies are the sorts of rules that Christians should readily adopt for such limited, though important, purposes. Some of the rules for getting along in a pluralistic academic situation are different from the rules within the Christian church, but not contradictory to them. So what may be appropriate to a church gathering may not be appropriate to an academic gathering. Preaching sermons and public prayer are not appropriate to teaching in state universities or to a session of the American Historical Association. As the body of Christ has many members, however, so Christians may have many callings. That means not only that some Christians are called to one task and others to another, but also that each Christian may be called to work in differing settings at different times. Some scholars may be called to serve strictly in the church and in its schools. Such academic communities are invaluable and can sustain a depth of sophistication regarding the implications of faith and scholarship that is unattainable in diverse settings.[27] Nonetheless most Christian scholars today have good reason also to be participating in pluralistic enterprises such as mainstream scholarship. In such settings it would be self-defeating to insist that the only rules one will follow are those that would be appropriate to the church. When one wants to speak to diverse audiences, one must be willing to accommodate to the language and rules designed for that community — to be all things to all people.

By the same token, however, if the rules of the academy are written in such a way as to exclude unnecessarily religious points of view, then religious people ought to try to point that out and change those rules. The contemporary academy is not, I think, wholly consistent on this matter. Not all religious views are discriminated against, and some parts of the academy discriminate much more than others. Nonetheless there is no denying that some parts of the contemporary academy do

---

27. Conventional wisdom today says that intellectual vitality can be attained only in diverse intellectual settings. Such settings, however, are also conducive to intellectual shallowness, since people who are working on differing principles usually cannot work together very long. I think that the level of scholarship attained at Calvin College, a theologically homogenous community, during the past forty years is evidence against conventional wisdom. Compare its scholarly production to that of other religiously based undergraduate institutions that have been more diverse.

discourage explicit religious expression. Such discrimination seems to me to be unjust, especially when the type of advocacy involved in presenting and defending religiously based views is directly parallel to some permitted advocacy of nonreligious views. So it is worth asking whether the rules of this game might not be improved.

Traditional Christianity and the Possibility of Historical Knowledge[1]

MARK A. NOLL

W HAT can we know about the past? About the shape and significance of the actions, thoughts, institutional creations, assumptions, and intentions of those who have lived before us? And how
should we think about efforts to describe and interpret the past? Given
the nature of the human mind, given the character of the evidence
linking our present existence with past lives, and given the relationship
of human thought, whether past or present, to the conceptual frameworks shaped by societies and cultures as a whole, what is possible
and what is not possible to affirm about our knowledge of the past?

These are questions which historians, surprisingly, have only recently addressed, and then only in a desultory fashion. Historians are
usually much more eager simply to set about their work than they are
to theorize about it. In recent years, however, casualness about the
broader intellectual implications of the effort to recover the past has
begun to change, and that for several reasons.

1. An earlier version of this chapter, presented first as the Timothy Dwight
Lecture in Christian Thought for the InterVarsity chapter at the University of Penn-
sylvania, was published in the *Christian Scholar's Review* 19 (June 1990): 388-406.
Brief sections of what follows are adapted from Mark A. Noll, "Contemporary
Historical Writing: Practice and Presuppositions," *Christianity and History Newsletter*
(University and Colleges Christian Fellowship, Great Britain), February 1988, 15-32;
and "Scientific History in America: A Centennial Observation from a Christian Point
of View," *Fides et Historia* 14 (Fall-Winter 1981): 21-37.

In the first instance, it has grown increasingly clear how "political" (in the broad sense of the term) historical writing is and always has been. The development of "professional history" in the universities over the last century and a half obscured the political character of historical writing for some time. Early leaders of academic history in Europe and in the United States prided themselves on a detachment and an objectivity that they felt defined their advance over earlier, amateur, and much more obviously partisan historians of previous generations.[2] The simple act of self-reflection during several generations of professional historical work has made it clear, however, that history writing has always served political purposes, not just in what historians write but also in how they conceive the nature of their tasks. This conclusion is the point of compelling formal studies, of which Peter Novick's *That Noble Dream: The "Objectivity Question" and the American Historical Profession* remains the most impressive.[3] In retrospect, it is evident that what the first great professional historians in nineteenth-century Europe wrote was harnessed in service to the rising sense of European nationalisms. Just as clear in our own day is the way that political considerations (again, in the broad sense of the term) shape historical writing. This generalization was most obviously true for works written by officially sponsored historians of communist countries and by dissidents within those countries. But it is just as true for Western chroniclers of the Cold War, where leftist historians follow the evidence and assign substantial responsibility for the Cold War to the United States and rightist historians follow the evidence and assign substantial responsibility for the Cold War to the Soviet Union. It is illustrated by historians of the Reconstruction period in American his-

2. On the scientific aspirations of early professional historians, see Ernst Breisach, *Historiography: Ancient, Medieval, and Modern* (Chicago: University of Chicago Press, 1983), 272-90; D. W. Bebbington, *Patterns in History: A Christian View* (Downers Grove, Ill.: InterVarsity Press, 1979), 68-91; and John Higham, with Leonard Krieger and Felix Gilbert, *History: The Development of Historical Studies in the United States* (Englewood Cliffs, N.J.: Prentice-Hall, 1965), 92-103.

3. Peter Novick, *That Noble Dream: The "Objectivity Question" and the American Historical Profession* (New York: Cambridge University Press, 1988). For a spirited rejoinder to Novick that argues for a larger range of mediating positions between simplistic objectivism and trendy relativism, see James T. Kloppenberg, "Objectivity and Historicism: A Century of American Historical Writing," *American Historical Review* 94 (October 1989): 1011-30.

tory, where a historian's degree of sympathy with the modern civil rights movement invariably correlates with that historian's interpretative conclusions about the efforts of radical Reconstructionists to bring about a better life for blacks in the postbellum South. It is true for historians of homosexuality, where gay liberationists find widespread acceptance of homosexual practice in the past and defenders of traditional values find persistent opposition to homosexual practice in the past. Political intent is also manifestly apparent in the writing of church historians. An immense distance, for example, separates the tone of Roman Catholic histories of the Reformation written before the Second Vatican Council and those written after the Council. Clearly it was the Council's charity in evaluating other groups of Christians, rather than fresh discoveries about the sixteenth century, that made the difference. Recently, in short, even historians with their noses deeply buried in the archives have come to sense that more is at work in reporting their findings than simply letting the facts fall where they may.

A second modern condition that has raised concern about our knowledge of the past is the proliferation in almost all academic disciplines of voices questioning the once widely shared ideal of detached, rational, scientific inquiry. The reasons for questioning that ideal are various — it is described as the tool of patriarchialist, capitalist, and racist oppressors; it is denounced as dehumanizing; it is depicted as intellectually incoherent. But in each case, the effect is to call into doubt the ability of researchers to move smoothly from a collection of facts to the presentation of universally valid truth.[4] In philosophy, a turn toward pragmatism, illustrated by revisionist works like Richard Rorty's *Philosophy and the Mirror of Nature* (1979), ridicules traditional quests for *the* truth about perception, being, and the good, and promotes in their place a picture of knowledge as the transient consensus of privileged intellectual communities. In literary theory, deconstruction à la Jacques Derrida or Stanley Fish denies the stable or systematic relationship between words and either the ones who write the words or the things the words are supposed to stand for. In cultural anthro-

---

4. The rest of this paragraph depends on the summary in Novick, *That Noble Dream*, 522-72; and Quentin Skinner, ed., *The Return of Grand Theory in the Human Sciences* (New York: Cambridge University Press, 1985), especially the chapters on Gadamer, Foucault, Derrida, and Levi-Strauss.

pology, the immensely influential work of Clifford Geertz is usually thought to undercut the notion of stable, universal conceptions of truth. In jurisprudence, proponents of Critical Legal Studies defend the multivalent nature of law and its interpretation, arguing, in the words of one such theorist, that "there are as many plausible readings of the United States Constitution as there are versions of *Hamlet*."[5] In psychology, a hermeneutical turn has called into question Freud's own pretensions about the scientific character of psychoanalysis. And in social theory, influential authors from the Continent like Michel Foucault and Jürgen Habermas define almost all cultural verities — whether about sexuality, mental health, diet, or the distribution of economic resources — as functions of shifting power relationships. Such voices, with their flat rejection of objective, value-neutral research, have become increasingly important among historians because of the growing trend to open up historical work to the concepts, materials, and strategies of the social sciences and humanities.

A third influence rousing historians from dogmatic slumbers has been even more unnerving. It is the conviction proposed most influentially by Thomas Kuhn in his 1962 essay, *The Structure of Scientific Revolutions*, that even natural science — the intellectual standard since Newton for hard, real, genuine knowledge — may itself be less fixed, less intellectually pristine, less value-neutral than once assumed.[6] Such a suggestion is significant because the goal of many professional historians once was to justify their existence by demonstrating that they too were scientific, that they were shedding the burdens of value-laden, subjective, and partisan history.[7] But Kuhn's shocker, though disconcerting enough, was only an opening salvo. His focus was on the internal operations of science, and his intent was to mount a backhanded defense of "normal science" on a pragmatic foundation more in line with the lived realities of scientific experience than with the self-gratifying myths of scientific heroism. Other, more radical histori-

5. Sanford Levinson, "Law as Literature," *Texas Law Review* 60 (1982): 391-92, as quoted in Novick, *That Noble Dream*, 555.

6. Thomas S. Kuhn, *The Structure of Scientific Revolutions*, 2nd enl. ed. (Chicago: University of Chicago Press, 1970).

7. An excellent discussion of that scientific ideal is found in Henry Warner Bowden, *Church History in the Age of Science: Historiographical Patterns in the United States, 1876-1918* (Chapel Hill: University of North Carolina Press, 1971).

ans of science went much beyond Kuhn. They argued that scientific knowledge was relative not only to intellectual shifts internal to the guild of professional scientists. It was also relative to the very social, political, racial, sexual, and economic conventions of culture that seem to have shaped so decisively the social sciences and the humanities.[8] These historians of the external relations of science have made an impressive case, as, for example, when studying the age of Boyle and Newton, the rise of Darwinism in Britain, or the American commitment to conceptions of commonsense, Baconian empiricism.[9] In these instances, along with many others, it has not been difficult to show that what scientists and awed nonscientists held to be the sanitized results of pristinely objective inquiry were in fact decisively shaped by religious or social preconceptions, competition for status, eagerness for warrants to justify influence, and still other factors having nothing directly to do with the study of nature as such. With the anchor of scientific objectivity drifting, if not lost altogether, aspirations to write history scientifically were cast loose on a very choppy sea.

This combination of influences has shaken historians into sober reflection on the nature of their enterprise.[10] The result is that murmurs about an "epistemological crisis" have reached even the out-of-the way landscapes that historians inhabit.[11] They are awakening to the fact that

8. For judicious commentary on these developments, see David N. Livingstone, "Farewell to Arms: Reflections on the Encounter between Science and Faith," in *Christian Faith and Practice in the Modern World: Theology from an Evangelical Point of View*, ed. Mark A. Noll and David F. Wells (Grand Rapids: Eerdmans, 1988), 239-62.

9. For example, Steven Shapin, *A Social History of Truth: Civility and Science in Seventeenth-Century England* (Chicago: University of Chicago Press, 1994); Margaret C. Jacob, *The Cultural Meaning of the Scientific Revolution* (Philadelphia: Temple University Press, 1988); James R. Moore, "Crisis without Revolution: The Ideological Watershed in Victorian England," *Revue de Synthèse* 107 (1986): 53-78; Adrian Desmond and James Moore, *Darwin* (New York: Warner Books, 1992); and Theodore Dwight Bozeman, *Protestants in an Age of Science: The Baconian Ideal and Antebellum American Religious Thought* (Chapel Hill: University of North Carolina Press, 1977).

10. A clear, general account of modern uncertainties is provided by Joyce Appleby, Lynn Hunt, and Margaret Jacob, *Telling the Truth about History* (New York: Norton, 1994).

11. For the phrase "epistemological crisis," see Novick, *That Noble Dream*, 573; and Joyce Appleby, "One Good Turn Deserves Another: Moving Beyond the Linguistic; A Response to David Harlan," *American Historical Review* 94 (December 1989):

the general chaos characterizing contemporary Western epistemology does not exempt the effort to understand the past.

This state of affairs presents a matter of pressing concern for everyone. The sense of who we are, what we are here for, and what we may hope for in the future are all dependent, to a greater than lesser degree, on our understanding of where we have come from, on who and what has contributed to our development. Upon the least reflection, almost everyone will admit to the sense of having been shaped by a multitudinous inheritance — ideals, scandals, patience, struggle, death, celebration, worship, love, disillusionment, hope, selfishness, altruism, and so much more — all experienced before we arrived on the scene, all having left some record that (we hope) can guide our existence, and all worthy of passing on in some fashion to our children. And so, in these general terms, the debate over how we know the past is a debate on how we define ourselves.

But if the crisis in historical knowledge is important in general, it is even more important for the members of Christian communities, since Christianity hinges critically upon an ability to understand the past.

At stake, first, is the foundation of Christian faith. Christians, at least those in the broad stream of orthodox Catholicism, Orthodoxy, and Protestantism, affirm that their very existence is defined by the meaning of purportedly historical events — an omnipotent deity who from nothing created the heavens and the earth, the same God who called Abraham to be the father of many nations, who threw the Egyptian horse and rider into the sea in order to preserve his purpose among a chosen people, and who showed himself and his loving intentions for humanity supremely in becoming a person himself. The historical record of Jesus, the incarnate Son of God, is for Christians even more foundational than the historical record of their own lives — that he was conceived by the Holy Spirit, born of the Virgin Mary, and lived a life of moral perfection; that he suffered under Pontius Pilate, was crucified, dead, and buried; that on the third day he rose again from the dead,

---

1326, 1328. The broader issues involved are the subject of an extensive series of essays in the *American Historical Review* 94 (June 1989): 581-698, and in "A Round Table: What Has Changed and Not Changed in American Historical Practice?" *Journal of American History* 76 (September 1989): 393-478.

ascended to heaven, and will come again to judge the living and the dead.

Implicit, moreover, in affirming these events in the history of salvation is a definite view of historical understanding. These events, Christians hold, may be known to be factual, and with less and less nuance with respect to the meaning of "factual" as we move from the Old Testament to the New. In addition, a reasonable degree of certainty and a reasonable degree of consensus among believers are possible about what these long-past events mean for life in the late twentieth century. Reliable records of these events, supremely in the Bible, present a basically accurate story.[12] The meaning of events described in the Bible has been handed down in lines of reliable tradition that show us (though at a distance of two thousand years and more) the significance of those ancient events today. Finally, by understanding the nature of those events and acting on that understanding, people may be reconciled to God, may be brought to see the infinite worth of other humans, and may become agents of God's work in the world.[13]

At stake in questions about historical knowledge is also, however, another range of issues besides those related narrowly to faith itself, for Christians have traditionally held that their picture of God and his works has far-ranging implications for more general knowledge. That is, the same sort of historical realism that undergirds Christian understanding of the gospel is matched by a general epistemological realism with respect to the creation. In a set of assumptions that takes different

12. Some of the clamor about the historicity of the Bible is muted once it is realized that Scripture presents its history as narrative rather than as "scientific" proposition. For an unusually perceptive accounting of Scripture in these terms, see Gabriel Fackre, *The Christian Story*, 2 vols., 3rd ed. (Grand Rapids: Eerdmans, 1996).

13. A strong challenge that questions whether the link between biblical past and modern interpretation can be as straightforward as I assert is provided by Van Austin Harvey, *The Historian and the Believer: The Morality of Historical Knowledge* (New York: Macmillan, 1966). Arguments similar to Harvey's, which expressed an earlier form of skepticism about the possibility of keeping anything supernatural in mind when practicing genuine history, were clearly expressed in F. H. Bradley, *The Presuppositions of Critical History* (1935; reprint, Chicago: Quadrangle, 1968). By contrast to Harvey and Bradley, John Lukacs finds nothing essentially incompatible between disciplined historical practice and the ordinary structures of supernatural religion; see John Lukacs, *Historical Consciousness, or the Remembered Past* (New York: Harper & Row, 1968).

shapes in different theological traditions, Christians have usually assumed that because God is the creator of the material world and of the institutions of civilization, because God has made human beings in his image, and because God wills for humans to subdue the earth, human beings may come to know some things about the material world and about human institutions. This epistemological confidence in general knowledge about the world also entails definite assumptions about historical knowledge, for it is based precisely on what the historical records of Scripture and Christian tradition tell of God's actions and of his character, and on what we may be assumed, even in a postmodern world, to draw reliably from those records.

These Christian assertions about historical knowledge have always been a challenge to searching minds. They were "foolishness" to "the Greeks" that the Apostle Paul described in his first epistle to the Corinthians. In the eighteenth century, their scandalous audacity offended Gotthold Ephraim Lessing, who described instead an "ugly ditch" between particular historical assertions and general truths of reason.[14] They stimulated David Hume, Immanuel Kant, and a whole host of their successors to propose alternative conceptions of knowledge, truth, and the past. But they have become even more of a challenge as modern currents undercut ever more persistently the conventions that citizens of the West once entertained about our ability to know and interpret the past.

What, then, may be said from a Christian point of view about the crisis in historical knowledge? The temptation may be great to slide around the issue. Some very capable historians have taken this approach, most notably the distinguished scholar of early modern England, J. H. Hexter, who made a kind of career out of pooh-poohing thorny issues of epistemology and who employed sympathetic common sense to cut through the Gordian knots of historical uncertainty.[15]

---

14. For sound Christian analysis, see Gordon E. Michalson, *Lessing's "Ugly Ditch": A Study of Theology and History* (University Park: Pennsylvania State University Press, 1985).

15. J. H. Hexter, *Doing History* (Bloomington: Indiana University Press, 1971); and *The History Primer* (New York: Basic Books, 1971). Gordon S. Wood's recent review of Simon Schama's *Dead Certainties (Unwarranted Speculations)* is an updated version of Hexter's commonsensical defense of traditional historical practices; see *The New York Review of Books*, 27 June 1991, 12-14.

The temptation for believers to sweep the challenges under the rug, simply to preach louder, to ignore these issues in hopes they will go away, is not necessarily foolishness, for the sort of people who most readily heed the Christian message seem also to have the fewest qualms about affirming that we can know quite a bit about the past.

Nonetheless, the security provided for Christian existence by intuitive, pre-critical practice should not be an excuse for turning aside from the epistemological dilemmas of modern history. So, while recognizing the great complexity of the subject, I would like to offer a Christian response to the issues posed by the contemporary crisis in historical knowledge, and to do so, moreover, in terms posed by those who have, with telling force, exposed the dimensions of that crisis.

The plan is, first, to describe briefly three widespread and influential twentieth-century attitudes toward knowledge of the past. These attitudes — which may be called the scientific, the ideological, and the relativistic — have predominated at different times over the last century. All also are defended today.

Second, an argument will be made that a Christian perspective on knowledge can provide not only *a*, but *the best* foundation for restoring confidence in the human ability to know the past reliably. By implication, this will also be an argument that the Christian faith provides a secure foundation for acquiring reliable knowledge about many other aspects of the material world and of human interactions.

Finally, the paper moves beyond a utilitarian recommendation of Christianity for its usefulness in recovering a certain degree of confidence in historical knowledge to suggesting that, even by the reasoning of relativistic theories of knowledge, Christianity should be regarded not just as historiographically useful, but also as true.

Three Attitudes toward the Past

The first attitude was one promoted by the founders of professional history in the United States. It is the conviction that genuine knowledge of the past must be derived through verificationist procedures modeled directly on a strictly empirical conception of the physical sciences. This position may be called positivistic, scientistic, or, with greater charity, scientific. It was the embodiment among historians of the Enlightenment ideal hailed by Alexander Pope in the eighteenth century: "Nature and nature's laws lay hid in night / God said, let Newton be, and all was light." If only those who wrote about the past could do so with the impartial objectivity of a Newton, the results would be as revolutionary in history as his had been in science. Among historians, this position enjoyed some vogue in England as early as the mid-nineteenth century, especially in the work of H. T. Buckle.[16] It flourished in America from the beginning of modern university study in the 1870s through the First World War as historians routinely promoted the idea that history should be a strictly empirical science. George Burton Adams summed up this general opinion in his presidential address before the American Historical Association in 1908. The job of historians, Adams argued, was "to ascertain as nearly as possible and to record exactly what happened." Questions concerning "the philosophy of history" were wisely left to "poets, philosophers and theologians." Historians knew, Adams went on, that "at the very beginning of all conquest of the unknown lies the fact, established and classified to the fullest extent possible." Others may yield to "the allurements of speculation," but "the field of the historian is, and must long remain, the discovery and recording of what actually happened."[17]

Conservative Protestants have a special reason for looking kindly upon this conception of scientific history, for over the last generation conservative Protestant historians have worked their way back into the ranks of university students of history by adopting objective standards. At least since the 1940s, a considerable number of British and American historians of confessional or evangelical Protestant conviction — among others, Herbert Butterfield, Patrick Collinson, and Margaret Spufford in Britain; Kenneth Scott Latourette, E. Harris Harbison, Arthur Link, Lewis Spitz, Timothy Smith, Martin Marty, and George Marsden in the United States — have won recognition in the academy for their work precisely by demonstrating their skill at writing objective history. To do so, these historians have abandoned — at least while working within university precincts — the church's long tradition of providential historiography that stretches back to Constantine's Euse-

16. Breisach, *Historiography*, 274-75.
17. George Burton Adams, "History and the Philosophy of History," *American Historical Review* 14 (1909): 223, 226.

bius. In theological terms, the historians have switched over to consider historical writing as situated in the sphere of creation rather than in the sphere of grace, as a manifestation of general rather than special revelation. Put differently, Christian historians in the modern academy have made the implicit confession that history is not theology. This confession means that they construct their accounts of the past from facts ascertained through documentary or material evidence and explained in terms of natural human relationships.

Christian historians may have exploited scientific history to reenter the academy, but the burden of Christian analysis also shows manifest shortcomings in extreme statements of the scientific ideal. The perversion of scientific history lies not in its use of empirical methods, but in its shortsightedness about the process that culminates in written history. The agents of history — those who act and who witness actions, those who make and transmit records, those who attempt to reconstruct past actions on the basis of those records — are people with worldviews, biases, blindspots, and convictions. Moreover, the most important human actions — responsible choices with consequences — are the very ones most resistant to the kind of replication and control required for a strictly empirical science. In short, the positivist presupposition about historical knowledge arises out of a good thing, but a good thing carried recklessly beyond its own limits.

A second contemporary presupposition about historical knowledge is much more widely shared among both academics and nonacademics. It is the assumption that historical writing exists in order to illustrate the truth of propositions known to be true before study of the past begins. This stance may be called the ideological presupposition. It could also be called the "whig" view of history, defined over a half-century ago by Herbert Butterfield as the telling of "a story which is meant to reveal who is in the right."[18] In simplest terms, this assump-

---

18. Herbert Butterfield, *The Whig Interpretation of History* (1931; reprint, New York: W. W. Norton, 1965), 130. For an application of Butterfield's wisdom to the world of American evangelicals, see Nathan O. Hatch, "'The Clean Sea-Breeze of the Centuries': Learning to Think Historically," in Mark A. Noll, George M. Marsden, and Nathan O. Hatch, *The Search for Christian America*, enl. ed. (Colorado Springs: Helmers & Howard, 1989), 145-55. On history as the servant of ideology, see Arnaldo Momigliano, "History in an Age of Ideologies," *American Scholar* 51 (Autumn 1982): 495-507.

tion holds that written history exists to illustrate two things: first, how similar all of the past is to the present; and second, how clearly the past reveals the inevitable emergence of the present conditions which most concern the historian. Western Christians often think of Marxism as the major proponent of such an ideological view, and with some justice. In crass and not so crass forms, Marxist history has had to fit.[19]

Ideological history, however, was not invented by Karl Marx. It rather began with the ancient Greeks and Romans, and then received an especially strong boost from early Christian historians. With the spread of Christianity, the content of history changed, but the form remained the same. The most influential early church historians, Eusebius and Orosius, specified how developments in Greece, Rome, and the Middle East demonstrated God's designs for the universal spread of the church.[20] This ideological conception of history prevailed among Christians in the Middle Ages, and then in competing versions among Catholics and Protestants into the nineteenth century.[21] It is still probably the dominant perspective in many religious traditions to this day, Protestant evangelicals more than most.

In other venues, ideological history has provided the form for the national histories written during the modern period. Under the influence of various romantic movements, it flourished during the nineteenth century as an effort to find the distinctive *Geiste* of the individual European *Völker*. This approach has always been important in the self-conception of Americans. Puritans tracing the rise of God's Kingdom in the howling American wilderness, nineteenth-century historians like the famed George Bancroft describing the rise of a free and democratic society, early professional historians who expounded the belief that "Democracy is the only subject for history," modern interpreters of America as the cradle of liberating capitalism or the source of imperialistic racism — all have shared an ideological approach to the past. More recently, feminist and black perspectives have generated a great amount of work exploiting innovative historical research for substan-

19. See, for example, Gordon A. Craig, "The Other Germany," *New York Review of Books*, 25 September 1986, 62-65.

20. Breisach, *Historiography*, 45-50, 63-69, 77-78; and Charles Norris Cochrane, *Christianity and Classical Culture* (New York: Oxford University Press, 1944), 183-86.

21. A fascinating discussion of that process is A. G. Dickens and John Tonkin, *The Reformation in Historical Thought* (Cambridge: Harvard University Press, 1985).

tially predetermined conclusions. In recent years, a particularly active form of ideological history in the United States has drawn together national, Christian, and political elements. It is the view that the American nation was created by special divine providence.[22]

A third modern attitude toward historical knowledge is the unsettling undermining of historical self-confidence noted above. It assumes that we cannot in any traditional sense really know the past, that all history is a creative reconstruction of how, for whatever reason, the historian would like things to have been. The theoretical denial of the objectivity of historical knowledge enjoys a robust life in the academy. We may call it the relativistic view, a position with important, even contradictory, manifestations.

In America, an influential view of historical relativism was first expressed by Carl Becker and Charles Beard, two of America's most influential historians of the century's first decades. Becker provided the most famous exposition of these views when he addressed the American Historical Association as its president in 1931. In that speech Becker gave full expression to the conviction that circumstantial predilections determine a vision of the past. History, he said, is "an imaginative creation, a personal possession which each one of us . . . fashions out of his individual experience, adapts to his practical or emotional needs, and adorns as well as may be to suit his aesthetic tastes."[23] Beard and Becker were recalled from solipsistic applications of their position by the events of World War II. Both were appalled by the thought that historical study, as they had earlier described it, could offer no principled reasons for favoring the Allies over the Axis Powers. Yet others soon arose to pursue the trail they had blazed.

Over the last quarter-century the number of serious proposals questioning the possibility of historical knowledge in anything like its traditional sense has increased dramatically. As noted above, these are now commonplace in philosophy, literary criticism, anthropology, jurisprudence, political theory, and psychology. Among historians, one

22. That view, with examples, is examined in Noll, Marsden, and Hatch, *The Search for Christian America*.

23. Carl Becker, "Everyman His Own Historian," *American Historical Review* 37 (1932): 228; and more generally, Cushing Strout, *The Pragmatic Revolt in American History: Carl Becker and Charles Beard* (Ithaca, N.Y.: Cornell University Press, 1958).

of the most visible proponents of the view is Hayden White, whose major study, *Metahistory*, argued already in 1973 that "the historian performs an essentially *poetic* act, in which he *pre*figures the historical field and constitutes it as a domain upon which to bring to bear the specific theories he will use to explain 'what was *really* happening' in it."[24]

The central argument underlying this view is that present circumstances and present realities so thoroughly define the vision of a historian that our supposed knowledge of the past is actually an expression of the historian's own longings, self-interest, ideology, or psychology. No path exists to the past which is not a disguised tour of the present.

In extreme form, the relativistic conception is a triple offense to Christian faith. Christians hold that a realm of reality beyond the immediate sensory perception of this generation is the fundamental reality which makes possible the perception of all other realities. They believe, furthermore, that this more basic reality was manifest with unique force in events and circumstances of history. And they affirm that this reality is supernatural as well as natural, that it stems originally from God. It is hard to imagine a sharper antithesis than that between such Christian views and the extreme statement of relativistic assumptions about historical knowledge.

At the same time, more modest statements of historical relativity turn out to comport surprisingly well with basic Christian teaching. In fact, insights from the relativistic and ideological approaches to history may be even more useful for a Christian effort to defend the reliability of historical knowledge than those associated with the notion of scientific history.

A Christian Defense of Historical Knowledge

Classical orthodoxy offers a conserving strategy with which to address the epistemological crisis of historical knowledge. It holds out the assurance that there is a past, real in itself, which we may actually study

24. Hayden White, *Metahistory: The Historical Imagination in Nineteenth-Century Europe* (Baltimore: Johns Hopkins University Press, 1973), x.

and genuinely come to know. To put the matter in altogether utilitarian terms: come to Christ and regain your confidence that historical research can lead to at least a measure of genuine knowledge about the past. Faith in God, rather than confidence in the capabilities of humans as defined in the Enlightenment, enables us to reach some of the goals advanced by defenders of scientific history.

To make this claim stick, we must begin by defining the kind of Christianity we are talking about. The sort of Christian faith that is best able to restore confidence in our ability to know the past is the full-blown theism of Augustine, the Catholic mystics, the Protestant Reformers, and, closer to the Enlightenment itself, the French Catholic Nicolas Malebranche, the British Bishop George Berkeley, and the New England Congregationalist Jonathan Edwards. This sort of Christian faith affirms that God is not just the creator and passive sustainer of the world, but also that his energy is the source of the world's energy and his will the foundation of its existence.

There are different ways of describing this kind of Christian belief, but all of them stress the world's radical dependency upon God, the human mind's derivative relation to the divine mind, and the benevolent intention of God to share with humans an understanding of the reality he sustains. A summary of Malebranche's arguments, for example, speaks of his convictions concerning "man's dependence on God. It is God who creates us and conserves us from moment to moment and who alone acts on us and for us. Owing our existence and actions as well as our knowledge to God, we are truly united with him."[25] Berkeley, J. O. Urmson summarizes, "certainly thinks that the metaphysical explanation of why some ideas have coherence, liveliness and independence of our wills is because God, the infinite spirit, causes them. Thus metaphysical reality is to be explained in terms of the activity of God."[26] Jonathan Edwards put it perhaps most directly: "that which truly is the substance of all bodies is the infinitely exact and precise and perfectly stable idea in God's mind, together with his stable will that the same shall gradually be communicated to us, and to other minds, according to certain fixed and exact established methods and

25. Willis Doney, "Nicolas Malebranche," *The Encyclopedia of Philosophy*, 8 vols. (New York: Macmillan, 1967), 5:140.
26. J. O. Urmson, *Berkeley* (Oxford: Oxford University Press, 1982), 37.

laws: or in somewhat different language, the infinitely exact and precise divine idea, together with an answerable, perfectly exact, precise and stable will with respect to correspondent communications to created minds, and effects on their minds."[27]

What these ideas of God and the world share is a rejection of the deistical notion that God made the world, established its laws, created humans with certain mental capabilities to understand the world, and then stepped back to see what would happen. Since the mid-eighteenth century, Christians, no less than nonbelievers, have been enamored of this Enlightenment view of God. That view fueled a passion for arguments from design to demonstrate the existence of God, which led to increasingly frenzied efforts at demonstrating the benevolence of God over against supposedly autonomous standards of justice, which heightened concern for the apologetic value of miracles as events in which God *intervenes* in a world proceeding normally under its own inner compulsion, and which placed a great burden upon believers to justify their faith rationally with the procedures that the great scientists used to reason about nature. The historian James Turner has well described the burden this view placed on orthodox Christianity from the time of the Enlightenment: "As Newton was deified, so the temptation was great to Newtonify the Deity. If science and rationalism had raised questions about God and unsettled belief, then, what more logical response than to shore up religion by remodeling it in the image of science and rationality? Accordingly, many spokesmen of the church — theologians, ministers, lay writers — enthusiastically magnified the rationalizing tendencies already apparent within belief, increasingly conceived assurance of God as a matter of the intellect and the grounds of belief as rationally demonstrable."[28]

Against these Enlightenment conceptions of God, believers like Malebranche, Berkeley, and Edwards postulated a deity who filled the universe he had created, who activated the minds he had made in his own image, who brooded over the world with constant love as well as

27. Jonathan Edwards, "The Mind," in *The Works of Jonathan Edwards: Scientific and Philosophical Writings,* ed. Wallace E. Anderson (New Haven: Yale University Press, 1980), 344.

28. James Turner, *Without God, Without Creed: The Origins of Unbelief in America* (Baltimore: Johns Hopkins University Press, 1985), 49.

distant power. This is the sort of Christianity that can rescue historical knowledge. The rescue operation consists of several steps, each resting on central teachings of the Christian faith. Together, these steps recognize a substantial contribution from relativistic as well as from scientific ideas of history, even if they are not in the end necessarily dependent upon either, or upon the practices of ideological historians.

(1) This view of God affirms that the divine creation and sustaining of the world is the foundation for epistemological confidence of whatever sort. Humans may have hope in their efforts to understand the world, past or present, because the reality of the world external to ourselves depends ultimately upon God rather than upon ourselves. Humans may have a reasonable degree of confidence that our minds can grasp some elements of reality external to ourselves because our minds have been made in the image of God, who is responsible for that external reality. And we may trust that there is some sort of meaningful correspondence between external reality and our own internal mental capacities because we, along with external reality, all flow from a single coordinate act of divine creation and all share in the same providential maintenance.

The doctrine of creation also shows why the analogy between historical study and scientific research is a fruitful one, if the analogy is taken in a general sense. Because of creation, the historian's reliance upon the empirical data of research resembles the scientist's reliance upon empirical data. In both cases scientists and historians do their work assuming the contingency of events — that is, they believe that knowledge depends more upon an ability to perceive the event in its own development than upon deductive explanations brought to the event. Christians like Malebranche, Berkeley, and Edwards contended that researchers were able to believe in the independent reality of events and circumstances beyond themselves, and in their mind's ability to follow the course of external developments, only because they were trusting, implicitly or explicitly, in God. Malebranche, Berkeley, and Edwards affirmed comprehensive theism in part because they felt that only such a theism was capable of sustaining the unusually productive potential of science. Theirs was an idealism in service to science. Their view of God is equally reassuring for efforts to understand the past. Early modern scientists and defenders of scientific history both overstated the degree to which they could be free from pre-understandings.

Yet they also displayed a laudable confidence in the world *extra nos* because God had made it, because God sustains it, and because God opens it to humans through mental abilities that also come from his gracious hand.[29]

(2) The analogy between scientific and historical research leads to a second consideration. If a Christian doctrine of creation looks in the first instance like a warmed-over version of scientific history, it also points in relativistic directions as well. If we say that humans may be confident about obtaining true knowledge in science or history because they are confident in God's creating power, we are conceding one of the most important principles of the relativistic approach to history. This concession is that arguments about the meaning of particular historical events, conditions, or circumstances must also be arguments, however implicit, about "the nature of things" more generally. The same is true for science. For example, when scientists discuss the nature of light, they must also display commitments about the reliability of human perception, the nature of probability, the meaning of human measurements, and many other meta-empirical subjects. Similarly, for historians to argue about what "caused" the Civil War or the Cold War, or about why the relationships between men and women in Western civilization have changed over time, is also to argue for certain views of human nature, ideals of social order, the nature of evil, and whether there is a possibility for human progress. In other words, when we affirm that a belief in creation stands behind the possibility of objective knowledge, we are also confirming a major tenet of relativism, that all knowledge, whether historical or scientific, is a function of some point of view, and in that sense ideological or relativistic.

There are still other ways in which Christian teaching points to the relativity of historical knowledge. The doctrine of the Fall and the resul-

---

29. This reading of early modern science is based on Michael B. Foster, "The Christian Doctrine of Creation and the Rise of Modern Natural Science," *Mind* 43 (1934): 446-68; Daniel O'Connor and Francis Oakley, eds., *Creation: The Impact of an Idea* (New York: Charles Scribner's Sons, 1969); Charles Webster, *The Great Instauration: Science, Medicine and Reform, 1626-1660* (New York: Holmes and Meier, 1976), 493-510; and Eugene M. Klaaren, *Religious Origins of Modern Science* (Grand Rapids: Eerdmans, 1977), 185-91. For a symposium raising serious questions about Foster's effort, see Cameron Wybrow, ed., *Creation, Nature, and Political Order in the Philosophy of Michael Foster (1903-1959)* (Lewiston, Maine: Edwin Mellen Press, 1992).

tant depravity of human nature suggest that the human moral condition obscures vision, presumably for historical as well as moral reasoning. The Scriptures are replete with warnings concerning the way that idolatry or willful disobedience of the divine law makes humans "blind" or "deaf" (e.g., Isa. 6:9-10; 42:18-20; 43:8; Matt. 15:14; 23:16ff.; 2 Cor. 4:4; 2 Peter 1:9), and they describe how sinfulness "darkens understanding" (Eph. 4:18). Except in those Christian traditions that teach human perfection in this life, the skewing of perspective caused by the bent toward self characterizes the vision of believers as well as those who are not believers. Christian doctrine about the human condition, in others words, calls into question the ability to understand the past without distortion.

There are, however, more positive Christian teachings that also lead to the conviction that God intends historical understanding to be relative to specific times, places, and circumstances. These teachings have to do with the dignity of particularities, with the awareness that God made humans in such a way that they could benefit from particular adaptation to particular cultural circumstances.[30] The story in the first chapters of Genesis about God's assignment to humans of stewardship for the earth certainly implies divine sanction for the particular adaptation to different landscapes, climates, and cultures that such a stewardship requires. And whatever one makes of the historical or moral implications of the Tower of Babel, it is clear that God ordained the multiplicity of human languages, with the consequent particularities of cultural understanding that the diversity of tongues entails. Again, these teachings indicate that, while we have come relatively late to consider the different perspectives created by differing cultural circumstances, it was God's determinate will that ordained those varying circumstances.

In addition, the Incarnation and the outworking of redemption in the particular culture of first-century Judaism suggests something — if only a dim shape within a mystery — about the dignity of human actions and perspective rooted in very specific historical circumstances.

---

30. On these points the missiologists Lamin Sanneh and Andrew Walls are superb. See, for example, Lamin Sanneh, *Translating the Message: The Missionary Impact on Culture* (Maryknoll, N.Y.: Orbis, 1989); Sanneh, "Gospel and Culture: Ramifying Effects of Scriptural Translation," in *Bible Translation and the Spread of the Church*, ed. Philip C. Stine (Leiden: E. J. Brill, 1990); and Andrew Walls, *The Missionary Movement in Christian History: Studies in the Transmission of Faith* (Maryknoll, N.Y.: Orbis, 1996).

If God accomplished redemption for humanity "when Cyrenius was governor of Syria" and "under Pontius Pilate," is not God also fully affirming the value of other particular sets of cultural circumstances? Christians traditionally have affirmed — and rightly so — the universal meaning for all people everywhere of those saving acts in first-century Judea under Roman rule on the edge of Hellenistic civilization. But could Christians not also confess that the cultural particularity of redemption affirms the appropriateness of cultural particularity? If so, the conclusion would have to follow that those who lived "when Ghengis Khan was governor of Mongolia" or "under President McKinley" — and who experienced the world from the particular cultural perspective of those times and places — would be fully justified in doing so because of the way that God himself had dignified the perspective of first-century, Judaic Palestine. On the basis of such reasoning, the writing of history from the point of view of a particular culture becomes not only inescapable, but also divinely ordained and good. Relativism, in other words, has a divine sanction.

(3) But, next, this kind of Christian relativism must not be mistaken for skepticism about historical knowledge or considered as support for nihilistic conclusions about the possibility of knowing the past. To race incautiously from this kind of Christian relativism — and perhaps from other forms of modest relativism as well — to skeptical or radically historicist conclusions is unnecessary. If we admit that our knowledge about the past (or about the world in general) is relative to our points of view, our characters, our particular perspectives, we are not necessarily saying that we are condemned to a merely imaginative grasp of the past. The Christian reason for this assertion includes doctrines concerning the unity of humanity and concerning humanity as the image-bearer of God.

The unity of human nature is built into the foundation of Christian teaching. In particular, it is the predicate of redemption: "As in Adam all die, so also in Christ shall all be made alive" (1 Cor. 15:22). For historiographical purposes, this Christian teaching means that all humans must be alike — not just in their moral nature, but also in their propensity to write about the past from within the perspective of their own particular cultures. That is, the relativity of historical understanding that arises from diverse perspectives, frameworks, and cultures is kept from historiographical solipsism by the fact that a common human nature underlies the production of different views of the past. Humans will conclude different things about the past, but the fact that all humans share God-given qualities of conscience, intellectual potential, and social capability means that differing views of the past will not differ absolutely. The differing conditions of human cultures mean that histories will never be the same; the commonalities of human nature mean that histories will never be absolutely antithetical.

As it happens, this extrapolation of Christian teaching fits fairly well with the logic of historical relativism. If all history is relative, due to the placement of the historian within the historian's own times, it must then follow that it is universally true that people write about the past in terms of their own present circumstances. And if this is true, then historical relativism yields one nonrelative reality: viz., all people write history the same way. If we put this in different words, we are led by relativistic arguments themselves to consider a second Christian doctrine that brightens the picture of historical relativism. Relativist views of historical knowledge depend upon the positive assertion that all humans in every time and every place construe the past relative to their own circumstances — that is, that humans are active and creative in similar ways as they draw meaning from their examination of the past. This assertion about what humans *do* variously assumes something about what humans *are* uniformly: agents who imaginatively create a mental picture of the world that they inhabit.

Such reasoning leads naturally to the Christian doctrine that humans are made in the image of God. Many of the traits and attributes that characterize God also characterize human beings. Such teaching is a constant in all Christian traditions, as is also the qualification that the image of God in humans is limited by our finiteness and distorted by our sin. But the positive statement of the doctrine is that human actions and human states of mind bear a resemblance to divine actions and divine states of mind. With this doctrine, and observing the imaginative energy that humans display in describing the past, we may conclude

---

31. The work of Dorothy L. Sayers offers several ways of formulating this assertion. Sayers's own account of how humans create in imitation of God (*The Mind of the Maker* [1941; reprint, San Francisco: Harper & Row, 1979]) is probably less helpful than her biographer's account of Sayers's own practice as a writer; see Barbara Reynolds, *Dorothy L. Sayers: Her Life and Soul* (London: Hodder & Stoughton, 1993), 307-40.

not that humans are *creative* in understanding the past, but that they are *re-creative*.[31]

The suggestion that people are and should be active re-creators of the past fits especially well with the full-blown theism of the Christian philosophers mentioned above: Malebranche, Berkeley, and Edwards. Their view was that the world, with all its regularities of physical nature and human society, continues to exist because God *thinks* it into existence moment by moment. These Christian philosophers were idealists, or tended in an idealist direction. The world simply is an extension of the mind of God. From that perspective, the element of human creativity in describing and evaluating the past becomes a creativity that explicitly imitates the divine creativity in sustaining the world. The human activity of re-creating the past images the divine activity that constantly engenders the world.

In trying to show how Christian doctrine supports confidence in our ability to know the past, but that it does so in ways closer in form to the principles of relativistic history than to scientific history, I have raced rapidly past far too many complicated and important questions. I have offered merely a sketch that has not even touched upon what might be called anomalies in the Christian paradigm, specifically the problem of evil and the nature of human free will.[32] But even from such a superficial and incomplete outline, perhaps it may be clear why it is possible to say that, from a Christian angle of vision, we are able to reach the scientific goal of reliable knowledge about the past only by embracing principles from the relativist depiction of historical knowledge.

In summary, from the perspective of the great Christian idealists of the eighteenth century, the correspondence theory of historical knowledge — the theory that the written product of research can correspond to the actual experience of what happened — is valid because of the correspondence God has ordained between our minds, the divine mind, and what God has caused to exist.

Next, we may progress in our understanding of the past not if we

---

32. The totalistic theism of Malebranche, Berkeley, and Edwards has special difficulty in accounting for God being able both to will and not will evil. Especially Jonathan Edwards' assertion that "free will" means the liberty to follow the last dictate of the inner self does not fully account for the persistent sense we retain of facing certain decisions as if, at least in part, the outcome depends upon our autonomous choice.

are confident in human autonomy (like the great proponents of scientific history), but if we celebrate our dependence upon God.

Then we may say we have objective knowledge about the past only because our knowledge is relative — relative to our circumstances, relative to our nature, and relative to God.

Last, we can reach toward a true picture of the past, not because we have abstracted ourselves from the influence of cultural bias, but because we embrace wholeheartedly the particularity of cultural situations.

(4) Finally, however, it is valuable to rehearse Christian reasons for why our knowledge of the past will never be entirely correct, fully true, or completely satisfactory. We might think that if historical knowledge depends upon the person and work of God, we would have the highest confidence in obtaining a perfectly true picture of the past. All that is necessary is to seek the divine perspective. But it is precisely Christian revelation that describes the effort to obtain the divine perspective as grossest idolatry and the source of profoundest evil. The height of foolishness is to confuse the tasks of creator and creature (Rom. 1). Humans are creatures, not the creator. As such we will always be limited by our finitude from seeing the whole picture. We will always be predisposed by our fallenness to misconstrue the results of historical inquiry for our own idolatrous satisfaction. We will always be trading the advantages that come from living in the God-ordained particularities of our own cultures for the blindness that comes from being unable to see what is so obvious to those who gaze upon the past from other frames of reference.

Historian Bruce Kuklick once helpfully illuminated the question of the historian's self-perception by arguing that many historians see themselves in the position of "ideal observers" — that is, individuals who through research make themselves nearly omniscient about particular historical episodes and who may then consider their evaluative reactions to be the normative reactions that all humans would experience if they too had carried out the investigation. However productive this self-portrait may be, Kuklick was quick to see its limits. As he put it, "Making an evaluation consists in part in *attempting* to put ourselves into a position of an ideal observer. Because this is ultimately impossible, however, there may be . . . disagreement about what is right or wrong. . . . [W]e have no guarantee that our reactions are similar to [others'] and thereby allow us to decide correctly. . . . [T]he conclusive answer to any evaluative question always eludes us and our evaluations will always be insecure. Men, in short, are only *like* God." But from his point of view as one examining the behavior of historians, Kuklick did not consider our inability to *be* God "a serious shortcoming."[33] There is still much of value to be discovered about the past through our efforts to act as though we could be ideal observers.

In Christian terms: We do see, but through a glass, darkly.

The historiographical conclusion, then, is that Christian teaching offers a solution to the crisis of historical knowledge, and indeed of scientific and other kinds of knowledge. The nature of the solution is to propose that we can have reliable knowledge and real understanding of the past, but that this knowledge and understanding must be modest. Christian teaching does not warrant the belief that we can obtain full and complete understanding, but it does provide reasons for a chastened realism about our grasp of history and indeed for other areas of research.

Relativist Arguments for the Objective Truth of Christianity

But this statement cannot really be the conclusion, for we must now ask — Is Christianity itself true? Christianity of the sort I have proposed may provide a theoretical defense for a modest realism, but that defense is of little consequence if Christianity itself is not true. Or at best such an argument might provide a bit of parochial reassurance for those already committed to faith, but will mean absolutely nothing to those who consider Christianity passé, outmoded, or false.

But how, if we have acknowledged that Christianity does not support naively objectivist modes of demonstration, can we recommend Christianity as true? One answer is to assert that an apology for Christianity must begin where our knowledge of the past begins, with understanding relative to our own perspectives. This strategy poses no

33. Bruce Kuklick, "The Mind of the Historian," *History and Theory* 8 (1969): 329.

difficulty for the religion of the Bible, since we read repeatedly in Scripture that the ability to rest in the truth of God depends upon a willingness to align our vision with the truth proposed. The Scriptures talk of a faith confirmed by experiencing it: "Taste and see that the Lord is good! Happy is the one who takes refuge in him!" (Ps. 34:8). They are frankly perspectivalist: "Whoever would draw near to God must believe that he exists and that he rewards those who seek him" (Heb. 11:6). They stress that even the ability to believe rests upon God's actions in changing the orientation of perspectives. In the words of Jesus, only when God alters our framework of reference are we then eager to come to God: "All that the Father gives me will come to me; and him who comes to me I will not cast out" (John 6:37). There is thus no Christian reason for expecting an apology for Christianity to fit the Enlightenment ideal of objective, scientific proof.

To be sure, believers and nonbelievers continue to share a common humanity, and that common humanity allows for a great deal of argument of the sort the Apostle Paul pursued on his missionary journeys and that other apologists have also advanced effectively. Yet the larger reality is that Christianity itself seems to suggest that the weight of value-neutral persuasion is slight. Instead, the faith seems to teach that if a person's perspective is defined by fixation upon the self, that person simply will not see why it is good to turn to God.

But what then is left for a believer to say to a nonbeliever who might be willing to concede that a Christian frame of reference offers a response to crises of historical knowledge, at least if one is a Christian? As it turns out, quite a bit may be said.

In biblical terms, the recognition that it is God who brings about belief is the source not of despair, but of hope. To recognize that my perspective is turned away from God, that I deny God, is to recognize that I am now numbered among those who are lost unless God draws them to himself. But this is not such a bad place to be in. So long as I think I have the capacity within myself to alter my own frame of reference by myself, I cannot be one whom God is changing to love and enjoy himself. When I come to see that only God can reorient my perspective away from lesser realities to supreme realities, then I am in a position to be drawn by God into his love. Only when I realize how bound I am by the particularities of my own experience can I come to sense how the particularities of the Incarnation open up a way of truth and love.

An apology for Christianity can also use the language of relativism.[34] Why become a Christian? Because of anomalies within other paradigms. To be sure, a person will not be able to experience the satisfactions of the Christian paradigm until that person undergoes a revolution, a gestalt shift from a paradigm defined by the centrality of the self to one defined by the centrality of God. But since all humans experience life within paradigmatic frameworks, we may confidently expect some common experiences to be present in all paradigms, however differently they are perceived. Within some paradigms the anomalies of historical knowledge when construed scientifically, relativistically, or ideologically may be enough to precipitate a personal revolution that leads to embracing a Christian paradigm and its confidence in reasonably secure knowledge of the past. But even for those who might find historiographical anomalies an occasion for embracing the Christian paradigm, there will be other anomalous experiences. Those anomalies will be shared by all humans who do not love and enjoy God, regardless of their interest in history. Of all such possible anomalies, the one that will recur with the greatest frequency and cause the greatest disquiet is the sense of beauty, truth, clarity, goodness, and holiness that is given to all men and women to glimpse, whatever their frames of reference and however obscurely, in the face of Jesus Christ.

34. An exquisite, though difficult, example of such an apology, which employs different, and much more learned, arguments than this chapter is John Milbank, *Theology and Social Theory: Beyond Secular Reason* (Cambridge, Mass.: Blackwell, 1991).

On Critical History

BRUCE KUKLICK

A T THE end of the nineteenth century there was a revolution in the way reflective Americans came to understand the world. Instead of serving as an assumption underlying one's knowledge, Protestant theism itself became a subject for study and analysis. This revolution was wide and deep. Theology virtually vanished as a discipline, ultimately to be replaced by religious studies. Philosophy ceased to provide intellectual support for religion, and eventually philosophical techniques were used to undercut old-time creeds. Historians and social scientists distanced themselves from the categories of the sacred: they began to study the supernatural as it manifested struggles for power, worldly perquisites, and psychic gratification.

This was surely not a phenomenon limited to the United States. Although religious matters other than Protestant theism were often at issue, the secular impulses one sees, for example, in John Dewey can also be found in Sir James Frazer, Max Weber, Sigmund Freud, and Emile Durkheim. The transition was not easy to make. Many ostensibly secular scholars imbued some dimension of their nonreligious beliefs with a sacred quality. Some, for example, gave to the humanities or to scientific method an eternal value that had previously been more openly and more sensibly attached to religion proper. Numerous academics had a thin surrogate for genuine faith — an unimpressive moralism puffed up with a vague spirituality. This tepid faith, indeed, was closely related to the explicit theological creeds of many religious liberals who also found the confrontation with modernism uncomfortable.

This appraisal is unsympathetic. Scholarly humanists, secularizing academics, and religious liberals forsook deep and important beliefs. From a psychological standpoint they could only be expected to find some sort of substitute, to rest for a while at a halfway house. We should give them the benefit of the doubt, just as we should take believers seriously. The former forswore the faith of their fathers not mainly because it was fashionable to do so or because they were thoughtless or because of peer pressure; but mainly because they no longer found religious beliefs credible. I myself don't like the nonreligious gentility that replaced religion in some quarters for a time in the 1880-1920 period, but we should understand it as perhaps necessary when we consider what was rejected.

It needs to be emphasized that the perceived *falsity* of the beliefs was a significant aspect of the revolution. Some religiously committed historians have found it comforting to suggest that we need not confront the empirical inadequacy of the Christian belief system in explaining "the secularization of the academy" but rather look at the causal factors at work in the early twentieth-century institutional life of the professoriate.[1] This sort of reduction of the intellectual to the social, so common to contemporary social history, is itself dubious. But it seems to me particularly dangerous for believing historians to engage in. This reductionism certainly can be used to show that secular ideas have their roots in a certain social milieu, but reductionism is a much more powerful weapon in the hands of secularists themselves. The religiously committed are legitimating a mode of analysis that is not a friend to them — somewhat like theologians at the end of the nineteenth century adopting certain liberal, modernist notions.

The collapse of religion, whatever its causes, was not empowering or ennobling. In many ways the collapse was disturbing and has carried with it many troubling consequences aside from, let's say, the decentering of the college curriculum. But one does not have to be a secular humanist or politically correct at least to feel uncomfortable about alternatives to this revolution. Even conservatives do not engage in a professorial nostalgia that would again place Congregationalist Protestantism at the forefront of higher education. Here we get at the nub of

1. See George M. Marsden and Bradley J. Longfield, eds., *The Secularization of the Academy* (New York: Oxford University Press, 1992).

the problem: the difficult place of the believer in higher education in general and in history in particular. If one thinks some religious beliefs are true and have a role in higher education, then we need to be told how they ought to be reflected in the university.

I think that these beliefs are false, and that it would be pernicious to put Protestantism, or even the common religious heritage of Judaeo-Christianity, back into the university. This would be an authentic step backward. I share, however, my Christian colleagues' concern with the intolerance of secular liberalism and its cousin, postmodernism. They have not delivered a creed to live by, and I'm troubled that there is *no* creed to live by. But none of these troubles can persuade me to believe what I think is not true. If believers are right, I can only wish that their God were a little less inscrutable so that his reasons for denying belief to so many reflective people in the West for the past one hundred years would be slightly less obscure.

These problems are especially acute for the committed Christian historian. And here it is appropriate to do a reprise on the meaning of the higher criticism of the Bible that was coterminous with the revolution I have just described. Scholars came to treat the Bible as they would treat any other book. In analyzing it *literarily,* they had an obligation to figure out if Moses did indeed write the Old Testament's first five books as many people asserted that he did. Whatever claims authority or tradition or convention made about Mosaic authorship, the learned were educated to use the best scholarly tools at their disposal and their reasoning powers to see if these claims held water. Since the Pentateuch itself spoke of the death of Moses, it strained credulity to assume he wrote it: there was something wrong with the view that someone could be the author of a text in which his death was proclaimed.

In analyzing the *truth* of Bible narratives, scholars came to be rightfully skeptical of the virgin birth, Jesus' feeding of the multitudes, and the resurrection. They did not believe that miracles occurred in their own culture, and what was possible in their experience became the criterion for what might occur in all possible experience. Scholars did not attack the integrity of the biblical authors — they may have believed in miracles. Indeed, higher critics made an effort to understand these authors in the context of their own time, perhaps to empathize with their prescientific ideas or their concessions to ancient local prejudice. For a full explanation scholars also needed perhaps to conjecture on what was really going on when, say, the resurrection was described. Maybe Jesus was still alive after he came down from the cross. Maybe he was dead but the body was stolen.

The fundamental assumption of higher criticism was that what occurred in the past was not radically dissimilar from what occurred in the present. What investigators believed could possibly happen in the contemporary period was a measure of what was acceptable as what could have happened in the past — no matter what the Bible or other venerated sources told us. The garden variety Western religious commitments that were being examined all postulated divine intervention in nature — the supernatural — and that was considered impossible in the present and so unacceptable as an explanation in the past. The principle that emerged in higher criticism was thus incompatible with traditional religious belief.

The higher criticism of the Bible was fundamental in reordering the worldview of twentieth-century thinkers, more crucial I think than Darwin. For what was at stake in higher criticism was what Van A. Harvey has called differences in the morality of the historian (or scholar) in contrast to the believer.[2] As an historian — and more significantly in every aspect of my experience — my duty is to establish the grounds of my beliefs not on what I wish or hope for; not on what I have learned from various authorities; but on what can be best established as true. The will to truth became primary.

In the philosophy of history, the enterprise of higher criticism came to fruition in F. H. Bradley's still stunning work of 1874, *The Presuppositions of Critical History*.[3] Bradley effectively unpacked the meaning of the phrases written above — "best scholarly tools at our disposal" and "our reasoning powers" — to lay out the criterion that historians must use in determining what beliefs about the past can be sound. Bradley said we examined the past and tried to figure out what was true of it in terms of our best sense of what would pass muster in the present. Contemporary authority — our own experience of the way the world worked, the prized truths of scientific investigation today —

2. Van A. Harvey, *The Historian and the Believer: The Morality of Historical Knowledge and Christian Belief* (New York: Macmillan, 1966).

3. Reprinted in Bradley, *Collected Essays* (Oxford: Clarendon Press, 1935), 1:1-70.

was the background to our analyis of the past. If we would not believe something today, we would not believe it for the past. We would not accept a story of the virgin birth today; we rule the supernatural out of the past. One reason that history is rewritten is that our sense of what is contemporarily acceptable changes as time goes on — the contemporary becomes the past; the present brings new authority to bear on what has transpired. Because our criterion of what makes for sound belief alters, our beliefs about the past change too.

In this sense it is a mistake to focus on the animus of historical criticism against traditional Christianity. For higher criticism was not a set of antireligious conclusions, or any substantive conclusions. It was rather the coming to clear consciousness of the way we reason (at least since the Reformation). The substance of belief changes and so too do the warrants we use in establishing belief. But for thinkers like Bradley, what could not change was the presuppositions — the *a priori* facts — that guided our thinking. These presuppositions brought the past to the bar of present conceptions of believability; they marked out determination to make what we credited about the past conform to what was appropriate in the present.

It may be true that Bradley's set of notions is in fact merely a limited "worldview" — a constellation of commitments that have a historical locus and that can be placed in an appropriate historical context. But the fact remains that it is *our* worldview and that we cannot think it away: we refuse to believe what is not believable to us. The Bradleyan notions are merely the spelling out of this presumption.

In their work, all professional historians have effectively accepted the Bradleyan notions — hereafter the critical conception of history. Bradley's ideas are at the core of history as a humanistic pursuit today — for secular liberals, for postmodernists, and for Christians. For Christian scholars it has been a pact with the devil necessary for them to have any credit in the scholarly community, and it has brought about bad faith. On the one hand, Christian scholars must, at bottom, reject the secularism that the critical conception now entails. Yet, on the other, they will get themselves laughed out of the profession unless they adopt a vision of history that they do not believe. They think that their convictions lend some special insight into the study of the past — for them history is, after all, in some measure the revelation of the divine and the eschaton is part of it. But how are Christians to show this?

How can they show how God peeps through in history? If Christian convictions lend no such insight, if they are not cashed out, they are worthless.

My notion of the decline of Edwardseanism may differ from that of a committed Christian historian. Each of us, however, will disallow an explanation that sees in the decline God's irritation at Congregationalists as opposed to Presbyterians — although this may be what the Christian truly believes. Christian historians really reject the position of critical history yet simultaneously argue as if it were true. Mark Noll has written that professional writing benefits from "a fiction" of religious neutrality. Yet he also writes that, in the study of the Bible, the book is "truth-telling" in "a cognitive, propositional, factual sense." This is bad faith.[4]

Some may want to suggest that we all get our biases on the table and learn to respect or disrespect them equally. After all, has not postmodernism shown the futility of the objective, disinterested observer-scholar? Should not we all own up to our prejudices, and then (a corollary of postmodernism?) spokespeople for different biases in the academy — or perhaps all the biased scholars — might be permitted to advocate the social, political, cultural, or religious ideas to which their biases lead. This strategy may seem appealing because of the great popularity of what I would call *perspectivalism* in the humanities today, a close kinsperson of postmodernism. The argument goes, as I have suggested, that the critical position emerged in a certain era — it has a history; it represents a peculiar *Weltanschauung*. Ultimately, however, competing worldviews are incommensurable and reflect incompatible ways of seeing the world, or even of talking about seeing a world. Christians — as well as perhaps feminists, Afrocentrists, gays and lesbians — may have insights that are irreducible to those of others, and experience has shown us that there is no rational way to adjudicate among such *Weltanschauungen*. The critical conception is only one of many webs of belief. It can be associated with a certain class of people with certain political and social commitments, and it has been just as effective (or ineffective) in grounding commitments as Christianity. Indeed, it is having trouble in maintaining what authority it has in the

4. Mark Noll, *Between Faith and Criticism: Evangelicals, Scholarship, and the Bible in America*, 2nd ed. (Grand Rapids: Baker Book House, 1991), 6-7.

contemporary world. Some feminists, for example, urge that it is a masculine form of reasoning.[5]

It must first be noted that these ideas were not invented in the aftermath of the 1960s. In an age that has forgotten the classics, it is useful to recall that the Sophists challenged Plato on these very grounds, most notably in the *Republic* and *Protagoras*. More systematically, since the time of Kant thinkers have worried about the role of the human subject in constituting knowledge and the way in which interests or relationships of power may (or even must) compromise belief. Perspectivalism is hardly new, nor is its point trivial even if literary critics now find it easy to teach the position to sophomores. C. I. Lewis, arguably the most influential American philosopher of this century, called himself a conceptual pragmatist. He contended that establishing claims to knowledge was akin to building an Empire State building out of toothpicks, "most of which we haven't got and cannot be given."[6] I am very fond of Lewis as a thinker and share his only modest hope of what cautious and careful inquiry can obtain.

Whatever the difficulties in gaining knowledge, perspectivalism as an option falls of its own weight. Its defenders never simply enunciate their position and say, "Well, there are other equally good alternatives." Instead, as positivist historian Lee Benson has repeatedly said, "Scratch a relativist and you find an objectivist."[7] In Alasdair MacIntyre's *Three Rival Versions of Moral Enquiry: Encyclopaedia, Genealogy and Tradition*, the author initially elaborates three irreconcilable views. But then one of them, it turns out, can suitably explain deficiencies in the others.[8] Surprise! The more inclusive perspective is the one to which MacIntyre adheres. Thomas Kuhn's landmark text does not end by saying that we cannot adjudicate among different scientific paradigms. He rather concludes that increasing human knowledge is mysterious fact and asks why paradigm change "invariably produce[s] an instrument more perfect in any sense than those

---

5. I draw this conclusion from Carol Gilligan's *In a Different Voice: Psychological Theory and Women's Development* (Cambridge: Harvard University Press, 1982).

6. C. I. Lewis, *An Analysis of Knowledge and Valuation* (LaSalle, Ill.: Open Court, 1946), 264.

7. In conversation, many times.

8. Alasdair MacIntyre, *Three Rival Versions of Moral Enquiry: Encyclopaedia, Genealogy and Tradition* (Notre Dame: University of Notre Dame Press, 1990).

known before."[9] Even Richard Rorty, who is not a sophomore perspectivalist, cannot muster much of an argument against the view that his own ideas are correct; and he gets irritated at "mindless defensive reflexes" and charges that have "no weight."[10] When he says that socialization goes all the way down, what does he mean?[11] What does his own position allow him to signify by these phrases?

Perspectivalists of various stripes believe that their views are true, or at least more adequate than those of others, and they try to persuade us of that fact. How do they do this?

Well, in historical studies they argue and use the modes of reasoning that have come to dominate the profession of historical research — they adopt the critical conception. The religiously inclined attempt to demonstrate that biases exist in supposed neutral learning, that there is discrimination against certain kinds of historical scholarship, that particular religious ideas do not get a fair hearing. The disciplines that comprise historical inquiry postulate a dispassionate forum where independent critics can all theoretically get a hearing. This forum is compromised in various ways, and surely its norms are honored more in the breach than in the observance. But even to make the intelligible claim that the academy is a Tower of Babel requires a *lingua franca*.

It is puzzling to me why perspectivalism is attractive to those with religious commitments. First, the biases of the religious concern the supernatural; they are different from the natural biases of everybody else, and we should not lose sight of that cleavage. For orthodox Christians to do so leads at once to theological liberalism. Second, the religiously committed believe explicitly in truth; they do not begin from the conceptually dubious starting point of the perspectivalist. Their adherence to this ideal seems an act of desperation at odds with their fundamental ideas. Third, true perspectivalists are not interested in preserving a place for religion; many of those who see language as the

9. Thomas Kuhn, *The Structure of Scientific Revolutions*, 2nd ed. (Chicago: University of Chicago Press, 1970), 173.

10. Richard Rorty, *Philosophy and the Mirror of Nature* (Princeton: Princeton University Press, 1979), 13; see also, crucially, Rorty's introduction to *Consequences of Pragmatism: Essays, 1972-1980* (Minneapolis: University of Minnesota Press, 1982), xliii-xliv.

11. For Rorty's recent thoughts, see "Towards a Liberal Utopia: An Interview with Richard Rorty," *Times Literary Supplement*, 24 June 1994, 14.

only reality simply refuse to talk to believers.[12] Finally, the commitments of most late twentieth-century perspectivalists — feminists, gays and lesbians, and multiculturalists — are morally repugnant to the would-be religious — mainly Christian — perspectivalist.

My puzzlement aside, I find that the attitude of some Christian historians is a mistake. Their position is not as weak intellectually as they fear it might be.

F. H. Bradley was not a conventional Christian, but he did not draw antireligious conclusions from his critical philosophy of history. Bradley was a philosophical idealist, the most significant Anglo-Hegelian metaphysician of the nineteenth century. Mind for him was an inescapable aspect of the world, its formative, shaping dimension; it constituted reality. Without mind, no world.

How did we know truths about this mind-infected world? Well, Bradley was something of a skeptic. All human thought was prone to error, confusion, and self-contradiction. We could never figure out *how* our ideas corresponded to their objects. The relationship was beyond our grasp, yet we knew *that* our judgments and nature were purposively linked.

Bradley was a metaphysician concerned about the nature of reality, and so for him historical understanding was a more specific dimension of our more general understanding of the real. Skepticism also applied to the past. In arguing that present frameworks must be used in the reconstruction of the past, Bradley also implied that the *advance* of knowledge in the present and future would also improve our understanding of the past. The progress of contemporary knowledge went hand in hand with progress in knowledge of the past. So historical knowledge evolved in a somewhat linear fashion, and Bradley believed it could comprehend its object. We might be able to know the truth about the past. But — a touch of skepticism — this could not occur in finite time and how it would happen was unintelligible to our intellects.

What Bradley was getting at is, I believe, something like this. Human beings do — even must — think in historical terms. History is of the nature of stories, of narrative. We inevitably construe our lives and that of our culture and that of others in such terms. Now, stories have a *point*, and we cannot conceive that history doesn't have a point,

12. See, e.g., Rorty, "Utopia," 14.

an aim. If all intelligent life were destroyed today forever — if history were to end — we would probably conceive its end as the conclusion to a failed enterprise; but we cannot not conceive its end. Stories imply a storyteller who stands outside the story and for whom the story has some meaning or other. Historians are, of course, human storytellers, but even supposing that the business of human history writing is over implies that a consciousness grasps that it is over. So historicity is not just a mandatory category of human understanding, but also implies a greater-than-human consciousness.

Our necessary ways of thinking about history suggest that if we ponder the human story at all, it must have a directionality that is grasped by a consciousness. But how this occurs, Bradley emphasizes, is beyond our ability to comprehend. Our reasoning powers are not the shipwreck of understanding, but our brains simply get lost when we try to press any farther. How different is this incomprehensibility from a belief in the undecipherable will of God in history that Christians ask us ultimately to take on faith? For the faithful, salvific religion is the *how* of the way our stories relate to the end — the aim or the finish — of history.

There is something nonrational in allowing that we have to think this way and yet urging that such thinking is wrong, an illusion. If story-like thinking is part of the furniture of the mind, if we reinstate it even in denying it, how can it be false? What we rather have is a puzzle or, better, a mystery of some large significance. We are required to think about ourselves historically but can't fully understand what is involved in such thinking.[13]

*   *   *

The common religious commitments that American academics have are false. They represent a failure of nerve, as I believe do the quasi-religious views of people in religious studies and comparative religion. Also unimpressive is the bad faith of Protestant evangelical scholars — the adherence to the critical position and the undercover complaints

---

13. Bradley's metaphysical system was elaborated in *Appearance and Reality* (London: S. Sonnenschein & Co., 1893); a companion piece is J. M. E. McTaggart, "The Unreality of Time," *Mind* 17 (1908): 457-74.

about it. I also think that the critical position rules out supernatural modes of historical explanation. Yet it is a mistake to infer that the critical position entails disbelief in religion. I am not myself religious, but the historical enterprise may not be a friend to atheism. There is something about history that makes me uncomfortable with unbelief. I would encourage religiously oriented historians to reflect on these issues in a more systematic way. I believe they can make a more persuasive, if not compelling, set of arguments for their views.

Advocacy and Academe

MURRAY G. MURPHEY

T HE university has traditionally been thought of as an institution whose raison d'être is the creation and dissemination of knowledge. It may be granted that this characterization does not apply to all institutions which call themselves "universities"; some are avowedly sectarian and make no secret of the fact that they seek to propagate a partisan view. But such sectarian institutions have been the exception in the United States in this century, and certainly the dominant view — the view upon which tax exemptions and such other modest benefits that universities enjoy is based — is that the university's goal is knowledge. Knowledge consists of beliefs that are true, or at least which can be asserted to be true with high probability on the basis of evidence. It is distinguished from opinion on precisely this basis — that it is true, or more probably true than any known alternative. The assumption has been that truth is nonpartisan, that rather than truth conforming to partisan views, it is partisan views that should conform to the truth.

Yet in recent years the universities have been besieged by groups which claim that their "unique perspectives" should be taught as a part of the curriculum. Feminists, gays and lesbians, racial groups, ethnic groups, religious groups — all now clamor for their special views to be included. No one can deny that in the past the histories and problems of these groups have not received adequate attention, and that is a failing which should be corrected since earlier studies were seriously incomplete. But that is not what the controversy is about; the assertion by these groups is rather that they have a special "perspective" on society and the world which has an equal, or superior, claim to be taught as any form of traditional knowledge. To the counterassertion that these "perspectives" are not knowledge, their answer is that there is no such thing as a true theory, that every theory is in fact an advocacy of the interests of some group, and that therefore every group should have an equal right to advocate its perspective through the curriculum of the university.

Such claims, if true, challenge what has been thought to be the fundamental mission of the university. Should they be granted, the university would become a bedlam in which the fantasies of every partisan would have to be given equal airing. The result would be a din in which the very concept of learning would become questionable, for in bedlam, what can be said to be "learned," and upon what basis? But even to ask if such claims are "true" seems self-contradictory, for if no theory is true, what does it mean to say these claims are true? One might think that if there is no knowledge — only the sociology of knowledge — then at least the sociological theory of knowledge must be asserted to be true, yet that very assertion lands these claims in an inconsistency. Such logical problems do not seem to bother the partisans of these perspectives, but they should bother us. I will therefore in this paper deal with the claims of one of these groups in the hope that by doing so the underlying difficulties of this sort of relativism may be exposed.

In a recent book, George Marsden has attacked the exclusion of religious perspectives from the twentieth-century university in the following terms:

> Few academics believed in neutral objective science any more and most would admit that everyone's intellectual inquiry takes place in a framework of communities that shape prior commitments. Such prior commitments might be arrived at on formal religious grounds or in some more informal way, but they were prior commitments nonetheless. Hence there is little reason to exclude a priori all religiously based claims on the grounds that they are unscientific.[1]

This does not lead Marsden to an embrace of postmodernism, since he condemns the postmodernists for being just as naturalistic as the ad-

---

1. George Marsden, *The Soul of the American University* (New York: Oxford University Press, 1994), 430.

herents of science. But it does lead him to conclude that, since science is merely one perspective among many, religious perspectives should now be given equal attention in the university.

There is a peculiar irony to this embrace of skeptical attacks on science. Anthropologists and historians have established beyond any reasonable doubt that different societies, both in the past and in the present, have held or hold widely different systems of belief. These systems of belief may be all embracing or they may deal with only a limited range of subjects, but they are fundamental components of the cultures into which human beings are socialized. We are all undeniably children of particular times and places, and unquestionably our thinking does embody premises drawn from our parent cultures, whether we are aware of that or not. From these platitudes, the conclusion has been drawn by some that all systems of belief are relative to the particular historical and cultural context in which they were born, and that therefore they can have no validity beyond those special circumstances. Indeed, many would hold that they are wholly arbitrary, since it is claimed that even within the particular situation which spawned it, any given worldview could have been replaced by a rival one which would have had an equal claim to acceptance. This form of relativism has been extended even to science, so that according to this view a scientific theory is merely a particular perspective which, for a brief interval in time and space, happens to win acceptance.

What is ironic about Christian adoption of this view is that it can obviously be applied to undercut the truth claims of Christianity itself. And it is surely clear that Christianity does make truth claims. When Augustine wrote "O Truth, Truth! how inwardly even then did the marrow of my soul pant after Thee,"[2] he was not describing a post-modern search for some community consensus but a quest to know reality as it is. In a more modern vein, fundamentalist claims that the Bible is "inerrant" surely involve the claim that the statements of the Bible are true.[3] Indeed, it is hard to imagine any committed Christian who would not claim that Christianity is true. Skepticism does not fit

2. St. Augustine, *The Confessions of St. Augustine,* trans. J. G. Pilkington (New York: Liveright Publishing Co., 1943), 48.
3. Mark Noll, *The Scandal of the Evangelical Mind* (Grand Rapids: Eerdmans, 1994), 133.

comfortably with Christian commitment. Why then have some Christian thinkers taken to flirting with the devil of doubt?

The answer is, I think, fairly obvious. At least since Darwin (and arguably well before that), Christianity has found itself engaged in a war, sometimes hot but more often cold, against science. The story of that war is too well known to need retelling here, and of course it is not over, as the recent crusade for Creationism shows. But the important point is that Christianity has been quite consistently the loser in this war. Evolution in the Darwinian tradition if not in Darwin's exact form has become the accepted account of human origins, despite fundamentalist opposition, and more evidence for it accumulates every year in fossil finds and laboratory experiments. Physicists now present us with a cosmology which has little relation to the book of Genesis, and a description of the universe which has led physicist Steven Weinberg to remark, "the more the universe seems comprehensible, the more it seems pointless"[4] — not a congenial view for committed Christians. In fact, while *religion* has survived, Christian *theology* has taken such a beating that Mark Noll was recently led to remark, "the scandal of the evangelical mind is that there is not much of an evangelical mind."[5] It is difficult to build systematic theology when the foundation keeps collapsing under one's feet.

During the last few decades, there has been a series of attacks upon science itself, coming not only from the European postmodernists but from historians of science such as Thomas Kuhn and from philosophers such as Richard Rorty, Paul Feyerabend, and Willard Van Quine. All of them have attacked the usual truth claims of science, although they have written from very different points of view. Kuhn has probably had the greatest influence in this country, partly because as a historian his work has been more accessible to a wide public than the more technical arguments of someone like Quine. Kuhn has denied that science is progressive, in the sense that he denies that successive scientific theories show any convergence to the "truth." Indeed, Kuhn has likened the course of scientific change to Darwinian evolution; just as evolution does not show any approach to a final type, so Kuhn holds

4. Steven Weinberg, *Dreams of a Final Theory* (New York: Pantheon Books, 1992), 255.
5. Noll, *Scandal*, 3.

that the history of science describes a directionless process of change in which theory succeeds theory without approaching any final form. The successor theories are not "truer" than their predecessors on this view; they are merely different.[6] It is the lure of this attack on science, the belief that the "dethroning" of science opens the way for religion, which has made this sort of view so attractive to Christian thinkers.

But the relativism of the committed Christians seems to be incomplete. Where relativism of this sort can be used to attack the claims of science, they have found it appealing. But one does not find among them an equal willingness to apply relativism to their own beliefs. Although the history of theology actually conforms more closely to the sort of Darwinian intellectual process described by Kuhn than does the history of science,[7] Christian thinkers have not made that application. When Noll writes, "The great truth of the Incarnation is that the Son of God became flesh and dwelt among us,"[8] one does not hear any echoes of relativism. Nor are other Christian thinkers less prone to assert the truth of their doctrine. But can one consistently be a relativist with respect to science and an absolutist with respect to theology?

What I find most unsatisfactory about this situation is not the Christian claims for truth but the relativist attack upon science. Why should one believe these skeptical arguments? Scientists certainly do not, and many academics dismiss them. While there are as many forms of relativism as there are relativists, and not all of them can be addressed here, it is worth commenting briefly upon Kuhn's very popular doctrine. Kuhn denies that science progresses. Nevertheless, Kuhn has never denied that as science has changed, particularly as it has changed over the last three centuries, the successive systems which have been adopted by scientists do show a quite steady increase in their adequacy as predictors of our experience and in their power to control and manipulate nature. If one compares modern medicine with that of the seventeenth century, or modern chemistry with that of the eighteenth century, or modern physics with that of the nineteenth century, the fact that modern theories possess greater adequacy and power than their

6. Thomas S. Kuhn, *The Structure of Scientific Revolutions* (Chicago: University of Chicago Press, 1970), esp. chap. 13.

7. Murray G. Murphey, "On the Relation between Science and Religion," *American Quarterly* 20 (1968): 275-95.

8. Noll, *Scandal*, 252.

predecessors is simply undeniable. In this sense, it is very clear that science has been progressive.

How is this progress of science to be accounted for? It is not accounted for by Kuhn's theory, or Feyerabend's, or Quine's, or Rorty's, or any of the other relativist theories now in vogue. I know of no other reasonable explanation for it than to suppose that there does exist a real world of which science is giving us a more and more adequate understanding as inquiry goes on. Surely it will be agreed that if there were a true theory of the real world, it would give us both adequacy and power; since our theories are increasing in adequacy and power, it is a reasonable explanatory hypothesis to account for that fact to suppose that our theories are approximating such a true theory. But it will be objected that this is contrary to the fact that successive scientific theories do not exhibit an apparent convergence toward a final form. I think not. What it does indicate is that reality must be sufficiently complex so that limited and partial data concerning reality will permit differing conceptualizations of it, depending upon how much and what sort of data we have. Like the blind men with the elephant, if each starts with a small section of the beast, the resulting theories of what it is will vary dramatically. But as the data are increased and inquiry goes on, each of the blind men will eventually explore the whole beast and their views will converge. And it is easy to find many examples in science where just such a process has occurred. In astronomy we have gone from Eudoxus's geocentric spheres to Aristarchus's heliocentric theory to Ptolemy's geocentric epicyclical theory to Copernicus's heliocentric theory. That is hardly a history of smooth convergence. Today we all know that the heliocentric theory is true, but the point is that the solar system could be conceptualized in radically different ways depending on which data were available. One should not expect under such a hypothesis about reality to see smooth convergence; what one should expect to find is that at some point in the course of inquiry a theory will emerge which will ever after be affirmed. And I have no doubt that the heliocentric theory will be affirmed as long as humans last.[9]

I do not believe that the lately popular skepticism concerning

9. Murray G. Murphey, *Philosophical Foundations of Historical Knowledge* (Albany: SUNY Press, 1994), chap. 6.

science holds water, because I can think of no other explanation for the demonstrable progress of science except to hypothesize that scientific inquiry does approach the truth about the real world as the process of inquiry goes on. But this does not mean that each theory adopted in the course of inquiry is "truer" than its predecessor — Ptolemy's theory was in crucial respects further from the truth than Aristarchus's theory. It is only in the long run that inquiry approximates the truth, and we can never be certain where we are in this process. Our current scientific theories may be true, or they may be among the many that will not survive the process of inquiry. But it does follow that our present theories must be regarded as the best *estimates* we now have of what the truth is. Recognizing our own fallibility does not imply rejecting all our present beliefs; it does imply a willingness to abandon them if better theories are forthcoming in the future.

Thus I think that the attempt of true believers to find salvation in the arms of a skeptical postmodernism is not successful, and cannot be successful. It cannot succeed because even if the skepticism of the postmodernists were true (and what does it mean to say that skepticism is "true"?), that would not help the Christian cause, if the Christian cause involves the claim of truth for Christian doctrine. It also cannot succeed because the skeptical attack upon science does not succeed. Any theory of science must account for the demonstrable increase in the adequacy and power of scientific theories as inquiry has continued. No skeptical or relativist theory has done so, and I do not believe any such theory can do so.

If this argument is correct, where does it leave religious belief? Religious beliefs will have to stand or fall on the basis of their claim to truth. But if the standard of increasing adequacy and power is applied to the process of religious inquiry, religious theories do not fare well. Can it honestly be affirmed that any series of religious theories can show increases in adequacy and power over the last three centuries, or the last three millennia? Have religious explanations of nature, or of the course of human affairs, become notably more accurate? Do we have greater predictability and power now than before? Did all the prayers of all the six million Jews that died in Hitler's camps do anything to save them? I know of no evidence that prayer has become more effective, or that religious rituals have altered the course of nature or of war or of the economy. Science can demonstrate, in the sense described above, grounds for believing that scientific inquiry does lead to truth about reality; religion so far as I can see cannot.

But this does not refute the truth claims of religion; it only shows that the standard being used is not appropriate to judging them. A committed Christian can perfectly well reply that religion should not be expected to result in increasing adequacy or power because religious inquiry concerns God and his will and God's acts are neither predictable nor controllable. This reply is neither ad hoc nor unreasonable, but it leaves it to the believer to specify upon what grounds religious theories can be held to be true.

Any theory of religion, like any theory of science, is a theory of belief. One may grant that the distinction between science and religion is not a distinction made in all cultures, but it is nevertheless a distinction made in our culture, and one which must be accounted for. It is customary to differentiate scientific theories from religious theories on the basis of the type of evidence used and the method in inquiry employed. Scientific theories are said to be based upon "empirical" evidence, meaning evidence obtained by observation with the five senses, and to employ a method of hypothesis testing in which hypotheses or theories, or more commonly consequences derived from those hypotheses or theories, are tested against those "empirical" observations. If this characterization is accepted, it appears that science is different from religion and that the sorts of evidence which support scientific theories do not support religious ones. Religion is not alone here; the same point can be made about moral theories. But if this is so, why are religious and moral beliefs found in all known cultures? Clearly there must be some reason why people believe them and some sorts of evidence that support them.

If there is an objective moral order in the universe, our moral beliefs may have as much of an objective reference as our scientific beliefs. But what grounds have we for supposing that such an objective moral order exists? It cannot be argued in the light of the horrors of this century that our moral knowledge has shown the same sort of progress as our scientific knowledge. Indeed, conflict over what is right and wrong seems as rife today as ever. Moreover, if there were an objective moral order, one might reasonably expect that theories of morality would show as much cross-cultural agreement as do theories of science. That, however, is not the case. Although morality is universal in the sense that every culture holds some moral theory, one finds that these theories differ radically from one culture to another. What seems to be universal is a belief in some moral theory, not in any one. Furthermore, there are alternative explanations for this universality. Human society is, and must be, a moral order. Since humans do not have a large repertoire of instinctive guides to behavior, they must acquire learned guides or rules, and rules are always normative. A society requires a morality as a condition of survival; without it social order cannot be maintained. But it does not appear to require any particular morality; any one of a number of moral codes will do as long as it is accepted within that society. And since society is necessary for human survival, there is every evolutionary reason to believe that a capacity for moral belief is hardwired into human beings. The fact that all societies have some moral code or other does not require postulating an objective moral order in the universe. It is sufficient to postulate a generic capacity for moral response. Like the Ur-grammar of the linguists which provides a linguistic capacity that is realized in a variety of different actual languages, this generic capacity finds many different realizations in the world's various moral codes.

Moral belief is universal in the sense that not only all societies but all normal individuals hold some moral beliefs. The same claim cannot be made for religion. While religion is a cultural universal in that all known societies contain believers in some religion, it is not true that all normal individuals believe in some religion. There are and have long been atheists, and these atheists are neither immoral people nor are they mentally impaired. Holding religious beliefs appears to be an optional matter in a sense that holding moral beliefs is not. One cannot therefore suppose some sort of hardwired predisposition to religious belief. Nor is it possible to argue that moral beliefs are derived from religious beliefs and that therefore the universality of moral beliefs proves the universality of religious beliefs. In fact, as Durkheim argued, causation likely runs the other way; moral beliefs are prior, and religious beliefs are at least in part attempts to account for them.[10]

What basis then do religious beliefs have? It has been common to say that science is supported by empirical evidence but that religion is

10. Emile Durkheim, *The Elementary Forms of Religious Life* (New York: Free Press, 1965), 236-45.

not. But that statement supposes a particular classification of experiences in which certain types of experiences are given the label "empirical" while others are denied that label. All that this shows is that scientific and religious beliefs are supported by different sorts of experiences. But what then are the experiences which support religious beliefs?

Doubtless there are people whose religion is based on no more than the fact that their parents taught them to believe a particular creed, just as most nonscientists believe in science because they have been taught that they should. But just as real scientists believe in science because they actually do it and see directly the evidence for it, so many religious people ground their faith not on tradition or on memories of their socialization but on their own experience. And if religion has a real claim to be taken seriously as a true system of belief, it must, I think, rest on actual experiences. It is not enough to say that in such matters, one must rely on faith; faith there may be, but it must be grounded on at least some concrete experience.

Anthropologists have often proposed that the essence of religion is ritual.[11] But when these claims are examined, it turns out that what is important about ritual is not the ritual per se, but the effects that the ritual produces in the participants. Thus Geertz's celebrated definition of religion runs as follows:

> Religion is (1) a system of symbols which acts to (2) establish powerful long-lasting and pervasive moods and motivations in men by (3) formulating a conception of a general order of existence and (4) clothing these conceptions with such an aura of factuality that (5) the moods and motivations seem uniquely realistic.[12]

This definition is excellent as far as it goes, but it does not go far enough. Particularly commendable is Geertz's emphasis on "moods and motivations." As evangelicals have always known, the essence of religion lies in emotional experience. As Jonathan Edwards put it,

---

11. Anthony F. C. Wallace, *Religion: An Anthropological View* (New York: Random House, 1966).

12. Clifford Geertz, "Religion as a Cultural System," in *The Interpretation of Cultures* (New York: Basic Books, 1973), 90.

But it is doubtless true, and evident from these Scriptures, that the essence of all true religion lies in holy love; and that in this divine affection, and an habitual disposition to it, and that light which is the foundation of it, and those things which are the fruits of it, consists the whole of religion.[13]

If religion has an experiential base, that base is emotional. But what the definition does not tell us is how "factuality" is produced. Geertz does, however, offer an explanation of this; he believes it is produced by participation in the performance of ritual. Thus the process as Geertz sees it appears to be one in which belief and experience mutually support each other, with ritual operating as a mediating factor through which the experiences are generated. Although this definition gives an appearance of circularity, that appearance is misleading; what is being described is a process relation not unlike that which exists in science between theory and experiment. Performance of scientific experiments produces sensible experiences which are interpreted by scientific theory as confirming evidence for the theory, and scientific theory provides the basis for designing the experiments which produce these experiences and explains their occurrence. Similarly, rituals produce emotional experiences which are interpreted as evidence for religious theories, and religious theories both determine the rituals and explain why the experiences are produced by them. In both cases, one is dealing with an integrated system of belief, practice, and experience in which each part supports the others.

But the notion of ritual employed by anthropologists needs to be expanded to deal with the evidence from countries like the United States. Ritual is, after all, a standardized procedure or process having a religious significance in which the believers participate. Studies of conversion in the United States, as well as religious accounts of it, both historical and modern, reveal fairly standardized sequences of stages culminating in the rebirth of the believer and his subsequent sanctification.[14] These sequences exhibit some variations among different religious confessions, but there are clear similarities among them. If

13. Jonathan Edwards, *Religious Affections,* ed. John E. Smith (New Haven: Yale University Press, 1959), 107.

14. Murray G. Murphey, "The Psychodynamics of Puritan Conversions," *American Quarterly* 31 (1970): 135-47.

"ritual" is understood in this more general sense, then much of the literature on Christian religious experience also seems to fit this model.

What are religious experiences? It is clear that different sorts of experiences are regarded as religious in different cultures. Those who experience visions today in our culture, or who hear voices others do not hear, are more likely to be hospitalized than viewed as messengers of the divine, yet the Christian tradition contains instances of such experiences, St. Paul's being a particularly well-known example. Visions still carry religious significance in some religions; possession, glossolalia, and similar phenomena are also so construed by some groups. An inventory of all the types of experience which have been interpreted as having religious significance in any of the world's cultures would be very long indeed. But with the Christian confessions of the United States at present, the most crucial experiences seem to be a feeling of connection to a greater power, often of surrender to that greater power so that one becomes a part of something greater than the self, feelings of liberation or freedom, of gratitude, awe, and love both to the divine power and to other people, a feeling of being accepted and of having greater worth, and one of understanding what was before obscure.[15] For those who have actually gone through the process of religious rebirth, these emotions carry an overwhelming power which certifies the reality of the divine beyond any reasonable doubt. These people know: they have been to the river and they have been baptized.

That these experiences do really occur is beyond question. Those who bear witness to them are not deluded; they are describing real experiences which they have had. But the interpretation of these experiences is not beyond question. The doctrines of evangelical Christianity do provide an explanation for these experiences, but that is not the only possible explanation. The challenge for those who doubt the Christian interpretation is to provide a naturalistic alternative explanation of these experiences which can account for them better than the religious explanation. And here it must be said that psychologists have failed to meet the challenge, at least so far. The poverty of the scientific work on the psychology of religion is really astonishing, and scandalous. That is part of a larger failing of contemporary psychology — a failure to

15. Luther P. Gerlach and Virginia H. Hine, *People, Power, Change: Movements of Social Transformation* (Indianapolis: Bobbs-Merrill Publishing Co., 1970), 124.

deal with the emotions. Compared to the work in cognitive psychology and learning theory over the last few decades, very little research has been done on emotion. That is in one sense fortunate for those who are committed to religious belief, because it means that alternative explanations of religious emotional experiences have not been produced. But it also means that when psychologists do turn seriously to the study of the emotions, as some are now beginning to do,[16] Christianity may face a new challenge. It will not, however, be an easy challenge to mount.

If social scientists are really to challenge the Christian account of religious experience, they will have to do more than show that these emotions can be produced by purely natural means. Emotions have objects: the joy of killing an enemy is not the same as the joy of seeing a child born. Religious experience, from the standpoint of the believer, is the result of an interaction between the human and the divine. The emotional response is not separable from that relationship. Seen from a naturalistic point of view, there is no divine person or entity with whom to interact. The interaction must therefore be construed as taking place between the human believer and an imaginary entity. There are studies of such interactions done chiefly by anthropologists, including studies of some imaginary social relationships which occur in the United States.[17] But the point is that generating such experiences requires that the human individual believe in the reality of the divine entity; it can only be from the viewpoint of the investigator that the entity is imaginary. It seems very nearly impossible that a situation involving such a combination of belief and experience *could* be created in a psychological laboratory, and it would clearly be unethical to do so.

Any such study would therefore have to be an observational study done in a natural setting. Such studies have in fact been done — for example, Gerlach and Hine's study of conversion among Pentecostals.[18] What is most striking about this study is the analogy the authors find between the commitment experiences of the religious converts and the commitment experiences of converts to the Black Power Movement, which is wholly secular. Gerlach and Hine are interested in the general

16. Cf. Thomas J. Scheff and Suzanne M. Retzinger, *Emotions and Violence* (Lexington: D. C. Heath and Co., 1991).

17. A. I. Hallowell, *Culture and Experience* (New York: Schocken Books, 1967); John Caughey, *Imaginary Social Worlds* (Lincoln: University of Nebraska Press, 1984).

18. Gerlach and Hine, *People, Power, Change.*

problem of how people become committed to social movements, not particularly in issues of religion. But their findings suggest a theory which provides a naturalistic account of religious experience.

Human life, as Hobbes pointed out, is nasty, brutish, and short. Looked at from a purely naturalistic viewpoint, it is an animal existence devoid of any cosmic significance at all. But as Santayana so brilliantly argued,[19] in the process of natural evolution, we have developed a consciousness that can objectify ourselves, that can think beyond our own time and place, and can create what Geertz called "webs of significance."[20] Humans try to endow their lives with some meaning beyond the simple animal existence of birth, growth, reproduction, and death, and one way — perhaps the only way — of doing this is to identify themselves with some ideal or object or cause which will endure beyond their brief lives and to which they can believe they have made or can make some contribution. That sense of being a part of and contributing to something beyond one's self is what permits us to regard our lives as meaningful.

What it is with which we identify seems to be largely arbitrary, so long as it is enduring and perceived as worthy. It can be a god, or a church, or a social group, or a cause such as social amelioration, or society itself. It is not, I think, an accident that things as diverse as nationalism and communism have often been referred to as "religions." The latter is a particularly interesting phenomenon since the official position of the communist party has been one of atheism, and yet communists have often been described as having a religious zeal and as making communism their religion. And communism, for its adherents, was a cause which could inspire such a devotion: it was both an ideology and a social movement, it claimed to be leading the world to a better life for all mankind, it was highly idealistic and demanded — and received — the self-sacrificing service of those captivated by its vision of history and the future. One could give one's self to communism, as women who become nuns give themselves to Christ. Thus, in his *Personal History*, Vincent Sheehan describes Rayna Prohme's decision to enter the Lenin Institute "to be trained as a revolutionary

19. George Santayana, *Realms of Being* (New York: Charles Scribner's Sons, 1942), 549-825.
20. Geertz, *Interpretation of Cultures*, 5.

instrument"[21] in just those terms. It was indeed a religion, but it did not involve a relationship to the divine.

What I am suggesting was that Durkheim was more right than he knew — that religion is a subclass of a more general phenomenon which is rooted in the human need to find meaning in a life which in fact has no meaning beyond that which we give it. Human beings seek to resolve this problem by identifying with some greater entity or idea, which may be a social group or movement or a cause or, in the case of religion, an imaginary entity of supernatural power and eternal existence. The most satisfying of these alternatives must be the latter, for such an entity can give to its believers all the love, the acceptance, the feelings of worth and value, and especially of cosmic significance for which all humans long.

This suggestion is nothing new, but it does offer an alternative explanation of the emotions which appear to form the basis of religious belief. It is not a direct refutation of religious belief; such beliefs cannot be disproven in any simple way. A committed Christian could perfectly well accept Gerlach and Hine's description of the conversion process, yet interpret it as a description of a spiritual process. Since in any such belief system, experience, practice, and belief are mutually reinforcing, a well-confirmed causal theory of religious conversion would simply be for the committed believer an improved method of bringing the lost sheep to God. Rather, the effect of such an alternative theory as I am suggesting, assuming it is well confirmed, is to undermine the plausibility of religious belief in general. Insofar as a commitment to secular entities or ideals produces the same sorts of experiences through the same sorts of processes that religion does, the belief in the uniqueness of the religious life is destroyed and the believer should be led to question the grounds on which he stands. To the degree that the special character of religious experience can be shown to arise from the identification of the self with some greater entity which can be natural or social, the plausibility of the claim for the existence of the divine should fade to be replaced by an understanding of the reasons why we have found this dream so compelling.

It seems to me that the position of the Christian intellectual is not

---

21. Vincent Sheehan, *Personal History* (New York: Doubleday, Doran and Co., 1937), 287.

a comfortable one. Any turn toward skepticism or relativism is sure to be self-defeating in the long run because even if it weakens the truth claims of science, it also weakens the truth claims of Christianity itself. Christianity does make truth claims; any defense of Christianity must therefore be a defense of those claims. But I doubt that those claims are really defensible. If the experiences which Christians interpret as religious are also produced by commitments to things which are purely secular, the supernatural explanation of those experiences becomes adventitious. And whatever the staying power of tradition, I do not believe that any vital commitment to a system of belief can be long maintained unless it is based upon experiences which clearly support its claims.

What then is one to reply to Marsden's claim that Christian "perspectives" should be taught in the university? It is certainly not the case that everything that is taught, or should be taught, in the university is true, or even our best estimate of the truth. Foreign languages are not true; neither is painting or architecture or creative writing. But such subjects do not make truth claims. If we restrict ourselves to those subjects in which theories do make truth claims, the charms of this perspectival relativism quickly fade. I have argued above that the current fads of skepticism with respect to science are not defensible, if indeed they are even coherent. There is such a thing as truth, and we do have knowledge, even if it is only highly probable knowledge. Truth is the *only* interest that the university can legitimately advocate, at least in those areas where the concept of truth is applicable. One cannot and should not banish partisanship; theories of physics have their partisans just as do the theories of social movements. But partisan theories, like all theories, must be tested against the standard of truth. Those which meet the test earn their place in the curriculum of the university; those which do not have no more business being taught there than the fantasies of the mad. The university is not bedlam and should not be, and what protects it from that fate — the only thing that can protect it from that fate — is its commitment to truth. That commitment must be preserved.

SECTION TWO

Advocacy and the Politics
of the Academy

Marxism, Christianity, and Bias in the Study of Southern Slave Society

EUGENE D. GENOVESE

THOSE who pretend to write an objective, value-free history charge those who frankly espouse a worldview with blind prejudice and contempt for evidence, but the charge itself betrays prejudice and contempt. Until recently, we primarily had to contend with the illusion that a historian could proceed without a worldview and attendant political bias and somehow arrive at an objectivity that one might have thought only God capable of.

That illusion stemmed from a narrow reading of such calls for objectivity as might be found in, say, Max Weber's plea for ethical neutrality in the social sciences. Weber spoke out boldly on politics in appropriate forums, while he advocated analytical rigor in specifically scientific work. He argued that a social scientist who wished to study syndicalism, for example, had to analyze its ideas and practices independent of a judgment on the validity of syndicalism itself.[1] We may reply that it is impossible to keep value judgments from distorting our most determined efforts at objective analysis, and we may suspect that Weber knew as much and primarily intended a warning. Our reply should itself warn us against our own biases and admonish us to try to hold the inevitable distortions to a minimum. Weber may well have

1. Max Weber, *The Methodology of the Social Sciences* (Glencoe: Free Press, 1949); Arthur R. Mitzman, *The Iron Cage: An Historical Interpretation of Max Weber* (New York: Gossett and Dunlap, 1969).

exaggerated the possibilities for objectivity, but he was right to insist that we must rein in our prejudices if we wish to do honest scientific work.

We cannot escape the intrusion of a worldview into our work as historians. Whether that worldview is Marxist, Christian, liberal, conservative, fascist, or other, the label tells us little. Giovanni Gentile, Italian fascism's ablest theorist, advanced a philosophy and even political policies that proved anathema to many prominent fascist intellectuals and party activists.[2] Similarly, Christian interpretations of history that derive from the theology of Calvin or Arminius, Schleiermacher or Hodge, Barth or Tillich are likely to diverge widely, and it would be extraordinarily presumptuous to declare all but one's favorite interpretation to be un-Christian.

Among Marxists no quarrels are drearier and less productive than those which focus on "what Marx really meant." As Eric Hobsbawm, the foremost Marxist historian in the English language, has long insisted, there have been "many Marxisms," for, in truth, Marx, like all great thinkers, left an ambiguous legacy, and mutually exclusive lines of thought may legitimately be developed from his many-sided work. It was, as I recall, Che Guevara, of all people, who demolished much nonsense when asked if he was a Marxist. We call ourselves scientific socialists, he replied. Well then, would you ask a physicist if he considered himself a Newtonian?

A quarter-century ago I wrote an essay entitled "Marxian Interpretations of the Old South," which led off with two quotations that identified my own stance. The first was from Alfred North Whitehead: "A science which hesitates to forget its founders is lost." The second was from Karl Marx: *"Je ne suis pas un marxiste."*[3] My interest in the Old South began when I was an undergraduate. As a committed Marxist, I naturally began by pondering Marx's writing on the subject and quickly decided that he did not know what he was talking about. He had clearly extrapolated from his limited reading on the slave societies of the Carib-

2. A. James Gregor, *The Ideology of Fascism: The Rationale of Totalitarianism* (New York: Free Press, 1969); Giovanni Gentile, *The Genesis and Structure of Society*, trans. H. S. Harris (Urbana: University of Illinois Press, 1960).

3. Eugene D. Genovese, "Marxian Interpretations of the Slave South," in *In Red and Black: Marxian Explorations in Southern and Afro-American History* (1968; new edn., Knoxville: University of Tennessee Press, 1984), chap. 15.

bean and mechanistically applied his conclusions to the slave society of the Old South. Marx relied heavily on Frederick Law Olmsted's travelogues and on the economic analysis of John E. Cairnes, who himself had engaged in dubious extrapolation from Caribbean sources. I therefore had to ask myself why I should pay attention to an analysis that was not being borne out by the empirical work I had begun to do.

Simultaneously, I saw much in Marx's *Capital* and *Theories of Surplus Value* — in his interpretation of history and political economy — that was heuristically arresting. I concluded that anyone who sought to construct a sound Marxist interpretation of the Old South had to begin by rejecting Marx's specific analysis of a subject with which he had only superficial acquaintance and, instead, proceed in accordance with Marx's own admonition to eschew ideological impositions on historical data and to reject attempts to construct a suprahistorical theory of human experience. Marx practiced what he preached, at least when he worked as a historian in such works as *The Eighteenth Brumaire of Louis Bonaparte* and in the great historical sections of *Capital* on the origins and development of capitalism.[4]

Here we come directly to politics. When today's radicals, in sharp contradistinction to Marx himself, condemn Western civilization and Christianity for racism, slavery, sexism, and imperialism without mentioning the slavery, racism, sexism, and imperialism of non-Western peoples, they promote distortions that can only lead to grave political errors. Among other things, radicals, many of whom call themselves Marxists, forget Marx's oft-made observation that Western imperialism spurred the only genuine social revolutions that Asia had ever experienced. Indeed, not necessarily to his credit, Marx notoriously supported the United States in its war on Mexico for a similar reason. In any case, only the Christian West extruded a profound theoretical opposition to those enormities, challenging their moral foundations and raising mass movements against them. It requires no genius to see that a politics based on mendacity will end badly.

The Left has repeatedly ruined its prospects by such opportunism.

---

4. Karl Marx, *The Eighteenth Brumaire of Louis Bonaparte* (New York: International Publishers, n.d.); Marx, *Capital: A Critical Analysis of Capitalist Production*, 3 vols. (Moscow: Foreign Languages Publishing House, 1961), vol. 1, pts. 7-8; vol. 3, pts. 4, 6.

For the moment I shall restrict myself to one observation. All sections of the Left claim that the people are constantly deceived by the ideological manipulations of their oppressors and that, therefore, the unveiling of the unvarnished truth about social, economic, and political relations constitutes the principal educational and ideological task of those who would fight for a more just and humane society. In its own way it proclaims: Know the truth, and the truth will make you free. That should mean that, since the people's cause is just, they must face any amount of evidence of their own weaknesses and errors, so as to be able to correct them and steel themselves for battle. The people can safely rest their case on the balance of the evidence in a telling of the whole story of domination and subordination in social relations. Conversely, if the struggle against injustice proceeds with lies, distortions, and swindles, who is so stupid as to think that a new society could emerge as anything except rotten to its core? The current game of denying the very possibility of objective truth or of the necessity to approximate it as closely as possible thus reveals itself as contempt for the people — for the allegedly oppressed — who apparently are incapable of facing unpleasantness and evidence of their own failings and who aspire to nothing better than to do unto others the horrors that have been done unto them. The self-proclaimed anti-elitists who sing such songs are practicing elitism with a vengeance.

Today we face the dangerous irrationality of a self-styled postmodernism. It is more dangerous than the pretense of ethical neutrality in social science and historical scholarship because, despite all pretense, it quickly passes into nihilism. Normally, cynicism and fanaticism combat each other and represent, as it were, opposing heresies. Yet, marvelous to say, they now march in lockstep. We are being told that since objectivity rests only with a God who does not exist, we should scorn it as the ideology of oppressors.

Those who denounce objectivity as a fraud in the service of oppression are offering flagrant mendacity as a Higher Law. And since just about everyone, except non-Hispanic, heterosexual, white males, is today a victim of oppression, we are invited to present our subjectivity — our "feelings," which usually appear as hatreds — as a substitute for a nonexistent truth. I make no apology for the harshness of these remarks. In accordance with the fashion of parading one's feelings as a contribution to every discussion of every subject, I shall admit to being outraged at hearing endless whines about oppression from American intellectuals — black as well as white, female as well as male. For since they (we) rank among the top one or two percent of the world's most privileged people, the whines may fairly be judged obscene. But then, I suppose I am merely revealing my own status as an oppressor by invoking an untenable standard of statistical objectivity, when I should be demonstrating my sensitivity to the precious feelings of the insulted and the injured. Unfortunately, never having met a human being who did not feel insulted and injured in this vale of tears, my capacity for compassion has been badly stunted. Atheist that I am, I learned that much from Christian teaching on original sin and human depravity, which has been confirmed by all historical experience of which I am aware, even if it is no longer in fashion in mainstream Protestant churches.

For a particularly destructive illustration of the consequences of fudging the political implications of historical scholarship, consider the relation of the admirable work on slave life to the problem of black nationalism. For the last few decades a large number of fine scholars, black and white, have investigated slave life (religion, folklore, family, material conditions, resistance) and have unanimously concluded that the slaves forged a vibrant culture under conditions of extreme adversity. Most have also acknowledged the centrality of religion to that achievement and demonstrated the unique features of the black religious experience. Taken as a whole, this work reveals a distinct Afro-American culture without analogue to the experience of any other ethnic group. Yet, with the exception of George Rawick, Sterling Stuckey, and only a few others, the scholars who have made these admirable contributions have remained silent on the political implications, which clearly support the black nationalist interpretation of the black experience in the United States and, at the least, call for serious qualification of the rival liberal-integrationist interpretation.[5] We are

5. See especially George Rawick, *From Sundown to Sunup: The Making of the Black Community* (Westport: Greenwood, 1972); Sterling Stuckey, *Slave Culture: Nationalist Theory and the Foundations of Black America* (New York: Oxford University Press, 1987) and *Going through the Storm: The Influence of African American Art in History* (New York: Oxford University Press, 1994); and Vincent Harding, *There Is a River: The Black Struggle for Freedom in America* (New York: Harcourt Brace Jovanovich, 1981).

entitled to suspect that the scholars whose work is supporting essential black nationalist contentions are themselves integrationists who are unwilling to face the political consequences of their own scholarship. As a result, the notion that black nationalism ought to be viewed as pathological rather than historically authentic remains widespread and inhibits frank discussion of the most pressing political problems.

Yes, our scholarly work, especially on subjects as explosive as slavery and racism, has inescapable political implications, some of which may, alas, contradict our intentions. Yes, a historian has the duty to make those implications clear. But, simultaneously, he has the duty to resist the imposition of his politics on the empirical record. Or to put it another way: It is one thing to lay bare the political implications of our analyses; it is quite another to whore in some ostensibly worthy cause.

Some years ago I devoted a decade of work to what became *Roll, Jordan, Roll: The World the Slaves Made,* a book on slave life.[6] That work constituted a detour in my lifelong special project — the history of the slaveholders and the slave society of the Old South over which they exercised hegemony. I embarked upon that detour not because of the emerging struggle against racial segregation, however much that struggle may have influenced the outcome, but because I found that I could not understand the slaveholders without understanding the slaves. Specifically, I had to evaluate the slaveholders' perception of slave life and consciousness in the light of the reality of that life and consciousness or as much of it as would prove amenable to empirical investigation.

The empirical investigations disturbed a historian with the biases of an atheist and a historical materialist who had always assumed, however mindlessly, that religion should be understood as no more than a corrosive ideology at the service of ruling classes. If, at the beginning, someone had told me that religion would emerge as a positive force in my book — indeed, as the centerpiece — I would have laughed and referred him to a psychiatrist. In the end, the evidence proved overwhelming, and I had to eat my biases, although not my Marxism. For while much went into the making of the heroic black

6. Genovese, *Roll, Jordan, Roll: The World the Slaves Made* (New York: Pantheon, 1974).

struggle for survival under extreme adversity, nothing loomed so large as the religious faith of the slaves. The very religion that their masters sought to impose on them in the interest of social control carried an extraordinarily powerful message of liberation in this world as well as the next.

The slaves interpreted the Word and experienced the Holy Spirit in their own way, and yet they did no violence to Christianity itself. True, they injected a strong dose of traditional African religion and Afro-American folk culture into their interpretation. But, as every historian knows, so did the peoples of Europe and the rest of the world. The vitality of Christianity — its very sense of being in accord with Word and Spirit — has depended upon the ability of the churches to respond to the positive elements in folk life while resisting heretical tendencies.[7] Recall that the decision of the early church in favor of the Trinity registered popular opposition to an intellectual elite that found irrational the concept of a triune God. The church, in effect, found the Holy Spirit in the consciousness of the faithful.[8] I find puzzling the decision of Nancey Murphy, in her remarkable book *Theology in the Age of Scientific Reasoning*, to bypass this history, which would seem to lend vital support to her principal thesis that theology has firm claims to rank as a science in accordance with the test of probability theory.[9]

Be that as it may, these musings bring us face to face with two questions: Can, in fact, a nonbeliever contribute anything of value to Christian thought? And can a confrontation with Christian thought and experience lead a Marxist or other nonbeliever to deepen his own worldview and help purge it of untenable features? Obviously, I would be the last person to be able to answer the first question with reference to my own work. But let me indicate what I tried to do, the conclusions toward which I was led, and some problems that that work may pose for believers.

To begin with, the overpowering evidence of religious faith aroused in me a skepticism about the reigning tendency in academia

7. Keith Thomas, *Religion and the Decline of Magic* (New York: Knopf, 1971).

8. See, e.g., Philip Schaff, *History of the Christian Church*, 8 vols. (1910; reprint, Grand Rapids: Eerdmans, n.d.), 3:720 and passim; William G. Rusch, ed., Introduction to *The Trinitarian Controversy* (Philadelphia: Fortress Press, 1980), 2, 9.

9. Nancey Murphy, *Theology in the Age of Scientific Reasoning* (Ithaca, N.Y.: Cornell University Press, 1990).

to, as it were, sociologize faith out of religion — to deny the reality of spirituality. That debilitating tendency may be observed even among scholars who profess Christianity but espouse an extreme theological liberalism that leads toward a denial of any claim Christianity may have to being not one religion among many but the Way and the Truth. I would not presume to tell Christians how to be Christians, but I must confess that I cannot understand how Christians, without ceasing to be Christians, can retreat one inch from a belief that Jesus is the second person of a triune God, the Christ, the redeemer. If other religions offer equally valid ways to salvation and if Christianity itself may be understood solely as a code of morals and ethics, then we may as well all become Jews, Muslims, Buddhists, or, better, atheists. I intend no offense, but it takes one to know one. And when I read much Protestant theology and religious history today, I have the warm feeling that I am in the company of fellow nonbelievers.

Theories derived from the sociology of religion proved indispensable to my own work, and I am sure that the influence of Max Weber and Ernst Troeltsch, among others, will appear obvious to anyone who reads it. For that matter, the Freudian bias in the psychological dimension of that work has probably not been lost on discerning readers. But no such theory or combination of theories could suffice to explain the power of the folk religion, as manifested, for example, in the spirituals. Mechal Sobel has criticized me for slighting the spiritual dimension of the slaves' experience, and she may well be right.[10] But if so, the error arose from a deficiency of talent, not of intention. For nothing could be clearer than that the slaves' successful struggle for survival as a people was more readily spiritual than physical. Christians are entitled to chide materialists with their inability to account for that dimension, for we have done poorly in response to the challenge.

Contrary to much current practice, the history of the slaves and of the slaveholders cannot be written independent of each other. It would have been astonishing if godless slaveholders had been able to introduce their slaves to Christianity. The hard truth is that the slaveholders, or at least the decisive figures among them, genuinely qualified

10. Mechal Sobel, *Trabelin' On: The Slave Journey to an Afro-Baptist Faith* (Westport: Greenwood Press, 1979).

as believers. Their belief contributed immeasurably to their social power and thereby lent itself to a sociological analysis of the ideological and political functions of religion. But we must still confront the ample evidence of piety among a considerable portion of the slaveholders. Probably half of all the proslavery and antislavery tracts written during the nineteenth century were written by ministers, and a large portion of the rest invoked scriptural arguments. That the Bible proved the principal terrain of ideological struggle over the slavery question demonstrates the centrality of religious thought to the American experience, both northern and southern.[11]

In defending slavery as a Christian social system, the proslavery divines and even the secular theorists appealed to Scripture. Regrettably, such formidable southern theologians as James Henley Thornwell and Robert L. Dabney — to say nothing of conservative antislavery northern theologians like Charles Hodge, who voted for Lincoln[12] — sustained themselves in scriptural exegesis with the abolitionists. Orthodox theologians demonstrated that neither the Old nor the New Testament condemned slavery as sinful. The abolitionists, some of whom displayed no small amount of intellectual dishonesty, never succeeded in making the Word say what they said it did, and eventually they had to spurn the Word for the Spirit. In consequence, they virtually reduced the Holy Spirit to the spirit (the conscience) of individuals. I do not say that an antislavery Christian theology remains an impossibility. I am prepared to hear that, say, the implications of Karl Barth's theology and Nancey Murphy's methodological work could yield an antislavery theology. But as a historian, I do insist that the abolitionists failed to construct one and that, so far as I know, no one has yet improved upon their performance. Note, for example, that Paul Tillich, in his *Systematic Theology*, introduces slavery only to assume its incom-

---

11. Eugene D. Genovese, "Slavery Ordained of God: The Southern Slaveholders' View of Biblical History and Modern Politics," Fortenbaugh Memorial Lecture, Gettysburg College, 1985; Genovese and Elizabeth Fox-Genovese, "The Religious Ideals of Southern Slave Society," *Georgia Historical Quarterly* 70 (1986): 1-16; Fox-Genovese and Genovese, "The Divine Sanction of Social Order: Religious Foundations of the Southern Slaveholders' World View," *Journal of the American Academy of Religion* 55 (1987): 211-33.

12. Charles Hodge, *Systematic Theology*, 3 vols. (Grand Rapids: Eerdmans, 1952).

patibility with Christianity, thereby assuming precisely what he needs to demonstrate.[13]

I undertook another task in *Roll, Jordan, Roll* and subsequent work on the religion of the slaveholders, and here my early training as a Marxist came to the fore. It is remarkable how little attention is paid to theology in most current work on religion. Today, most historians of religion, believers or no, proceed as if theology were the special province of a small portion of a well-educated elite. They thereby separate the religion of the elite from the religion of the common people, apparently on the assumption that only a handful of theologians and sophisticated ministers and laymen know or care about theology. I proceeded on the contrary assumption — that even folk religion, the religion of the least sophisticated, necessarily had a theological content with ideas of God, sin, soul, and salvation, and that the historian's task was to extract those ideas from the mass of the seemingly incoherent beliefs inevitably found in the thoughts of everyman. For if, as I believe with Antonio Gramsci, that "the philosophy of every man is contained in his politics," so is his theology, which is no less contained in his philosophy.

I may have gotten the answers wrong for the slaves — that remains a matter for further empirical investigation — but I stand by the assumption. And similarly for the slaveholders. Historians who posit a chasm between the "high culture" of the theologians and the "popular culture" of the least educated of the southern whites run into a serious problem. For the principal themes and ideas of the theologians, whether Calvinist or Arminian, including their defense of slavery and a hierarchical natural and social order, clearly resonated through the country preachers and their flocks. In few if any modern societies has the intelligentsia, clerical and lay, been so clearly in harmony with the common people.

The political ramifications of southern Christian theology were enormous. For at the very moment that the northern churches, albeit with stiff internal resistance, were embracing theological liberalism and abandoning the Word for a Spirit increasingly reduced to personal subjectivity, the southern churches were holding the line for Christian

13. Paul Tillich, *Systematic Theology*, 3 vols. (Chicago: University of Chicago Press, 1951-63).

orthodoxy, whether in Calvinist or Arminian form. Not for nothing was Thornwell called "the Calhoun of the Church." He, as well as Calhoun, recognized, indeed proclaimed, that the southern insistence upon the Word of the Bible had its direct counterpart in the southern insistence upon the word of the United States Constitution. In politics, as in theology, the overwhelming majority of southerners were strict constructionists.

The study of the religious life of both slaves and slaveholders thus encourages an atheist to hope that he can contribute something to a subject generally slighted by his ideology and can even position him to challenge Christians to clarify their theology. By extension, it encourages a Marxist to reexamine fundamental tenets of his own interpretation of history. Let us proceed, *arguendo*, to accept the idea that social relations lie at the core of historical development. Marx died before he could write all but a few introductory lines on social classes for the final chapter of the third volume of *Capital*. Many Marxists could therefore be excused for having relied on a few sweeping generalizations in *The Critique of Political Economy* and other works and to view social classes as economic entities.[14] Yet Marx himself did no such thing in his own historical writing, most notably in his analyses of the emergence of capitalism and his studies of the class struggles in nineteenth-century France. One thing is clear: as every serious Marxist has understood, Marx was not an economic determinist.

During the twentieth century, Marxists, especially those influenced by Gramsci, have discarded the mechanistic dichotomy of a social base and a derivative ideological superstructure. Two grave weaknesses nonetheless continue to plague Marxist thought: an underestimation of nationalism and of religion. These are big subjects, and I can only touch upon the second here. The study of religion in the Old South reveals that the churches largely succeeded in binding social classes to each other, most impressively among the whites. But neither Marxism nor any other historical or sociological theory can fully account for the dynamics — for the alacrity with which the well-to-do and the lowly accepted the "good news" about Jesus.

We can no longer close our eyes to the centrality of the Christian

14. Marx, *A Contribution to the Critique of Political Economy* (New York: International Publishers, 1970).

message to the formation of the slaveholding class, as well as of the yeomanry, and to the bond it created between them. Marxists, then, are compelled to reconsider their very notion of social class — or, more broadly, of social relations — to include much more than the economic relations that undoubtedly loomed large. Slaveholders may have been slaveholders and yeomen may have been yeomen in the sense that all such classes have much in common with their equivalents elsewhere. But the Protestant slaveholders and yeomen of the Old South may be equated with their Catholic counterparts in Brazil only at the risk of misunderstanding the essentials of their history.

For the political Left there is an especially dark side to the question of ideological bias and its attendant contempt for religion. Conservatives have long charged us with the espousal of Christian heresy. Most tellingly, Eric Voegelin has identified our worldview as a modern gnosticism. There is too much truth for comfort in the charge. Having substituted what may fairly be called a gnostic vision for Christianity and scoffed at the moral baseline of the Ten Commandments and the Sermon on the Mount, we ended a seventy-year experiment with socialism with little more to our credit than tens of millions of corpses. The bourgeois slave traders of Europe and New England and the slaveholders of the South committed terrible atrocities and have much to answer for, especially to their black victims. But did they overmatch our own atrocities? For that matter, has a radical-egalitarian party ever come to power on a significant scale and not plunged into mass murder and the establishment of tyranny? On this ground alone, we can no longer postpone a reconsideration of the Christian idea of justice and equality before God and of our own blood-drenched romance with the utopia of a man-made heaven here on earth.

As we are tirelessly reminded these days, the history of Christianity has been strewn with blood, but, as we are rarely reminded, that same history has contributed a body of teaching that has made possible a line of resistance and counterattack. If Christianity, in the days in which it took itself seriously, stressed human depravity and capacity for evil, it also insisted on an element of divinity in everyman. Secular liberals, invoking Locke's blank slate, like to say that man is neither beast nor angel. It would seem safer to say, in the spirit of Christian orthodoxy, that man is both beast and angel. Christianity therefore denies the right of any individual or state to treat human beings as objects of social engineering rather than as a discrete personality sacred in the sight of God. Until nonbelievers can match that performance they would do well to temper their criticism and to look to their own moral responsibilities.

For myself, I have no idea whether I have been able to contribute anything of value to the study of religion. I do know that the effort to come to terms with the history of Christianity has contributed much to my understanding of what my preferred political movement and ideology have been and what they must become if we are to contribute to the more just and humane world we have devoted our lives to fighting for.

Advocacy and the Writing of American Women's History

ELIZABETH FOX-GENOVESE

I

Since American women's history as a discrete subject emerged in direct response to "second wave" feminism, it has, virtually without apology, developed as an explicit effort of advocacy. Beginning with modest claims about the need to "restore" women to their rightful historical place, it rapidly moved to the more ambitious claim that any serious restoration of women to the historical record would necessarily entail the reconsideration of fundamental historical assumptions, notably about periodization and significance. After all, if one adopts the perspective of women, is it not reasonable to argue that the advent of reliable contraception represents a more important historical milestone than, say, one or another of the wars that have so preoccupied the male imagination?[1] By the same token, might one not plausibly argue that the married women's property acts or women's suffrage were more significant events than the election of, say, Abraham Lincoln or Franklin D. Roosevelt?

These escalated claims, independent of the intentions of their proponents — and many, but not all, intended precisely what ensued

---

1. Gerda Lerner has played a leading role in developing the theory and claims of this tendency in women's history. See, for example, her *The Creation of Patriarchy* (New York: Oxford University Press, 1986).

— explicitly privileged social history over such rival forms as political, military, diplomatic, or even economic or intellectual history. Proceeding on the assumption that there was little to be gained from emphasizing activities that had largely excluded women and frequently contributed to their oppression, those American women's historians who have been most influenced by feminism have focused upon the private relations of everyday life as a way of bringing women's experience to the center of the historical stage. Along the way, they have increasingly attended to the distinct "culture" and "values" that women had developed from their discrete experience, thus implicitly mounting a challenge to prevailing assumptions about the ways in which history should be written and, especially, to the possibility for any historical objectivity. This challenge, with its inherent predisposition to open advocacy, arose as poststructuralist literary criticism and postmodernist cultural studies began to penetrate historical writing. A new emphasis on multiculturalism, normally taken to include women and homosexuals as well as national and ethnic groups, merged with these tendencies to promote the view that most canons of historical scholarship, notably objectivity and the identification of facts, should be dismissed as inherently suspect if not intentionally oppressive. According to this view, all history should recognize the inherent partiality and partisanship of any historical perspective and openly reclaim oppressed people's unmediated perceptions of their own condition. More portentously, the advocates of history from the subjective perspective increasingly conflated attention to the experience of oppressed peoples with the promotion of their own careers. The ultimate spoils emerged as less the production of a compelling or comprehensive narrative than as the advancement of scholars who spoke in the name of specific groups of the oppressed with whom they personally identified and whom they personally claimed to represent. Thus did women's history move from the recovery of women to the celebration of feminist advocacy to the advancement of the careers of feminist historians.[2]

2. See especially Joan Wallach Scott, "History in Crisis?: The Other's Side of the Story," *American Historical Review* 94, no. 3 (June 1989): 680-92, and her *Gender and the Politics of History* (New York: Columbia University Press, 1988). Patricia Hill Collins takes the position to its logical conclusion, arguing that "living life as an African-American woman is a necessary prerequisite for producing Black feminist thought." See her "The Social Construction of Black Feminist Thought," *Signs* 14,

Within a remarkably brief period, the identification of women's history with feminism was authoritatively effected. Women's history must be understood, by definition, as an act of advocacy and must claim as its mission the defense of women's interests. But these seemingly straightforward, if contestable, propositions masked a number of more dangerous implications, many of which challenged the very nature of history as an intellectual, and even a moral and socially accountable, enterprise. For those who most vigorously defended the imperative of what was increasingly being called feminist history claimed a monopoly on the interpretation of women's experience and interests. As women's history became feminist history, it embraced many of the more dubious features of feminism itself, notably the pretension that those who spoke in its name were entitled to tell women who they were and what they wanted. And, in the measure that feminist historians explicitly claimed authority in the interpretation of women's past, which they explicitly read to advance women's prospects as they defined them in the present and future, they increasingly tended to subordinate what (probably) had been to what (incontrovertibly) should be. They thereby sought to transform history into serviceable propaganda.

In the ensuing discussion I shall frequently refer to feminism in the singular on the assumption that there is a dominant feminist position, the proponents of which disquietingly tend to silence, reject, or ignore competing positions. Let me therefore acknowledge frankly that this simplification does some injustice to the many disparate tendencies within feminism, which emphasize different goals and aspects of women's experience. Feminists divide between those who emphasize spiritual and those who emphasize economic and social concerns; between those who defend and those who attack heterosexuality; between those who emphasize women's equality with men and those who emphasize their difference from men; between those who favor the maximum sexual freedom and those who favor severe restrictions upon male sexuality, including pornography; between those who emphasize civil liberties and those who favor speech and discriminatory harassment codes. The list could be extended almost indefinitely. Ecofeminists

---

no. 4 (Summer 1989): 770. For a fuller discussion of the issues, see Elizabeth Fox-Genovese, *Feminism without Illusions: A Critique of Individualism* (Chapel Hill: University of North Carolina Press, 1991).

tend to regard most of what is wrong with our world from the destruction of the environment to the eating of meat as attributable to men. Gynofeminists tend to favor female separatism and a radical revision of our language as necessary antidotes to men's centuries-long abuse of authority that lacked legitimacy in the first place. Some feminists celebrate an original world of female power, including hegemonic female deities; some celebrate women as witches.[3]

Given these varieties within feminism, not to mention the others I have not listed or heard of, what is the justification for referring to a singular feminism as if agreement on all feminist issues indeed prevailed? That justification, I believe, lies in the recognition that feminism, notwithstanding its complexity and internal divisions, does rest upon a series of common assumptions about women's subordination throughout history, the need to improve women's situation, the essentials of what that improvement must entail, and, above all, about the legitimacy of any inherited form of authority, including and perhaps especially religious and moral authority. The hegemony of these assumptions within feminist circles helps to explain why so many women who care passionately about specific women's issues refuse to call themselves feminists.[4] That hegemony also helps to explain why we so rarely, if ever, encounter feminists who would agree that feminists-for-life can be feminists at all. Thus the justification for the use of feminism in the singular primarily derives from feminism's own negative, in

3. For a few examples of different feminist perspectives, see Marianne Hirsch and Evelyn Fox Keller, eds., *Conflicts in Feminism* (New York and London: Routledge, 1990), Seyla Benhabib, Judith Butler, Drucilla Cornell, and Nancy Fraser, *Feminist Contentions* (New York and London: Routledge, 1995), Catharine A. MacKinnon, *Toward a Feminist Theory of the State* (Cambridge: Harvard University Press, 1989) and her *Only Words* (Cambridge: Harvard University Press, 1993); Susan Estrich, *Real Rape* (Cambridge: Harvard University Press, 1987); Judith Butler, *Gender Trouble: Feminism and the Subversion of Identity* (New York and London: Routledge, 1990) and her *Bodies That Matter: On the Discursive Limits of "Sex"* (New York and London: Routledge, 1993); Wendy Kaminer, *A Fearful Freedom: Women's Flight from Equality* (Reading, Mass.: Addison-Wesley, 1990); Susan Moller Okin, *Justice, Gender, and the Family* (New York: Basic Books, 1989); Patricia Hill Collins, *Black Feminist Thought: Knowledge, Consciousness, and the Politics of Empowerment* (Boston: Unwin Hymen, 1990); Jean Bethke Elshtain, *Power Trips and Other Journeys: Essays in Feminism as Civic Discourse* (Madison: University of Wisconsin Press, 1991).

4. See Elizabeth Fox-Genovese, *"Feminism Is Not the Story of My Life"* (New York: Nan A. Talese, 1996).

contradistinction to its positive, positions. Feminists may not always agree about what they are for, but they do fall into line with respect to what they are against and, especially, whom they exclude.

II

Feminists' certainty about what they are against decisively colors feminism's relation to the writing of history. Feminist historians have never doubted that all historical writing is a form of advocacy, primarily because they readily assert that history as we know it has been fashioned by men to celebrate their triumphs and values and has overwhelmingly focused upon realms from which women have largely been excluded, notably those of power and prestige. Starting from this premise, feminist historians have generally claimed the right and responsibility to redress that imbalance. But the feminist sense of righteous advocacy has too often led to the projection of contemporary values upon the past. The problem does not lie with the commitment to advocacy so much as it lies with an openly partisan view of the form that advocacy must take, as the case of the religious history of American women clearly illustrates.

The central problem in the religious history of American women lies in the uncomfortable truth that religion has played a major role in the lives and values of countless American women — more women than men, in fact — yet most religious institutions, notably the most prestigious and authoritative, and most of the religious life of the mind, notably theology, have been dominated by men. Feminist historians are thus challenged to understand why so many women have sought spiritual guidance, moral standards, and personal consolation in a faith that worshiped a male God and his Son and from religious institutions and practices that were officiated by men. Some, notably believers trained in theology, respond to the challenge by recovering the religious roles that women did play, as nuns, spiritual leaders, and even as preachers, or by elucidating the persistent female imagery that informs the core of the Christian tradition.[5] Their work unambiguously demonstrates

5. See, for example, Carolyne Walker Bynum, *Jesus as Mother: Studies in the Spirituality of the High Middle Ages* (Berkeley: University of California Press, 1982),

that, however we ultimately assess the evidence, Christianity was never as blind or hostile to the female aspect of all humanity as its critics commonly assert.

Other women's historians, many of whom also consider themselves feminists but not necessarily believers, have focused upon the recovery of women's religious lives and, especially, practices. It is to this group that we owe most of the work on women's moral, charitable, and reform organizations within and without churches. The historians who have focused upon these topics have tended to argue that women, notwithstanding their exclusion from priesthood and ministry, became central agents of religion, as much in leading the members of their families to conversion and church membership as in seeking to promote the education of ministers, the general amelioration of society, and even political causes such as the abolition of slavery.[6] Women emerge from most of this work as embodiments of a special sense of moral obligation and personal responsibility — as the custodians of more humane values than the men's world of business and politics normally fostered. Indeed, these and related considerations led Ann Douglas to argue that, during the antebellum period, American religion underwent a "feminization."[7]

The implications of Douglas's work continues to deserve widespread attention, especially from those who are concerned with the role of religion in contemporary American society. Sadly, it has hardly received the attention it merits from other feminist historians, presumably because Douglas treats feminization, which she discerns in ministers' growing dependence upon the values and approval of female parishioners, as a falling off from the most demanding and heroic aspects of American culture. In other words, she gently reproves antebellum

---

Elisabeth Schüssler Fiorenza, *In Memory of Her: A Feminist Theological Reconstruction of Christian Origins* (New York: Crossroad, 1983).

6. See, for example, Mary Ryan, *Cradle of the Middle Class: The Family in Oneida County, New York, 1790-1865* (Cambridge: Cambridge University Press, 1981) and her "A Woman's Awakening: Evangelical Religion and the Families of Utica, New York, 1800-1840," *American Quarterly* 30 (1978): 602-23; Janet Wilson James, ed., *Women in American Religion* (Philadelphia: University of Pennsylvania Press, 1980); Rosemary Radford Ruether and Rosemary Skinner Keller, eds., *Women and Religion in America: A Documentary History*, 2 vols. (San Francisco: Harper & Row, 1981-86).

7. Ann Douglas, *The Feminization of American Culture* (New York: Knopf, 1977).

women for pulling religion down from the heights of stern authority, demanding morality, and the recognition of the inevitable sin and tragedy of the human condition to the trite realm of sentimental deaths and cozy domesticity. Douglas never doubts that women generally operated in a different moral universe than men, especially the Puritan divines, but she emphatically does not regard them as men's moral superiors. Rather, she views them as engaged in a wholesale attempt to cut religion down to their own size, to trivialize what was inherently grand and difficult in order to make it easily palatable.

Douglas traces an important aspect of what other feminist historians have described as the growing divorce between home and work — domestic and public or male and female spheres — with the rise of industrial capitalism. But, unlike others, she does not concur that women's morality should necessarily be seen as superior to that of men. The problem is not that she sympathizes with the ethos of industrial capitalism, which she sharply chastises. The problem is that she refuses to agree that women escaped from its clutches to create a distinctly separate and superior vision. Douglas is not, in fact, primarily concerned with the costs of these developments to religion itself. Like most of the leading feminist historians and activists, her values and concerns are distinctly secular. Notwithstanding her grudging admiration for the demanding vision of the Mathers, she is primarily interested in what she takes to be the obvious declension in intellectual quality from a Hawthorne or a Melville to a Harriet Beecher Stowe or a Fanny Fern. In other words, she agrees with Hawthorne's stern assessment of the domestic sentimentalists as a bunch of scribbling women and attempts to explain the rapidity with which their vision conquered popular cultural sensibilities.

Douglas's successors, most of whom either have been reluctant to accept her conclusions or even to engage her work, interpret women's place in nineteenth-century society and culture differently. Most important, they more often than not tend uncritically to endorse women's moral superiority. This is especially the case among those who have studied the connections between women's culture and abolition or, more generally, women's culture and various reform movements. In this respect, even those who most bitterly protest women's exclusion from power are quick to take women's powerlessness relative to men as a sign of their special moral virtue. There is a delicious irony here, for this "progressive" feminist interpretation carries forward the views of those antebellum supporters of male prerogatives, most notably the slaveholders, who invoked the moral superiority of women to justify their exclusion from public life. And there is another irony: for feminists, it is but a short step to the position that the triumph of women's values in the world would indeed correct the wrongs that capitalism have wrought.[8] And the corollary to this view is the frequently rather mindless identification of women's values with the essence of religion. Thus, at least some feminist historians tend to claim for women a special relation to a religion in which many of the historians themselves apparently do not believe and which they frequently blame for its contributions to women's second-class status.

III

The secularism of most feminist historians has made it difficult for them to take religion seriously or even to credit women of previous eras with having taken it seriously. In the measure that they have stressed the importance of religion in women's lives, they have normally done so as a way of underscoring women's alienation from the dominant (male) values of their society. Moreover, they have focused on specific aspects of women's religious experience and, especially, upon the religious views of specific women on the assumption that women of previous periods would necessarily have thought pretty much the way secular women think today. These attitudes admittedly find reinforcement in the writings of some of the most important early advocates of women's rights, notably Elizabeth Cady Stanton. For Stanton charged man, in his oppression of woman, with having "usurped the prerogative of Jehovah himself, claiming it as his right to assign for her a sphere of action, when that belongs to her and to God." Thus has man not merely disenfranchised but degraded women, by using every means at his disposal "to destroy her confidence in her own powers, to lessen her

8. An especially interesting and influential version of this line of thought may be found in Jane Tompkins, *Sensational Designs: The Cultural Work of American Fiction, 1790-1860* (New York: Oxford University Press, 1985).

self-respect, and to make her willing to lead a dependent and abject life."[9]

With this as a starting point, it is hardly surprising that feminism as advocacy has had difficulty in coming to terms with the religious aspect of women's experience. The difficulty emerges with special clarity from the unwillingness of feminist historians to take seriously the beliefs of conservative women, most of whom took religion seriously indeed. The white southern women whom I have studied, especially the slaveholding women, regularly turned to religion not merely for consolation and a guide for their practical and spiritual lives, but for confirmation of their political convictions, which almost invariably included the legitimacy of slavery and of women's subordination to men in the world.[10] As often as not, when I have spoken or written of these women, I have encountered fierce hostility and repudiation. On one occasion, an especially irate feminist asked me why I could not leave slaveholding women in the oblivion they so richly deserved. More often, I am simply rebuked for having too much sympathy for them — for too easily tolerating their unpalatable views. And many of those who reject my interpretation, which includes the judgment that they were by no means feminists, much less overt or covert abolitionists, suggest that my willingness to treat them with respect betrays my own reactionary and elitist views.

As it happens, I do believe that my interpretation of the religious experience and beliefs of southern women hews as closely as my own human imperfections permit to the historical evidence. Claiming this much, I should also be the first to admit that there is room for honest disagreement. But however considerable that room, it probably does

9. Elizabeth Cady Stanton, "Declaration of Sentiments," in *The Concise History of Woman Suffrage: Selections from the Classic Works of Stanton, Anthony, Gage, and Harper,* ed. Mari Jo and Paul Buhle (Urbana: University of Illinois Press, 1978), 94-95.

10. Elizabeth Fox-Genovese, *Within the Plantation Household: Black and White Women of the Old South* (Chapel Hill: University of North Carolina Press, 1988) and "Religion in the Lives of Slaveholding Women of the Antebellum South," in *That Gentle Strength: Historical Perspectives on Women in Christianity,* ed. Lynda L. Coon, Katherine J. Haldane, and Elisabeth W. Sommer (Charlottesville: University Press of Virginia, 1990), 207-29. For a thoughtful perspective on the religious lives of southern women, see also Jean E. Friedman, *The Enclosed Garden: Women and Community in the Evangelical South, 1830-1900* (Chapel Hill: University of North Carolina Press, 1985).

not encompass the possibility that a majority of the slaveholding women who have left written records did not regard religion as an important aspect of their lives and an important bulwark for their proslavery political views. To claim otherwise is unacceptably to distort the historical evidence — the testimony of their own words — to fit contemporary feminist views. And, withal, I am not exempting myself from the rule that each of us, independent of our standards of historical objectivity, does, in some measure, write from a position of advocacy.

In part my advocacy stems from a commitment to history itself, to the notion that history matters and that historical responsibility and honesty are possible, even if scientific precision is not. In part it stems from theories to which I was drawn because of my prior commitment to history and which influenced my coming to intellectual independence, notably Marxism and Freudianism, although it is worth noting that my understanding of both has always struck many Marxists and Freudians as idiosyncratic. And in part it stems from my allegiance to feminism itself, and especially from my conviction that the most visible manifestations of feminism may not faithfully capture the values that women have derived from their experience, much less serve their best interests in the present and future. Finally, I was reared in accordance with stern Calvinist traditions by parents who were no longer believers and a grandmother who was. From my earliest years, that Calvinism fueled my sense that both intellectual honesty and personal accountability were not only possible but necessary. But both, according to those who most influenced me, required an unflinching willingness to look unpleasant truths, notably about oneself, in the face and to respect strenuous demands as the ultimate test of human mettle.

Each of these commitments informs my advocacy — or what some would call point of view — as a historian, and together they account for my most serious quarrels with the dominant tendencies in feminism. Feminism's relation to and attitudes toward the religious past, present, and future of American women lies at the heart of these quarrels. If nothing else, the religious history of American women should teach us respect for history itself and humility in the face of other women's ability to make sense of their lives. For religion did, preeminently, help women to make sense of their lives — to turn the recurrent routine of domestic life into a narrative of purpose and service, to turn the subordination of one's own feelings and needs to the feelings and needs of others into a calling.[11] Too frequently, it seems to escape feminist historians that if we deny previous women that commitment to service and self-discipline, we trivialize their lives. Worse, we subordinate the meaning of their lives to our own historically specific and self-serving dreams.

Traces of what we now call feminism may be found among women of vastly different conditions in vastly different historical epochs. But traces do not an ideology make, even when they are passionately held — even when they are, as in the case of Saint Teresa or Joan of Arc, acted upon. The first signs of the modern ideology of feminism emerged in tandem with bourgeois individualism, notably the language of individual political rights. The immediate origins of and catalysts for modern feminism were distinctly secular, and they concerned the position of women in this world. Many of the more diffuse origins were religious, but they rarely acquired the same impatience with the conventions of the world. For they assumed that the ultimate worth of the individual soul would be realized in another world and would not be measured by the things that are Caesar's. Throughout the early centuries of Christianity, women were not alone in pursuing a truth that freed them from, rather than bound them to, the goods of the world. Nor were they alone in recognizing service to the Lord and his Son, the Savior, as the highest human calling. Only with the triumph of individualism in politics, secularism in intellectual life, and capitalism in social relations and economics did the majority of the most gifted men decisively throw in their lot with the goods and powers of this world rather than the next.

Women's *de facto* custody of and, some would claim, enforced association with religion thus unfolded in tandem with the early glimmerings of modern feminism. Since religion proved one of the heaviest chains that bound women to domestic responsibilities, it has made it difficult for feminist historians to come to terms with its meaning in women's lives. Many, to be sure, have eagerly seized upon the ways in which women drew a sense of empowerment and mission from their

11. Rosemary Skinner Keller, "Calling and Career: The Revolution in the Mind and Heart of Abigail Adams," in *That Gentle Strength*, 190-206, has written thoughtfully of the role of calling in women's internal lives, although she argues that in the specific case of Abigail Adams calling led to a concern for secular individual rights for women.

association with religion, but, as a rule, have chosen only to focus upon the ways in which that sense of empowerment moved women to reform the world in the light of their own distinctly female standards.[12] Feminist historians have displayed considerably less interest in the many women who drew upon religion in order to reinforce their fundamental satisfaction with their own condition and responsibilities. Here and there, for example, we learn of women who opposed suffrage, but even then the emphasis normally falls upon the social prerogatives they were trying to protect, as in the case of southern white women who feared that women's suffrage would dangerously increase the black vote. We rarely see explored, much less sympathetically explored, the views of women who genuinely believed that the differentiation of male and female roles articulated a worthy, biblically sanctioned order.

IV

Recently, during a visit to one of my graduate students' sections of our introductory course in Women's Studies, I listened to a group of undergraduate women explain what they had learned during the semester. Knowing my student to be a devout Catholic and an admirably independent thinker, I did not expect to hear clichés about women's liberation, but even these expectations did not prepare me for the response of the first student in the group to speak. A semester of Women's Studies, which she had very much appreciated, had, she told us, convinced her that, after all, women should not be ministers. Her intensive reading and reflection in a demanding course had, she elaborated, sent her back to her Bible and to a new consideration of traditional male and female roles. She hastened to add that, of course, she expected to work, to be paid the same as men for the same work, and to be spared sexual harassment. But, having read so much of what feminists were offering, she had come to the conclusion that women ministers represented a dangerous challenge to the Christian tradition and teachings in which she anchored her life.

12. This has been especially true in the cases of women's role in antislavery and temperance. See, for example, Ruth Bordin, *Women and Temperance: The Quest for Power and Liberty, 1873-1900* (Philadelphia: Temple University Press, 1981).

I do not share her doubts about women in the ministry or priest-hood, but I do respect what she was trying to say. For this young woman, feminism as advocacy embodied a revolutionary agenda that threatened to cut women and men loose from the past and thus sever their moorings to the heritage of their families, communities, nation, and faith. What she had, in effect, learned from her introduction to Women's Studies was that feminism and religion were engaged in a combat to the finish — that to side with feminism was to side against religion. Many feminist teachers and scholars would doubtless be aghast at the conclusions she drew from their teaching. They would certainly counter that many feminists view themselves as deeply reli-gious and have directed their best efforts at bringing the churches into line with feminist teachings. But this student, who had also been intro-duced to feminist writing on religion, refused to accept their interpreta-tion. From her perspective, the problem lay precisely with feminist revisions of religion, which she saw as eviscerating if not radically uprooting the faith she cherished. Seeing feminism as an unequivocal effort to force a choice, she chose against it — or chose against what feminists had taught her that feminism stood for.

Even without extensive instruction, this student instinctively grasped that feminist theologians, following the lead of secular femi-nists, have "exalted the importance of women's experience in matters of Biblical and theological interpretation."[13] This emphasis upon the primacy of women's experience has led feminist theologians to chal-lenge the authority of biblical texts, which have traditionally been taken as authoritative. Thus Letty Russell has argued that the "word of God is *not* identical with the biblical texts," and those texts may not be regarded as the sole authority in the practical theology of a Christian life.[14] In so arguing, Russell, like other feminist theologians, has fol-lowed the path traced by the abolitionists, who, when confronted with the biblical sanction of slavery, insisted that if the Bible defended slavery, which their consciences told them was wrong, then their con-sciences must supersede biblical authority. That is, they identified their

13. Mary A. Kassian, *The Feminist Gospel: The Movement to Unite Feminism within the Church* (Wheaton, Ill.: Crossway Books, 1992), 169.

14. Letty Russell, "Household of Freedom: Authority in Feminist Theology," in Letty Russell, ed., *Feminist Interpretation of the Bible* (Philadelphia: Westminster Press, 1985), 17.

own conscience or spirit as the Holy Spirit, the objective existence of which they implicitly denied. Feminist theologians' insistence upon the primacy of experience pushes their initiative to its logical conclusion by elevating experience over the vestiges of conscience and insisting that whatever divine spirit exists must derive from it.

This student's instinctive rejection of individual experience as the ultimate Christian authority confirmed my own deepest sense that the most important struggle lies within feminism rather than for or against it. And this is where my own advocacy as a skeptical feminist and especially as a historian comes into play. For feminism, especially in its poststructuralist and postmodernist variants, has emerged above all as a war against history — as much a war against what many women have felt to be societies that men (supposedly by themselves) have wrought. The evidence permits no doubt that religion has mattered to women — mattered as practice and perhaps even more as identity. Religion has structured and sanctified women's efforts at individual worth and their efforts on behalf of others through which they have attempted to enact the convictions that inspired their lives. In the measure that feminism has repudiated those personal and social identities, dismissing them as painful evidence of the confinement in which men (and implicitly children) forcibly held women, it has simultaneously repudiated women's capacity for an independent spiritual relation to religion.

An important element of the Christian tradition has always included the celebration of sacrifice, most notably the willing self-sacrifice of Jesus on behalf of the salvation of humanity — a sacrifice that represented a supreme act of obedience to legitimate authority. No, the most powerful of the Christian churches have not always lived up to that example themselves. Yes, there has been a tendency to foist the practice of sacrifice off onto others while church leaders enjoy as many of the prerogatives of the world as the appearance of decency permits — and in some notorious cases, more than it permits. But withal, the ideal has persisted. And through the ages, parish priests and country ministers wrestled with its demands, even as theologians have wrestled with its implications in a changing world. In the United States, a fluid society, a dynamic economy with devastating fluctuations, and a sense of opportunities for the seizing have discouraged clerical leaders from asking too much of the faithful out of fear of losing them entirely. Thus emerged a pronounced tendency to attribute the gentler and more self-abnegating virtues to women, perhaps in the hope that women's assumption of them would ensure their perpetuation for the community as a whole.

The great danger in this solution — this *de facto* divorce between morality and power — has only emerged in our own time when feminism has led many women to insist that their first need must be an appropriate share of power. For some that power means corporate incomes, for others a share of the most lucrative political spoils, for still others an equal share of the professions. But some women's pursuit of the brass ring has been accompanied by a disastrous erosion of the material and spiritual support for women who prefer more traditional paths. As a result, some women's goal of economic independence has increasingly become all women's necessity. The specialization in charity and service has moved from being a worthy choice to being an almost certain sentence for the woman and her children of comparative or absolute social and economic deprivation. And these developments have unfolded in the absence of any serious effort to reknit the bonds between morality and power.

Tacitly accepting that divorce, feminists have increasingly focused on power at the expense of morality. Even those who claim a special moral sensibility for women rarely suggest that women should draw upon that sensibility to assume the special obligations of charity and service. Thus even within religion, feminism more often than not focuses upon women's right to ordination or upon dismantling the "sexist" language of hymnals, prayer books, the Bible, and Christianity. Not surprisingly, the very idea of a male God and his Son has emerged as the ultimate target. The supposed pretension that God is male brutally exposes the measure in which Christianity has always embodied a plot to discredit, devalue, and disempower women. No longer may any reasonable person expect women to worship a God who has not been cast in their image. And herein lies the ultimate revolution. According to the Bible, God made man in his own image. According to feminism, woman must make God in hers. That the faithful rather than God do the making reverses the central meaning of Christianity, thereby destroying Christianity. By the same token, it realizes the most radical implication of feminism — not merely for women but for our society and culture. And lost is what every Christian knows — that God is spirit and that the literal ascription to him of maleness or femaleness is simply ludicrous. More than a century ago, the slaveholding polemicist

Louisa S. McCord proposed that the real goal of her feminist opponent Harriet Martineau was "(as some of her recent works seem to indicate) to have it decided that she is *Le Bon Dieu* himself."[15]

In the end authority and its legitimacy constitute the problem. The divorce between power and morality opens the way to the charge that power must be understood as brute force. It thus invites the complacent assumption that authority must, by definition, lack legitimacy. This conflation of power and authority in turn permits the self-serving conflation of robber barons and God, since both represent power. Once that conflation has been effected, it becomes child's play to discredit history, religion, morality, objectivity, logic, rationalism, and even traditional notions of individual freedom as self-serving embodiments of male power. Thus, by one broad stroke, does all authority go by the board, and with it any reason to subordinate one's immediate desires to any consideration or circumstance. This assumption then invites us to reread the history of women's experience as an unending saga of subordination and oppression, which precludes our understanding that many women may have taken pride and comfort in the fulfillment of their "ordained" roles. And this dubious historical revision supports the comfortable feminist assumption that all women must want and need "liberation" from the authorities that have constrained them, notably Christianity and other "traditional" religions.

We may doubt that most women see things that way. And their willingness to accept some measure of self-sacrifice in the service of a higher good does not mean that they are, by some extraordinary exercise of false consciousness, wallowing in their own oppression. Most women recognize their own vulnerability all too clearly. They also suspect that the further destruction of legitimate authority will only worsen their condition. Those who act on this suspicion are as likely as not to opt for tradition, notwithstanding its admitted inadequacies for our current situation, as for a feminism that promises only an exacerbation of their problems. For me, the responsibilities of advocacy above all entail the willingness to attend to their concerns, which means a willingness to understand the history that has shaped their values and aspirations and to accept that history as a valuable force in what we are today.

15. L. S. McCord, "Enfranchisement of Women," *Southern Quarterly Review* 21 (April 1852): 330.

In Search of the Fourth "R": The Treatment of Religion in American History Textbooks and Survey Courses

PAUL BOYER

IS RELIGION systematically excluded from U.S. history textbooks and survey courses? Are educators and textbook authors in the grip of an "antireligious bias" that leads them to ignore or downplay religious piety as a shaping force in American historical experience? These are the questions I should briefly like to explore in this essay.[1] First, however, some background may help place this volatile issue in context.

The 1980s and 1990s have seen a flood of books by Christian believers, especially evangelicals, commenting on the status of religion in American public life. Glenn Tinder's *The Political Meaning of Christianity*, Stephen Carter's *The Culture of Disbelief*, George Marsden's *Evangelicalism and Modern America* and *The Soul of the American University*, Mark Noll's *One Nation Under God?* and *Religion and American Politics*,

1. This essay appeared in *The History Teacher* 29 (February 1996): 195-216. An earlier version was presented at the Conference on Faith and History, Messiah College, October 8, 1994. My thanks to Professor James Lorence, University of Wisconsin Center–Marathon County, for sharing references and materials relating to this topic, and to Professor Charles Cohen for a critical reading of the essay. I should also at the outset declare my own vested interest as the author or co-author of several high school and college U.S. history textbooks, including *Todd and Curti's American Nation* (Austin: Holt, Rinehart & Winston, 1994); *The Enduring Vision: A History of the American People*, 3rd ed. (Lexington, Mass.: D. C. Heath, 1995) (co-author); and *Promises to Keep: The United States Since World War II* (Lexington, Mass.: D. C. Heath, 1994).

Cal Thomas's *The Things That Matter Most,* Gene Edward Veith Jr.'s *Postmodern Times: A Christian Guide to Contemporary Thought and Culture,* William J. Bennett's *The De-Valuing of America,* and Ralph Reed's *Politically Incorrect: What Religious Conservatives Really Think* are only a few of scores of books exploring the interface between religious faith and the "secular" culture. One evangelical publisher commented in 1994, "Cultural studies [are] . . . very big for us right now. . . . [P]eople want to find out what's shaping the way we live and whether there are any bridges we can use to cross over to the present culture."[2] These books have attracted notice not only in the religious press but in such publications as the *New York Times,* the *Economist* of London, and the *Chronicle of Higher Education.*

A common theme in these works is the charge (or lament) that religious perspectives are systematically excluded from, or downgraded in, the public sphere. Our legal and political systems "trivialize" religious belief, Stephen Carter claims, despite the fact that such beliefs undergird millions of Americans' views on some of the most vital issues of the day.

One aspect of this general charge of cultural marginalization is the accusation that religion is virtually ignored in all levels of public education, from the primary schools to the research universities. George Marsden finds religion downgraded in America's institutions of higher learning. American higher education arose out of deep religious piety, and U.S. colleges and universities once actively engaged religious issues,

2. Leonard Goss, editor-in-chief of Crossway Books, quoted in Gayle White, "Battle Plans for the Culture Wars," *Publishers Weekly,* 11 July 1994, 35. Glenn Tinder, *The Political Meaning of Christianity: An Interpretation* (Baton Rouge: Louisiana State University Press, 1989); Stephen L. Carter, *The Culture of Disbelief: How American Law and Politics Trivialize Religious Devotion* (New York: Basic Books, 1993); George M. Marsden, ed., *Evangelicalism and Modern America* (Grand Rapids: Eerdmans, 1984); George M. Marsden, *The Soul of the American University: From Protestant Establishment to Established Nonbelief* (New York: Oxford University Press, 1994); Mark A. Noll, *One Nation Under God? Christian Faith and Political Action in America* (San Francisco: Harper & Row, 1988); Mark A. Noll, ed., *Religion and American Politics* (New York: Oxford University Press, 1990); Cal Thomas, *The Things That Matter Most* (New York: HarperCollins, 1994); Gene Edward Veith Jr., *Postmodern Times: A Christian Guide to Contemporary Thought and Culture* (Wheaton, Ill.: Crossway Books, 1994); William J. Bennett, *The De-Valuing of America: The Fight for Our Culture and Our Children* (Colorado Springs: Focus on the Family, 1994); Ralph Reed, *Politically Incorrect: What Religious Conservatives Really Think* (Dallas: Word, Inc., 1995).

Marsden insists, yet that same faith is virtually absent from the higher reaches of academia today. Garry Wills in *Under God* (1990) similarly accused intellectuals and educators of writing religious believers out of the national experience. "[How can so many scholars] keep misplacing such a large body of people?" he writes; "Every time religiosity catches the attention of intellectuals, it is as if a shooting star had appeared in the sky." Stephen Carter agrees. "It ought to be embarrassing, in this age of celebration of American diversity," he says, "that the schools have been so slow to move toward teaching about our nation's diverse religious traditions." Michael Novak adds to the chorus: "A large majority of American students and professors come from Christian homes, and all of us, Christian or not, live within a predominantly Christian history. . . . Yet the way in which our philosophers neglect the intellectual implications of Christianity for our politics, economics, and moral life is nothing short of scandalous. It is as if Christianity does not exist." Martin Marty, discussing the upsurge of religious fundamentalism worldwide, observed in 1993; "Certainly, impulses that are so strong, that attract so many millions of people and disturb the peace on all continents, should be noticed by the academy, which has long neglected them." As for the public education scene, Marty lamented in 1989: "[T]he study of religion on elementary and high school levels remains neglected."[3]

Much evidence, both statistical and anecdotal, supports the claim that religion is the Black Hole of American public culture, noted episodically and intermittently at best. During the 1993 Branch Davidian standoff in Waco, Texas, I received many calls from radio stations, newspaper reporters, and magazine editors across the United States and Canada. Having written a book on prophetic belief in modern America,[4] I was presumed to have some insights that might help the journalists make

---

3. Garry Wills, *Under God: Religion and American Politics* (New York: Simon & Schuster, 1990), 15; Carter, *Culture of Disbelief*, 208; Michael Novak, "Christianity's Place in Political Life," *Christian Science Monitor*, 2 February 1990, 12; Martin E. Marty, "Fundamentalism and the Scholars," *The Key Reporter* 58, no. 3 (Spring 1993): 3, and "The Academic Study of Religion," *Humanities* 10 (January-February 1989): 29. For a historical perspective on intellectuals' view of religion from the 1920s to the 1950s, see Lewis Perry, *Intellectual Life in America: A History* (New York: Franklin Watts, 1984), 385-403.

4. *When Time Shall Be No More: Prophecy Belief in Modern American Culture* (Cambridge: Harvard University Press, 1992).

sense of Waco. But then the calls stopped. Once the crisis ended, media interest in my work fell to its normal level: zero.

The summer of 1994 brought another flurry of calls, triggered this time by the comet striking Jupiter; the death of Rabbi Schneerson, the Lubavitchers' designated Messiah; and the Rev. Harold Camping's bold prediction of the world's end in September 1994.[5] And, sure enough, the mass suicide or murder of the Order of the Solar Temple cultists in Switzerland in early October brought another short-lived round of journalistic queries.

But if the media's attention to religion is short-lived, what about academia, and specifically, what about historians? Here, I would argue, generalizations are risky. As we shall see, the historical guild, despite charges to the contrary, has in fact devoted much scholarly attention in recent years to religious history, including religion's role in America's past. But the more specific charge addressed in this essay — that religion continues to be largely absent from U.S. history textbooks and survey courses, especially at the high school level — cannot be so easily dismissed. This claim, often advanced as part of a broader discussion of the alleged exclusion or marginalization of religion in academia, is a serious one, and it merits a serious response.[6]

5. Harold Camping, *1994?* (New York: Vantage Press, 1992).

6. This question has, in fact, received much attention from scholars and educators. See, e.g., Robert Michaelson, *Piety in the Public Schools* (New York: Macmillan, 1970); David Engel, ed., *Religion in Public Education: Problems and Prospects* (New York: Paulist Press, 1974); Peter Bracher et al., eds., *Religious Studies in the Curriculum: Retrospect and Prospects* (Dayton: Public Education Religious Studies Center, Wright State University, 1974); James E. Wood Jr., "Religion and Education: A Continuing Dilemma," *Annals of the American Academy of Political and Social Science* 446 (1979): 63-77; Robert Bryan, "History, Pseudo-History, Anti-History: How Public School Textbooks Treat Religion," *Policy Studies in Education,* Washington, D.C.: LEARN, Inc., 1984 (ERIC Document Reproduction Service No. ED-249575); Donald Oppewall, *Religion in American Textbooks: Review of the Literature* (Washington, D.C.: National Institute of Education, 1985); Frederick W. Jordan, "Religion in United States History Textbooks: Some Preliminary Reflections," *New England Journal of History* 48, no. 3 (1991-92): 22-32; James J. Lorence and James G. Grinsel, "Amen: The Role of Religion in History Teaching," *Perspectives* (American Historical Association newsletter), October 1992, 20-23; Edwin S. Gaustad, "American History, With and Without Religion: '. . . the whole truth . . . so help me God,' " *Magazine of History* (Organization of American Historians) 6, no. 3 (Winter 1992): 15-22; and — an older study of one state — Harold Pflug, "Religion in Missouri Textbooks," *Phi Delta Kappan* (April 1955).

*   *   *

The charge that textbooks and survey courses slight religion has been made by many individuals and organizations, including the indefatigable Texas gadflies Mel and Norma Gabler, and Robert L. Simonds's Citizens for Excellence in Education.[7] Perhaps its most vehement and widely disseminated elaboration, however, came in a 1985 study contracted by the National Institute of Education, the research arm of the U.S. Department of Education, during William Bennett's tenure as Secretary of Education. The principal investigator, Paul C. Vitz, a professor of psychology at New York University, offered a popularized version of his findings in a 1985 paperback published under the provocative title *Censorship: Evidence of Bias in Our Children's Textbooks*.[8]

Citing data from some sixty textbooks, Vitz buttressed his claim that religion is rarely mentioned in grade school social studies texts and high school U.S. history books, especially as one moves from the early Spanish missions and the seventeenth-century Puritans toward the present. None of the history textbooks, he writes, "came close to adequately presenting the major religious events of the past 100 to 200 years . . . , the large role that religion has always played in American life, . . . [or] the great religious energy and creativity of the United States."[9]

Vitz's explanation for this state of affairs is summed up in his title's references to "censorship" and "bias." Textbooks downplay religion, he charges, because of the "liberal and secular prejudice" of an

7. Mel and Norma Gabler, *What Are They Teaching Our Children?* (Wheaton, Ill.: SP Publications, 1985). On Citizens for Excellence in Education, see Sonia L. Nazario, "Crusader Vows to Put God Back into Schools Using Local Elections," *Wall Street Journal*, 15 July 1992; Rob Boston, "Educational Odyssey: How a North Carolina Town Fought the Religious Right — and Won," *Church and State* 46, no. 5 (May 1993): 4-7; Anti-Defamation League, *The Religious Right: The Assault on Tolerance and Pluralism in America* (New York: Anti-Defamation League, 1994), 101-5.

8. Paul C. Vitz, *Censorship: Evidence of Bias in Our Children's Textbooks* (Ann Arbor: Servant Books, 1986). The original study on which the paperback is based, entitled *Religion and Traditional Values in Public School Textbooks: An Empirical Study* (Washington, D.C., National Institute of Education, 1985), is available only in photocopied or microform editions.

9. Vitz, *Censorship*, 2-3, 56. Discussing an earlier edition of *Rise of the American Nation*, a high school textbook of which I am now the author, Vitz finds its religious coverage "seriously inadequate," and cites a long list of neglected events, including "the Holiness or Pentecostal movement of 1880-1910." *Censorship*, 50.

116

unholy alliance of authors, publishers, selection boards, and bureau-crats who run the National Education Association, the teachers' union. The Ur-villain is that perennial whipping boy, John Dewey. Offering an action strategy for rectifying the situation, Vitz advises: "[T]he publish-ers should hear from the millions of Christians and Jews that if God and the Bible are left out, the publishers will also lose sales. And, God willing, lots more sales will be lost than when publishers leave God and the Bible in."[10]

Vitz's larger ideological agenda, formulated at the high noon of the Reagan era, emerges as he blasts the textbooks for other sins as well:

> Are public school textbooks biased? Are they censored? The answer to both is yes. . . . Religion, traditional family values, and conserva-tive political and economic positions have been reliably excluded from children's textbooks.[11]

Vitz's survey of social studies readers for the earlier grades found conditions just as shocking: "[B]usiness was ignored. No Horatio Alger stories appear. . . . [M]any aggressively feminist stories . . . openly deride traditional manhood."[12]

Vitz denies that all this reflects "a deliberate and large-scale con-spiracy,"[13] but a conspiratorial tone pervades the book. And Charles Colson, who should know a conspiracy when he sees one, agrees in a jacket blurb praising Vitz for his "shocking revelations about the elimi-nation of moral and religious ideas from the nation's textbooks."

How shall we evaluate all this? First of all, I do not question the general accuracy of Vitz's data for the early to mid-1980s. While the intervening decade may have seen some improvement, I suspect the general pattern he describes still exists. Religious history is, indeed, only slowly filtering into the textbooks and the survey courses. This is especially true of high school textbooks and courses, but impressionistic evidence suggests that college-level texts and survey courses reveal the same deficiency, though perhaps to a lesser degree.[14]

10. Ibid., 78-87; quoted phrases, 80; on Dewey, 86.
11. Ibid., 1.
12. Ibid., 3.
13. Ibid., 80.
14. Jordan, "Religion in United States History Textbooks," 23; Lorence and

This neglect is particularly puzzling in view of the recent outpouring of scholarly work in this field. Early in 1992, preparing for an October 1994 lecture on this topic, I began a file of ads and reviews for new books on U.S. religious history. The file soon bulged and overflowed. A bibliography prepared in 1993 by my Wisconsin history department colleague Charles L. Cohen on recent work in American religious history down to 1860 ran to fourteen densely filled pages. As early as 1989, the *Encyclopedia of the American Religious Experience* spoke of "a veritable renaissance of historical writing about American Christianity."[15] And Yale professor Jon Butler commented in 1992:

> Among college and university-based historians, especially Americanists, religion could scarcely be getting more attention. The meetings of the American Historical Association, the Organization of American Historians, and the American Studies Association overflow with sessions on religion.[16]

In fact, Butler insisted, "evangelicalism" is much overworked as a causal factor in historical interpretation! Much evidence confirms the outpouring of scholarship Butler described. Whether one looks at scholarly reviews, conference programs, Internet databases, publishers' advertisements in the historical journals, or the *Journal of American History*'s regular listing of newly published articles and dissertations, the evidence for a burgeoning of scholarly work in American religious history is ubiquitous.[17]

Deepening the puzzle is the fact (again despite critics' charges to the contrary) that professional education associations and state boards of instruction have for years been urging more coverage of religion in

---

Grinsel, "The Role of Religion in History Teaching," 20; Gaustad, "American History, With and Without Religion," 15.

15. Henry Warner Bowden, "The Historiography of American Religion," in *Encyclopedia of the American Religious Experience,* 3 vols., ed. Charles H. Lippy and Peter W. Williams (New York: Charles Scribner's Sons, 1988), 1:9.

16. Jon Butler, "Born-Again History?" Paper presented to the American Historical Association, Washington, D.C., December 1992.

17. For a roundup of one decade's output, see Martin E. Marty, "American Religious History in the Eighties: A Decade of Achievement," *Church History* 62 (September 1993): 335-77.

history textbooks and survey courses. In 1964, the American Council of School Administrators declared:

> A curriculum which ignored religion would itself have serious religious implications. It would seem to proclaim that religion has not been as real in men's lives as health, politics, or economics. By omission, it would appear to deny that religion has been and is important in man's history — a denial of the obvious. As an integral part of man's culture, it must be included.[18]

From the 1970s on, numerous state educational boards and professional organizations of educators adopted guidelines or issued reports advocating greater attention to religion in public instruction.[19]

In 1987, the Association for Supervision and Curriculum Development (ASCD), a 180,000-member, Virginia-based organization of principals, teachers, supervisors, and professors of education, called for "decisive action . . . to end the current curricular silence on religion." Following through on this tocsin call, the ASCD issued a series of specific curricular recommendations. In 1990, it followed up with *Religion in American History: What to Teach and How*.[20]

The "Religious Studies Guidelines" issued by the Wisconsin De-

---

18. American Association of School Administrators, *Religion in the Public Schools* (New York: Harper & Row, 1964), quoted in Wisconsin Department of Public Instruction, "Religious Studies Guidelines," Bulletin no. 2385 (Madison, 1982), 3.

19. See, e.g., H. Michael Hartoonian, "Religion and the Public Schools" (Madison: Wisconsin Department of Public Instruction, 1978); Henry Hoeks, *Studying the Sacred in the Schools: A Handbook for the Academic Study of Religion* (Council of the Study of Religion in Michigan Schools, 1976); California Board of Education, *Handbook on the Legal Rights and Responsibilities of School Personnel and Students in the Areas of Moral and Civil Education and Teaching about Religion* (Sacramento, 1973); State of Minnesota Guidelines Steering Committee, *Guidelines for Teaching about Religion in Public Schools* (1978). For general surveys of such guidelines and recommendations, see Lynn Taylor, *Religion and Culture in Education: Open Door for the Fourth "R"* (Lawrence: University of Kansas, Division of Continuing Education, 1977); *Religious Studies in the Curriculum: Retrospect and Prospect, 1963-1983* (Dayton: Public Education Religious Studies Center, Wright State University, 1974).

20. *Religion in the Curriculum* (Alexandria, Va.: Association for Supervision and Curriculum Development, 1987); Charles C. Haynes, *Religion in American History: What to Teach and How* (Alexandria, Va.: Association for Supervision and Curriculum Development, 1990). The ASCD's 1987 "decisive action" call quoted in Gaustad, "American History, With and Without Religion," 15.

partment of Public Instruction (DPI) in 1982 summed up the case that many agencies and organizations were making the way for more attention to religion in public school instruction. While "the restrictions of the Constitution in the matter of indoctrination" should be observed, the Wisconsin DPI's guidelines said,

> [T]he schools surely cannot fulfill adequately their educational function without including instruction concerning the impact of religion upon people, cultures, political systems, and world history.
>
> If the public schools are truly to educate for responsible citizenship . . . , they certainly cannot ignore the influence of religious values in forming democratic institutions and in shaping contemporary society.[21]

Yet despite the flood of recent historical scholarship on the role of religion in American history, despite the urging of educational associations and state instructional agencies, and despite a green light from the courts (see below), religion still remains largely absent from the textbooks and survey-course syllabi. As historian Edwin S. Gaustad wrote in 1992,

> Both the judicial and the pedagogical establishments have made bold statements in favor of academic attention to religion at every level of the school curriculum. But bold announcements have been generally followed by timid actions on the part of publishers, principals, parents, and teachers. . . . Religion remains a classroom pariah.[22]

Why this apparent anomaly? Does the pedagogues' neglect of religion in fact reflect a secularist bias — what George Marsden provocatively calls "the antireligious heart of modern academia"?[23] Perhaps, to some degree. Religious belief — especially evangelical belief — *is* weaker among academics, particularly at the research-university level,

---

21. "Religious Studies Guidelines," ii.

22. Gaustad, "American History, With and Without Religion," 15.

23. Marsden, *Soul of the American University,* 442. See also George Marsden and Bradley J. Longfield, eds., *The Secularization of the Academy* (New York: Oxford University Press, 1992); "Scholar Calls Colleges Biased against Religion," *New York Times,* 26 November 1993, A14; Carolyn J. Mooney, "Devout Professors on the Offensive," *Chronicle of Higher Education,* 4 May 1994, A18, A21-22.

than among the general populace. Stephen Carter cites poll data to show that "the devoutly religious [are] . . . grossly underrepresented on campus." James Davison Hunter, drawing upon research conducted in 1978-79, finds that thirty-eight percent of Americans with only a high school education are evangelicals, while the figure drops to about nine percent for those with a university degree.[24]

Certainly while researching *When Time Shall Be No More* (to resort again to anecdotal evidence), I repeatedly had to justify the project's importance to uncomprehending colleagues, including specialists in American culture utterly at ease in discussing the gender implications of TV's *Roseanne* show, the semiotics of Disneyland, or the cultural meaning of rock 'n' roll, but mystified when I mentioned Cyrus Scofield, Hal Lindsey, the Rapture, or the Mark of the Beast.

While American historians have quite properly been much preoccupied in recent years with rectifying glaring omissions in the "master narrative," this much-needed corrective effort has rarely focused on the neglect of religion as a causal factor in history or of religious believers as a major yet largely invisible population group. At a 1991 conference at the University of North Carolina on historical understanding in contemporary America, a succession of historians called for a rethinking of how the guild approaches race, gender, science, foreign policy, and the literary canon — but remained silent on how historians treat (or fail to treat) religion.[25]

But does neglect translate into hostility and willful suppression? Are we dealing with deliberate misrepresentation undertaken by aggressively "secular" scholars, teachers, and textbook writers infected with an "antireligious bias"? The full explanation, I think, is more complex. Let me suggest several factors that may help explain the thinness of the treatment of religion in U.S. history textbooks and survey courses.

24. Stephen L. Carter, "Conservatives' Faith, Liberals' Disdain," *New York Times*, 15 August 1993, E15; James Davison Hunter, *American Evangelicalism: Conservative Religion and the Quandary of Modernity* (New Brunswick, N.J.: Rutgers University Press, 1983), 54. For more recent demographic data confirming the point, see Barry A. Kosmin and Seymour P. Lachman, *One Nation under God: Religion in Contemporary American Society* (New York: Harmony Books, 1993).

25. The conference papers are reprinted in Lloyd Kramer, Donald Reid, and William L. Barney, eds., *Learning History in America: Schools, Cultures, and Politics* (Minneapolis: University of Minnesota Press, 1994).

*   *   *

First, some textbook writers and survey teachers may avoid religion out of a confusion between advocacy and analysis. To emphasize religion as a factor in historical explanation or to stress the religious beliefs of historical actors might be seen as *promoting* religion and thus breaching the constitutional "wall of separation." This is clearly a misreading of the separation-of-church-and-state principle derived from the First Amendment, as construed by the Supreme Court, with its carefully counterbalanced provisions: Congress may neither *establish* religion nor prohibit the *free exercise* of religion. Addressing the issue of religion and public education in *Engel v. Vitale* (1962) and again in two 1963 cases, *Abington School District v. Schempp* and *Murray v. Curlett*, the high court firmly forbade prescribed prayers and Bible reading, but gave a constitutional clean bill of health to teaching about religion "when presented objectively as part of a secular program of education." Indeed, Justice William J. Brennan Jr., in a concurring opinion in the 1963 cases, underscored the difficulty of "teach[ing] meaningfully about many subjects in the social sciences or the humanities without some mention of religion." This position, in turn, echoed that of Justice Robert H. Jackson, who wrote in the 1948 case *McCollum v. Board of Education:*

> [I]t would not seem practical to teach . . . the arts if we are to forbid exposure of youth to any religious influences. Music without sacred music, architecture without the cathedral, or painting without the scriptural themes would be eccentric and incomplete, even from a secular point of view. . . . One can hardly respect the system of education that would leave the student wholly ignorant of the currents of religious thought that move the world society. . . .[26]

In short, far from imposing constitutional restraints on teaching about religion (other than prohibiting advocacy), the Supreme Court has

26. Joseph Kobylka, *"Abington School District v. Schempp"* and *"Engel v. Vitale"* in Kermit L. Hall, ed., *Oxford Companion to the Supreme Court of the United States* (New York: Oxford University Press, 1992), 1-2, 254-55; Wisconsin Department of Public Instruction, "Religious Studies Guidelines," 6. For overviews, see Donald E. Boles, "Religion and the Public Schools in Judicial Review," *Journal of Church and State* 26 (Winter 1984): 55-71, and Thayer Warshaw, *Religion, Education, and the Supreme Court* (Nashville: Abingdon Press, 1979).

repeatedly underscored the subject's centrality to a well-rounded education. Nevertheless, lingering uneasiness and confusion about the precise pedagogical status of religion in the aftermath of the school prayer and Bible-reading decisions may be one factor in retarding the flow of historical scholarship into the textbooks and the public school classrooms.

A second reason may be simply our uneasiness with controversy. Religion touches the profoundest emotions and most bedrock beliefs of students and teachers, not to mention parents, newspaper editors, trustees, school-board members, and textbook adoption committees. Classroom instructors, textbook authors, and publishers are understandably nervous in treating a subject where one's words are sure to be minutely scrutinized. In the 1920s, the Irish-American mayor of Chicago, William "Big Bill" Thompson, standing on the steps of City Hall, publicly burned history textbooks that he considered tainted by anglophilia. Fear of similar if less incendiary reactions may subtly influence teachers, textbook writers, and publishers, already besieged on many fronts, when they approach the touchy subject of religion.[27]

A possible instance of this avoidance of the potentially controversial was provided by a public school history teacher who participated in the 1991 conference on history teaching at the University of North Carolina. Clearly a resourceful and imaginative pedagogue, this teacher offered a variety of suggestions for bringing history alive for students. "In a seminar on the 1920s," she commented, ". . . one might find the classroom set up as a speakeasy and students dressed as characters of the era." Or, again, the classroom might be transformed into Harlem's legendary Cotton Club for a session on the Harlem Renaissance. Encouraging the use of music to supplement the study of history, she proposed singalongs with tapes of protest songs from the American Revolution and the civil rights movement.[28]

27. For a taste of the controversy that the subject of religion in textbooks can arouse, see John Orr, "California's Textbook Controversy: Religious Studies in the Public Schools," *Religious Studies News*, May/June 1991. I should note, however, that I have never experienced any pressure, subtle or otherwise, from my textbook publishers, including D. C. Heath, publisher of *The Enduring Vision*, whose concluding chapters deal extensively with recent religious trends, including the evangelical resurgence and the political mobilization of conservative Christians under the banner of Jerry Falwell's Moral Majority and Pat Robertson's Christian Coalition.

28. Alice Garrett, "Teaching High School History Inside and Outside the Historical Canon," in *Learning History in America*, 72-73.

These are imaginative suggestions, but note the absences. Along with speakeasies, many thousands of Americans of the 1920s also attended the revivals of Billy Sunday or the Los Angeles services of Aimee Semple MacPherson. Harlem of the 1920s had its storefront holiness churches as well as its jazz clubs. Hymns and gospel songs have played at least as important a role as protest music in the American historical experience. Yet it did not occur to this teacher to suggest classroom exercises built around such religious material. Similarly, the end-of-chapter materials in high school U.S. history textbooks and the available supplementary readings rarely offer primary documents or role-playing opportunities drawn from the nation's religious experience.[29]

But again the more interesting point is not simply the empirical one of documenting religion's absence from the history classroom, but the question of *why* the realm of the sacred is downplayed, not only in the textbooks and survey-course lectures, but even in the supplementary activities and pedagogical aids. One reason, I suspect, is simply most teachers' commonsense awareness that to enter this realm is to venture into a briar-patch of potential controversy and parental reaction.

This uneasiness has surely been intensified in recent years by the bitter, highly polemical controversies that have swirled around public education. As early as the Supreme Court's school-prayer rulings of 1962-63, many Protestant evangelicals (as well as some Roman Catholic prelates) became convinced that the nation's judicial, political, intellectual, and media elites had become actively hostile to religion. Francis Cardinal Spellman denounced *Engel v. Vitale* for striking at "the very heart of the Godly tradition in which America's children have for so long been raised." New York Congressman Frank Becker called it "the most tragic [ruling] in the history of the United States." Seventy-six percent of Americans told pollsters they favored a constitutional amendment permitting school prayer.[30]

In the years since, the contentious wrangling over the nation's public school system has only increased in vitriolic stridency. The class-

29. One exception is Robert Mathisen, ed., *The Role of Religion in American Life: An Interpretive Historical Anthology*, rev. ed. (Dubuque: Kendall/Hunt Publishing Co., 1994), a collection for secondary-school students that includes readings from William Bradford to Charles Colson and Ronald Reagan.

30. Kobylka, *"Abington School District v. Schempp,"* 1.

room has become a major front in what James Davison Hunter has called our contemporary culture wars.[31] Like Paul Vitz, conservatives convinced that "secular humanists" control America's public education, politics, and media have adopted an accusatory, polemical tone as they lambast what they see as a deliberate plot by "secularists" to eradicate religion from the past just as they denigrate it in the present.

Numerous conservative religious organizations, including Lou Sheldon's Traditional Values Coalition, James Dobson's Focus on the Family, and Pat Robertson's Christian Coalition have targeted the public schools for special attention. The California-based Citizens for Excellence in Education, claiming more than 200,000 members in some 1,700 local branches across the nation, has dedicated itself to restoring prayer and "creation science" to the classroom, banishing the "immoral sex education curriculum," stopping "the homosexual/lesbian invasion" of the schools, and in general routing the forces of "secular humanism" from American education. The overall aim, says CEE head Robert L. Simonds, is to "return faith to our public schools." One step toward this goal, he adds, is to persuade adoption committees to "select good textbooks." Through his *Education Newsline* newsletter, his weekly "Issues in Education" broadcasts heard on seventy Christian radio stations, and his campaign to elect evangelicals to local school boards, Simonds and his CEE have effectively pursued these sweeping goals, dismissing critics such as the National Education Association and the American Civil Liberties Union as "union goons" and "anti-Christian hate groups."[32]

The line the Supreme Court has attempted to draw between permissible instruction and impermissible advocacy is often far from clear in the lurid prose of conservative critics of American education, as in Paul Vitz's loosely worded demand that publishers restore "God and the Bible" to the textbooks or face the retribution of an outraged citizenry. For some who advocate "return[ing] faith to the schools," merely

31. James Davison Hunter, *Culture Wars: The Struggle to Define America* (New York: Basic Books, 1991). See also Robert Lekachman, "New Wars of Religion," in *Visions and Nightmares: America after Reagan* (New York: Macmillan, 1987), 205-53.

32. Anti-Defamation League, *The Religious Right*, 101-5. In Austin, Texas, a CEE-dominated schoolboard banished *Little Red Riding Hood* from the open shelves of school libraries because Ms. Hood's grandmother is portrayed as drinking wine (ibid., 104).

teaching about the historical importance of religion is no more than a feeble halfway measure, and even a dangerous one if it appears to place all religions on an equal plane as social phenomena meriting study. This uneasiness became explicit in a 1989 letter to the *Christian Science Monitor* objecting that such a historicizing approach turns religion into "a relic, a museum piece — for study, but not for use today." "This is reverse discrimination — away from faith," the letter writer charged; "It is a secular religion in which all religions are treated as objects of study, not belief."[33]

In fact, the call for more attention to religion in the schools has emanated from two quite distinct sources. On the one hand, many historians and educators of diverse religious faiths or no religion at all advocate this position on intellectual and pedagogical grounds: religious belief has obviously been central in human experience and human history, and the textbooks and survey courses should reflect this fact. On the other hand, conservative polemicists use this issue to bludgeon and demonize "secular humanists" and their alleged conspiracy to drive "God and the Bible" from the classroom as from all other realms of life. For these polemicists, this issue is simply part of a much larger, highly divisive political/cultural agenda.[34]

When the demand for more attention to religion in textbooks and history courses is combined with a litany of other religio-political aims, including instruction in "creation science," a school-prayer amendment, tuition credits for sectarian schools, an end to sex education, and the banning of books such as *The Catcher in the Rye* or the stories of Judy Blume, the uneasiness of textbook writers and teachers becomes understandable. In such an overheated climate, it is hardly surprising that some educators and publishers choose to downplay religion altogether,

33. Kelley Vincent, Elm Springs, Arizona, letter to the editor, *Christian Science Monitor*, 8 March 1989, 20. Vincent was responding to an earlier essay in the *Monitor* ("A Glaring Omission in History Texts," 23 January 1989) deploring the inadequate coverage of religion in history textbooks.

34. I recognize, of course, that this overly schematic bifurcation of the two groups excludes many Americans who believe that religion merits more coverage in the textbooks and survey courses, but who do not necessarily embrace the larger agenda of the New Religious Right. Unfortunately, in the contemporary arena of what is generously called "public discourse," the broad-brush polemicists receive the most attention, while those who draw careful distinctions and avoid inflammatory language are often marginalized.

rather than venture onto such a dangerous minefield. Ironically, then, one reason that religion continues to receive insufficient attention in textbooks and survey courses may be that the issue has been so politicized by those who profess to care about it most deeply. In a cultural climate marked by lurid rhetoric, emotional exaggeration, and conspiratorial accusations, it becomes difficult to address dispassionately any single issue — even a valid one — that has become so hopelessly entangled in the raging *Kulturkampf* that agitates our public life.

* * *

Other reasons for the paucity of religious history in our textbooks and survey courses, however, relate more to pedagogical conventions and to the evolution of the discipline of history itself than to our contemporary culture wars. For example, this inadequate coverage is, in part, a by-product of the continued pedagogical tenacity of the "presidential synthesis."[35] In the endless quest for interpretive coherence, the presidential term has proven a perennial favorite. Thus, we have "The Age of Jackson," not "The Age of Finney"; the "Eisenhower Era," not the "Billy Graham Era," though an evangelist can embody an epoch as well as a president. Despite the emergence of social history, the presidential synthesis remains strong, especially at the introductory-textbook and survey level, obscuring aspects of the past that do not conveniently fit this framework.

Worsening the problem is the conservative nature of the history-textbook genre; not *political* conservatism, but stylistic conservatism. Textbooks evolve with glacial slowness, as authors and publishers make incremental changes rather than radically revising. A similar conservativism affects history teaching. As beginning teachers, we replicate the courses we took in college, and assign the books we read in graduate school. As the years pass, we cherish our lecture notes, now yellowing with age. To rethink our approach from the ground up is a scary, time-consuming undertaking. This, too, checks the flow of new scholarship on religion — or any other topic — into the textbooks and the introductory courses.

35. On this point, see Lorence and Grinsel, "Role of Religion in History Teaching," 21.

And pity the poor U.S. history textbook writer struggling to include an ever-growing body of material. Not only does history keep happening, but the material to be covered expands as well. Paralleling the new religious history is pathbreaking new work on women, blacks, Hispanics, Native Americans, Asian-Americans, the environment, the West, technology and science, gays and lesbians, working class culture, and on and on. Sometimes as a textbook author I feel like a driver facing a crush of people trying to board an already jammed bus. The pressure to add content is endless — and endlessly frustrating. American religious history, in short, is only one among many passengers clamoring for a seat on the bus.

More substantively, many textbook writers, like other historians — whatever their own religious beliefs — tacitly accept the secularization paradigm when conceptualizing U.S. history. With Darwinism, the rise of modern science, the emergence of a heterogeneous urban society, the spread of the mass media, and the influence of advertisers seeking the broadest possible market, so the story goes, religious loyalties weakened. Among American social thinkers, Walter Lippmann articulated this view as early as 1914 in *Drift and Mastery*. Like Auguste Comte earlier, Lippmann saw the old faiths fading, and a new secular order taking their place.[36]

The secularization paradigm, often linked to "modernization" theory, can serve to justify diminished attention to religion as one nears the present. Everyone concedes the importance in American history of Puritanism and the Great Awakening, the role of evangelicalism in antebellum reform, the Social Gospel's influence, and perhaps the modernist-fundamentalist controversy. But after a paragraph or a few minutes of lecture time on the Scopes Trial, attention to religion thins out dramatically, perhaps to resurface fleetingly, if at all, in the personae

---

36. Walter Lippmann, *Drift and Mastery: An Attempt to Diagnose the Current Unrest* (New York: Mitchell Kennerley, 1914; reprint, Madison: University of Wisconsin Press, 1985), esp. 113-19, 146-57; Mary Pickering, *Auguste Comte: An Intellectual Biography*, vol. 1 (Cambridge: Cambridge University Press, 1993), 98, 236-37, 540, 665. For useful discussions, see Melvin L. Adelman, "Modernization Theory and Its Critics," in *Encyclopedia of American Social History*, 3 vols., ed. Mary Kupiec Cayton, Elliott J. Gorn, and Peter W. Williams (New York: Charles Scribner's Sons, 1993), 1: 347-58, and James A. Henretta, " 'Modernization': Towards a False Synthesis," *Reviews in American History* 5 (1977): 445-52.

of public figures like Martin Luther King Jr., Jerry Falwell, and Pat Robertson.[37]

Of course, the secularization paradigm has value, but like many useful paradigms, it can also mislead. What U.S. history in fact reveals is not a straight-line "secularization" process but a complex pattern as religious energies ebb and flow, fade, and reemerge in new forms. And the post-1970 era has clearly been a time of renewed energy, whether measured in terms of church growth, public activism, or (self-reported) personal piety and church attendance, with evangelical and charismatic Protestants leading the way.[38] Also, as R. Laurence Moore reminds us in *Selling God: American Religion in the Marketplace of Culture*, the boundary between secular and sacred has been highly permeable in America, as religious leaders from George Whitfield to Pat Robertson have exploited the vocabulary and techniques of the marketplace to further their cause.[39]

37. Lorence and Grinsel, "Role of Religion in History Teaching," 20.

38. Inverting the secularization paradigm, sociologists Roger Finke and Rodney Starke in *The Churching of America, 1776-1990* (New Brunswick, N.J.: Rutgers University Press, 1992) find *increasing* rates of church membership from the late colonial era to the present. They view America's open, *laissez-faire* religious environment as a key to this vitality, with "upstart sects" from the Methodists and Baptists to the Assemblies of God and the Church of God as the engines of renewal. Similar arguments appear in Robert Wuthnow, *The Restructuring of American Religion: Society and Faith Since World War II* (Princeton: Princeton University Press, 1988) and Dean M. Kelley, *Why Conservative Churches Are Growing: A Study in the Sociology of Religion* (New York: Harper & Row, 1972). Boyer, *When Time Shall Be No More*, also stresses the contemporary vitality of evangelical faith, including belief in biblical inerrancy and Bible prophecy (pp. 1-8). See, however, recent studies that question the reliability of self-reported poll data on church attendance and religious fervor. For example, a 1992 research project headed by political scientist John C. Green of the University of Akron concludes that only about nineteen percent of adult Americans regularly practice their religion — though the study finds significantly higher rates of active observance among evangelical believers: "The Akron Survey of Religion and Politics in America" (1992), discussed in Mark A. Noll, *The Scandal of the Evangelical Mind* (Grand Rapids: Eerdmans, 1994), 9, and "The Rites of Americans," *Newsweek*, 29 November 1993, 80-82. Useful general sources on American religious life include Kosmin and Lachman, *One Nation under God*; Garry Wills, *Under God*; Mark A. Noll, *A History of Christianity in the United States and Canada* (Grand Rapids: Eerdmans, 1992); and Lippy and Williams, eds., *Encyclopedia of the American Religious Experience*.

39. R. Laurence Moore, *Selling God: American Religion in the Marketplace of Culture* (New York: Oxford University Press, 1994). See also Frank Lambert, *"Pedlar in Divinity": George Whitefield and the Transatlantic Revivals, 1737-1770* (Princeton: Princeton University Press, 1994).

PAUL BOYER

Another paradigm shapes historical scholarship as well: the centrality of *change*. The events and processes that alter history's course and reshape society grip our attention more than the forces of stability and continuity. For Paul Vitz, this is further damning evidence of the textbooks' bias against "traditional values." Of the social studies books written for the primary grades, he writes: "Not one . . . features a homemaker — that is, . . . a woman principally dedicated to acting as a wife and mother — as a model."[40] And of course the same is true of the history textbooks: they highlight the likes of Susan B. Anthony, Jane Addams, and Eleanor Roosevelt, not the women who continued in traditional domestic roles; the New England farm girls who came to the Lowell mills, not their sisters who stayed behind tending cows; the African American ministers who led the civil rights revolution, not the more cautious black clerics who held back from challenging Jim Crow. If this is "bias," it is less a "liberal" or "secular" bias than an analytic one that privileges change over stasis. We may no longer believe in progress, but we do believe in change.

To be sure, the founders of the French Annales school — Lucien Febvre, Marc Bloc, Fernand Braudel, and others — rejected *l'histoire eventuelle* — the history of events — in favor of the *longue durée* — time's stately flow measured in centuries rather than in years, and the great underlying continuities of human experience. The *Annalistes* focused on *mentalité* — the deep structures of thought and culture beneath the surface turbulence of politics and ideological contention. Such an approach obviously pays close attention to religious institutions and beliefs.

But the *longue durée* and *mentalité* approach has not taken root in America, where the scholarly tropism in favor of change receives strong cultural reinforcement, as Alexis de Tocqueville recognized long ago in describing Americans' fondness for pulling up stakes, moving on, beginning afresh.[41] In any event, the Annales model does not adapt well to textbooks and survey courses, where the dynamism

40. Vitz, *Censorship*, 38.
41. James A. Henretta, "Families and Farms: *Mentalité* in Pre-Industrial America," *William and Mary Quarterly*, 3rd series, 39, no. 1 (January 1978): 2-32. For a general introduction see Christopher Clark, "*Mentalité* and the Nature of Consciousness," in *Encyclopedia of American Social History*, ed. Cayton, Gorn, and Williams, 1: 387-95.

of change is central. A U.S. history text that simply repeated the phrase "Things continued much as before" would test students' patience, accurate though it might be in describing large tracts of history's glacial flow.

Thus, our textbooks and survey courses *do* pay attention to religion when it is clearly linked to social or political change. Antebellum evangelicalism gains notice as a stimulus to the antislavery cause and other reforms. Religion's importance in the civil rights and antiwar movements of the 1950s and 1960s, and in our contemporary political and cultural wars, at least sometimes makes its way into the textbooks and the survey courses as an aspect of the discussion of these social movements.

But historians have difficulty with religion's autonomous role as a source of comfort and meaning for individuals, as an anchor of social and cultural stability, and as the animating force underlying great institutions that possess their own historical autonomy and dynamic. Again, I suggest, this arises not from a secularistic hostility to religion, but from analytic assumptions shared by most historians.

Finally, if contextualization can help us understand the campaign for more attention to religion in history teaching, so, too, it can shed light on historians' *response* to that campaign. Part of the reason history teachers and textbook writers have steered away from religion, I suspect, lies in the history of the discipline itself.

In the nineteenth century, history instruction and historical writing in the United States were *steeped* in religion. Christianity — and, specifically, evangelical Protestant Christianity — was treated not merely as a social phenomenon worthy of scholarly attention and pedagogical notice, but as a basic framework of meaning for interpreting the national experience, and as a font of moral guidance. Henry Barnard, the first U.S. commissioner of education (1867-70), advocated Bible reading in the public schools as a means of inculcating Christian principles, and few protested.[42]

Such prescriptions were often linked to the cultural wars of the nineteenth century, which frequently pitted Protestants against Roman

---

42. June Edwards, "Civil Religion and the American Public Schools," in Thomas C. Hunt and Marilyn N. Maxon, *Religion and Morality in American Schooling* (Washington, D.C.: University Press of America, 1981), 179.

Catholics. In 1854, for example, a prominent figure of the day, Stephen Colwell, urged the teaching of (Protestant) Christianity in the public schools as a way of counteracting "papist" influences. In terms strikingly similar to those often heard today, Colwell warned that for the schools to fail to inculcate a "knowledge of Christianity . . . would be to abandon more than one-half the children of the nation to practical heathenism." He continued:

> In the present state of civilization and national intelligence, the question of national instruction for children cannot be left to the action of parents. . . . [T]he most indispensable feature of wise national policy in a Christian country [must be] to give all the children of the nation that training which will fit them for Christian citizenship.[43]

Religion also pervaded nineteenth-century historiography in the form of an unabashedly patriotic, nationalistic, and quasi-theological dogma. According to this interpretive schema, America from the days of the Pilgrims onward had enjoyed special divine favor, and God had directly intervened time and again in guiding the nation's unfolding history. As an 1867 textbook put it, commenting on the recent Civil War: "We cannot but feel that God has worked in a mysterious way to bring good out of evil. It was He, and not man, who saw and directed the end from the beginning."[44] This view pervaded not only the textbooks of the period, but the work of the era's best-known historians. George Bancroft's great multivolume U.S. history, pub-

43. Stephen Colwell, *The Position of Christianity in the United States, in its Relations with Our Political Institutions and Specially with Reference to Religious Instruction in the Public Schools* (Philadelphia: Lippincott, Grambo & Co., 1854), 91-92. On Colwell (1800-1871), a Pennsylvania industrialist, lawyer, Presbyterian lay leader, and writer on social and economic topics, see *Dictionary of American Biography* (New York: Charles Scribner's Sons, 1929), 2:327. The anti-Catholicism that pervaded nineteenth-century textbooks is discussed in Ruth Miller Elson, *Guardians of Tradition: American Schoolbooks of the Nineteenth Century* (Lincoln: University of Nebraska Press, 1964), 47-54.

44. Marcius Willson, *History of the United States* (New York: Ivison, Phinney, Blakeman and Co., 1867), 434, quoted in Elson, *Guardians of Tradition*, 41. For a general discussion of the providentialist theme in nineteenth-century history textbooks and in broader currents of intellectual history, see ibid., 59-62; Boyer, *When Time Shall Be No More*, 226-29; and Ernest Lee Tuveson, *Redeemer Nation: The Idea of America's Millennial Role* (Chicago, University of Chicago Press, 1968).

lished between 1834 and 1874, for example, is replete with instances of divine intervention.[45]

This tradition of providentialist historical interpretation survives in the rhetoric of politicians — from Woodrow Wilson to Ronald Reagan — and in popularized history writing marketed through Christian bookstores and the religious press. The perspective of one such work emerges clearly in its title: *One Nation under God: The Story of America's Dependence on God's Guidance — From Columbus to the Astronauts*. The Bible-prophecy popularizers, whose paperbacks sell by the hundreds of thousands of copies, routinely offer providentialist readings of America's past — and future.[46]

In a partially secularized guise, as a component of what Robert Bellah and others have called America's "civil religion," this view of the United States as a divinely chosen nation, or at least as a special instrument of God's unfolding plan for humanity, proved extremely tenacious even in ostensibly "secular" historical writing, encouraging an uncritical and triumphalist tone. In the U.S. history textbooks published as recently as the 1950s, Francis FitzGerald has observed, "America was perfect: the greatest nation in the world, and the embodiment of democracy, freedom, and technological progress. For them, the country never changed in any important way: its values and its political institutions remained constant from the time of the American revolution."[47]

Present-day historians, acculturated in the discipline's scholarly methodology, evidentiary standards, and vastly broadened social and

45. Boyer, *When Time Shall Be No More*, 312-13; Dorothy Ross, "Historical Consciousness in Nineteenth-Century America," *American Historical Review* 89 (October 1984): 909-28; Elson, *Guardians of Tradition*, 59-62.

46. Boyer, *When Time Shall Be No More*, 225-53; Norman Vincent Peale, *One Nation under God: The Story of America's Dependence on God's Guidance — From Columbus to the Astronauts* (Pawling, N.Y.: Foundation for Christian Living, 1972). See also, in the same vein, James C. Hefley, *America: One Nation under God* (Wheaton, Ill.: Victor Books, 1975), and Peter Marshall's *The Light and the Glory* (Old Tappan, N.J.: Revell, 1977) and *From Sea to Shining Sea* (Old Tappan, N.J.: Revell, 1986).

47. Frances FitzGerald, *America Revised: History Schoolbooks in the Twentieth Century* (Boston: Little, Brown & Co., 1979), 10; Robert N. Bellah, "Civil Religion in America," in *American Civil Religion*, ed. Russell E. Richey and Donald G. Jones (New York: Harper & Row, 1974); Tuveson, *Redeemer Nation*, 209-12; Boyer, *When Time Shall Be No More*, 229.

demographic coverage, and shaped by the social movements of recent decades, are made understandably uneasy by rose-tinted versions of history in which everything unfolds for the best and in which divine intervention becomes the central causal dynamic.

This is not to suggest that more emphasis on the historical importance of religion would logically or necessarily entail a return to older providentialist or triumphalist modes of historical explanation. But historians' awareness of the intellectual and ideological evolution of their discipline may well be a subtle factor in the much-noted reluctance, at the textbook and introductory survey-course level, to emphasize religious belief. Some historians may harbor the justifiable suspicion that the demand for more attention to religion in our textbooks and survey courses also implies, as an unspoken subtext, a return to the earlier celebratory, uncritical, and even providentialist view of the American past. And, indeed, as we have seen, the rhetoric of some conservative polemicists gives substance to the suspicion. Some (certainly not all) of the criticism directed against historians and history teachers for slighting religion is clearly part of a broader reaction against the discipline's shift from a laudatory, super-patriotic, and providentialist tone to a more complex and critical perspective.

Whatever their flaws, the history textbooks and survey courses of today unquestionably present a more comprehensive, balanced, and empirically grounded view of America's past (and a more accurate picture of the nation's racial, ethnic, gender, geographic, and class diversity) than did their predecessors in early generations. Insofar as the campaign to "restore religion to history" is perceived as part of a broader reactionary drive to reverse the processes that have transformed historical scholarship in the past half-century, one can readily understand that historians remain wary.

*   *   *

But simply because the demand that historians pay more attention to religion has become entangled with the political agenda of the so-called New Religious Right does not mean that the call itself can be dismissed as nothing but rhetorical hyperbole. When one moves beyond the realm of ideologically driven polemic to the specific issue at hand — the failure of textbooks and survey courses to deal adequately with the role of religion in American history — the question becomes considerably clearer.

To suggest *reasons* for the failure of many textbook writers and survey-course teachers to treat religion adequately is not to *justify* that failure. Without question, history textbook writers and teachers at all levels need to provide a fuller picture of religion's role in our history. As church historian Edwin Gaustad has observed, for the student of American history, "religion is a datum and point of reference as omnipresent and inescapable as the rivers and the mountains, the laws and the courts, the trade routes and the labor unions, the political parties and the national presidents."[48]

To begin to correct this record of neglect, we need to treat religion not only as an adjunct of political and social change, but on its own terms: as the foundation of great and enduring social institutions, as a force for continuity as well as for change, and as a source of meaning and solace for hosts of Americans in the past and present.[49]

To be more than merely a sop to yet another pressure group, this deepened coverage must convey the complexity of a religious tapestry comprising not just the familiar triad of Protestant, Catholic, and Jew, but also Mormons, Christian Scientists, Jehovah's Witnesses, Muslims, Buddhists, New Age mystics, Eastern Orthodox, and — yes — the ag-

---

48. Gaustad, "American History: With and Without Religion," 17.

49. Note, for example, the phenomenal growth of American Methodism in the early national era: "Rising from three percent of all church members in 1776 to more than 34 percent by 1850, Methodism was far and away the largest religious body in the nation, boasting over a million members" — "The Puzzle and Promise of American Methodist Scholarship," *Asbury Theological Seminary Wesleyan Holiness Studies Center Bulletin* 2, no. 2 (Summer 1994): 1. A similar point could be made about indigenous religions such as Mormonism, Seventh Day Adventism, Christian Science, and the International Watchtower Society (Jehovah's Witnesses); the arrival of millions of Roman Catholic, Jewish, and Orthodox immigrants; the emergence of the Assemblies of God and other pentecostal groups early in the twentieth century; the explosive growth of evangelical churches since 1970; the enormous vitality of televangelism and religious publishing; and the spread of evangelical and charismatic Protestantism (as well as Mormonism) in Africa and Latin America through U.S. missionary effort. (The number of Mormons in Mexico and Central and South America, for example, increased from 797,000 in 1980 to 2.7 million in 1993, an explosive growth whose implications historians have not even begun to assess. See "A Ceremony in Mexico City Shows Growth in Mormonism," *New York Times*, 11 December 1993.)

nostics, the atheists, the indifferent, and those shadowy but much-vilified "secular humanists." Even when dealing with American Protestantism alone, historians must somehow suggest the dizzying array of denominational traditions, splinterings, fusions, and splits, as well as the differing perspectives shaped by gender, race, and class. They must document and seek to account for the periodic surges of religious energy and the shifting loci of that energy, as it bursts forth sometimes at the liberal end of the theological spectrum, sometimes at the conservative end. This is a tall order, especially as historians juggle everything else that must be covered. But it is a challenge we must address. If America is, indeed, "a nation with the soul of a church," as G. K. Chesterton once observed, the meaning and implications of that insight demand our best analytic efforts.

What's So Special about the University, Anyway?

D. G. HART

THE fortunes of evangelical scholarship have never been better. Well, maybe never is a bit strong. But since the rise of the modern research university in the United States, evangelicals — those Protestants usually differentiated from the mainline variety — have not been as comfortable walking down the corridors of the academy as they appear to be today. Evangelicals now boast a number of colleges which by a variety of measures offer a good if not excellent education. The movement has also produced any number of scholars who if not leading their respective fields command the respect of their colleagues. And evangelicalism itself has become a cottage industry among scholars who study American history and culture, so much so that a Yale historian warns of an "evangelical thesis" taking over the study of the United States' past.[1]

1. Jon Butler, "Born-Again America? A Critique of the New 'Evangelical Thesis' in Recent American Historiography," paper delivered at the annual meetings of the American Historical Association, December 1992. On the improving prospects for evangelical scholarship, see Mark A. Noll, *Between Faith and Criticism: Evangelicals, Scholarship, and the Study of the Bible* (San Francisco: Harper & Row, 1986); idem, *The Scandal of the Evangelical Mind* (Grand Rapids: Wm. B. Eerdmans, 1994), chap. 8; George M. Marsden, "The State of Evangelical Scholarship," *Christian Scholar's Review* 27 (1988): 348-52; and as an example of evangelical historiography, the essays in D. G. Hart, ed., *Reckoning with the Past: Historical Essays on American Evangelicalism from the Institute for the Study of American Evangelicals* (Grand Rapids: Baker Book House, 1995).

The rise and influence of evangelicals within American higher education since World War II is a remarkable development. During the first half of the twentieth century, evangelicalism was synonymous with fundamentalism, a movement with a reputation for anti-intellectualism. Few observers of conservative Protestantism during the 1920s and 1930s would have thought the tradition capable of producing any qualified scholars, let alone ones who might have some influence upon an academy assumed to be hostile to religion. Yet, a small group of "progressive fundamentalists," tired of the movement's separatism and simple-mindedness, went off to graduate school at some of America's better universities, made a credible case for the importance of Christian scholarship, and pumped academic blood into a tradition lacking intellectual vigor. It may be too much to attribute the success of the contemporary evangelical academy solely to the labors of such neo-evangelical leaders, but the vitality of evangelical scholarship clearly owes a great debt to the shift effected at mid-century by such figures as Harold John Ockenga, Carl Henry, and Edward Carnell, all of whom were associated at one time with Fuller Theological Seminary.[2]

Given this change in fortunes, it comes as no surprise to hear evangelical scholars calling for even greater and better engagement with the contemporary university. The triumvirate of evangelical historians, Nathan O. Hatch, Mark A. Noll and George M. Marsden, have been especially vocal in prodding the evangelical academy to produce scholarship that rivals the work done at research universities. Over a decade ago on his way to a splendid study of antebellum religion, *The Democratization of American Christianity*, Hatch observed the negative effects of a deeply ingrained populism on evangelical scholarship. The evangelical commitment to evangelism and missions has fostered, he argued, hostility to educated elites, an inability to engage in first-order thinking, and the habit of evangelicals, in the rare cases when they do produce scholars, to speak and write for a popular rather than scholarly audience. The result, Hatch laments, has been a singular failure to sustain serious intellectual life. Evangelicals have "nourished millions

2. On the rise and influence of neo-evangelicalism, see Joel A. Carpenter, "From Fundamentalism to the New Evangelical Coalition," in *Evangelicalism and Modern America*, ed. George Marsden (Grand Rapids: Wm. B. Eerdmans, 1984), 3-16; and George M. Marsden, *Reforming Fundamentalism: Fuller Seminary and the New Evangelicalism* (Grand Rapids: Wm. B. Eerdmans, 1987).

of believers in the simple verities of the gospel, but have abandoned the universities, the arts and other realms of 'high' culture."[3] More recently Hatch has criticized evangelical colleges, particularly their administrators, for "shackling" evangelical scholars and failing to provide environments where intellectual questions may be pursued with the openness and candor found at mainstream universities, where Christian scholars may "confront intellectual issues with intellectual responses."[4] Hatch's concerns about the evangelical academy explain in part his leadership in the Pew Evangelical Scholars Initiative, a program established to "bring a distinctly Christian voice to critical scholarly problems in the humanities, social sciences and theological disciplines."[5]

Wheaton College's Mark Noll has been equally vociferous in pointing out the failings of evangelical scholarship and intellectual life, the title of his most recent book, *The Scandal of the Evangelical Mind*, giving some indication of his perspective. Though critical, Noll does not call for better scholarship from evangelicals in order merely to ape the university and receive the plaudits of the wider culture. Rather, his case for first-rate Christian scholarship is rooted in the conviction that believers are called to love their God not only with their hearts and souls but also with their minds. Protestant theologians such as Jonathan Edwards, John Wesley, and Charles Hodge all believed that diligent, rigorous mental activity was a way to glorify God. But now evangelicals not only do not know how to love God with their minds but find themselves far removed from the centers of first-rate academic life. If they are going to win the world for Christ and make all areas of life subject to his lordship, Noll warns, evangelicals will have to devote concerted effort to nurturing and sustaining the mind.[6]

Noll's explanation of the collapse of the evangelical mind points to fundamentalist habits of thought such as creationism and dispensationalism. Both of these pieces of twentieth-century evangelical theology stem from the movement's historic ties to popular revivalism, American democratic individualism, and the crisis — both intellectual and social — of fundamentalism. The net effect has been that evangeli-

3. Marsden, "Evangelicalism as a Democratic Movement," in *Evangelicalism and Modern America*, chap. 6, quotation on 81.

4. "Our Shackled Scholars," *Christianity Today*, 22 November 1993, 13.

5. Quotation from Hatch in 1993 brochure for the ESI program.

6. Noll, *Scandal*, 35-49.

cals think more about the next world than they do about living responsibly in this one. Yet by escaping the world, evangelicals find themselves unknowingly and uncritically being shaped by the contemporary university, an institution that sets the standards for so much of modern life, according to Noll. The only hope for evangelicals to obey God's command to love him with their minds is to turn afresh to the cross, where the message of Christ's death for sinful humanity reveals a God who loves the material world as much as the world of spirit. If evangelicals can add the urgency of humankind's need for salvation to older Christian intellectual traditions, Noll concludes, they may be able to develop a tradition of scholarship undertaken as a spiritual discipline.[7]

Noll's call for robust Christian learning of the first order surely raises the stakes for believing academics who care about bringing faith to bear upon their vocations and who desire to use their gifts for God's glory. Yet, as inspiring and as provocative as Noll's argument is, there are features of it that should give pause to believers who want to cultivate the Christian mind. A strong and reappearing theme throughout Noll's argument is a high estimate of the modern university and the kind of learning it nurtures and produces. Not only does he call upon evangelical institutions to provide the support — both financial and intellectual — that secular universities offer, but Noll seems to regard many of the norms and practices of the university world — reduced teaching loads, advanced research, and the like — as necessary soil for cultivating the Christian mind.

George Marsden's recent book *The Soul of the American University: From Protestant Establishment to Established Nonbelief*[8] gives some grounds for those believers, evangelical or not, who have second thoughts about the modern university and the scholarship it produces. On the one hand his book reiterates what historians of American higher education have long argued, namely, that the triumph of research universities in the late nineteenth century secured the secularization of advanced learning. On the other hand — and this is why Marsden's book is so valuable — he also shows how the secularization of the academy was not merely the result of atheistic scientists and secular humanists. Rather, the mainline

---

7. Ibid., chaps. 5 and 9.
8. George Marsden, *The Soul of the American University: From Protestant Establishment to Established Nonbelief* (New York: Oxford University Press, 1994).

Protestant churches generally oversaw the demise of religious influences upon the university. Mainline Protestants contributed to the process of secularization both through the ideal of serving the public, a commitment which made it more difficult to maintain distinctive Christian doctrines, and through the theology of liberal Protestantism, which broke down the historic Christian distinction between the sacred and the secular. The moral of the story is that for over a century now Christians have had a very difficult time holding together commitments to both theological orthodoxy and first-rate scholarship.

Despite the seemingly stark prospects for Christian scholarship in today's academy, Marsden still holds out hope for the university and the place of Christians in it. On the basis of arguments for intellectual diversity and academic freedom, Marsden contends that colleges and universities with religious missions, rather than being forced to conform to the standards that prevail in state and nonreligious private institutions, be recognized as legitimate partners in the enterprise of American higher education. He also believes that greater diversity in the academy will allow believing scholars to be more forthright about their religious convictions both at public and nonreligious private institutions and in the various scholarly guilds.[9] Consequently, even though Marsden recognizes and documents well the structures and ethos of modern learning which make religious perspectives objectionable, he does not question fundamentally the aims and products of the modern university. For this reason Marsden has seconded the challenges of Hatch and Noll for evangelicals to be more engaged with higher learning and more active in recovering "a commitment to Christian scholarship of the highest order." He has also proposed a strategy for pursuing this scholarship, namely, the establishment of research institutes which would perform all of the tasks which universities perform in the way of producing advanced research, except in this case the scholarship would be done "for the kingdom of God."[10]

9. Ibid., 429-40.

10. "Why No Major Evangelical University? The Loss and Recovery of Evangelical Advanced Scholarship," in *Making Higher Education Christian: The History and Mission of Evangelical Colleges in America*, ed. Joel A. Carpenter and Kenneth W. Shipps (Grand Rapids, 1987), 294-303, quotations on 301 and 302. See also George M. Marsden, "The State of Evangelical Christian Scholarship," *Christian Scholar's Review* 27 (June 1988): 347-60.

D. G. HART

To their credit, Hatch, Noll, and Marsden have practiced as well as they have preached. They have produced work on the history of American Protestantism of the highest caliber. Furthermore, they have been very instrumental in the renaissance of evangelical historiography that now threatens or sustains — depending on one's perspective — the study of American religious and cultural history.[11] Not only has their scholarship been a source of inspiration to graduate students and younger scholars, but they have helped to construct a small but nonetheless significant institutional network on the margins of the university world that supports the kind of work for which they call.[12] To their list of accomplishments must also be added their willingness and ability to write for more popular audiences, thus avoiding the age-old complaints of irrelevance and inaccessibility so often registered against professional history.

Yet, having acknowledged the insights and inspiration that Hatch, Noll, and Marsden provide for Christian scholars, one may still ask whether the life of the mind for which these historians call is in the best interests of the evangelical academy. On the one hand, is it possible to add the spiritual vitality of the evangelical soul, the many recruits which evangelicalism uncannily attracts, together with systems of Christian theology, both Protestant and Catholic, which value the work of believing scholarship, dump in four cups of leave time and heaps of research grants, bake for a generation or so, and come up with an evangelical mind? The fact that evangelicalism appears to thrive better as a low- to middle-brow movement, more in sync with the rhythms of the marketplace and popular culture than the habits of the library and seminar room, suggests that an evangelical mind may be too much to ask. On the other hand, while the current generation of evangelical scholars may be better equipped theologically to overcome the congenital indifference of their tradition to intellectual matters, there appears

---

11. For differing assessments of evangelical historiography, see Jon Butler, "Born-Again America?" 6, and Leonard I. Sweet, "Wise as Serpents, Innocent as Doves: The New Evangelical Historiography," *Journal of the American Academy of Religion* 56 (1988): 397-416.

12. The author bears a special debt to Hatch, Noll, and Marsden because of the advice and support they supplied to him while a graduate student, a postdoctoral fellow at Duke University's Divinity School, and director of the Institute for the Study of American Evangelicals.

to be little consideration of the socioeconomic foundation that sustains the contemporary university. And when the material apparatus of modern scholarship is factored into calls for an evangelical mind, one is confronted with the possibility that the way intellectual life is currently constituted may in fact pose a significant barrier to the life of the mind. In other words, is the modern university really a fit place for cultivating the mind?

Before pursuing this question, some concessions need to be made to the university as we now know it. Rooted as it is in the general trend of the democratization of learning, the university has made it possible for many individuals and families to read and enjoy good books, to be exposed to important artistic expressions, to ponder questions about the meaning and purpose of human existence, and, generally, to think about the true, the good, and the beautiful. The expansion of higher education over the last century has also allowed men and women whose ordinary vocational prospects would have been limited to enter the ranks of professional academics and relish the perks and privileges that go with scholarly pursuits. In other words, the modern university has some accomplishments to its credit; it has made contributions which may not have existed otherwise.

Yet, for all of the possibilities that the university opens, the institution has clearly not lived up to its potential. To use but one example, perhaps too anecdotal, despite the remarkably high number of university graduates in the United States compared to other Western countries, it is not at all clear that American intellectual life has been enriched by the efforts of the modern academy. By one measure of learning — admittedly an odd one at that — roughly 28,000 people in North America subscribe to the *American Scholar*. Granted, this journal is edited by a humorous yet cranky neoconservative and so leans to the right in intellectual and cultural matters. But it is a journal for people of modest intelligence who are interested in books, the arts, and intellectual life. Yet only a fragment of the general population subscribes to (let alone reads) the publication. Statistics like this suggest that despite the proliferation of degrees, books, journals, and research institutes, intellectual life is no healthier today than it was before the advent of the research university. What is more, the stranglehold which the university now has on what Americans generally regard as the life of the mind means that the ascendancy of the university over matters intellectual has come

143

at a significant cost. Whereas intellectual life once bore fruit in a hodge-podge way through various literary clubs, chautauquas, lyceums, education societies, denominational colleges, and other local organizations, the university now monopolizes most fields of artistic and cultural endeavor and has made virtually extinct the independent scholar or scientist.[13] For all of the talk about hegemony by modern academics, few seem ready to consider whether the modern university's eclipse of intellectual and cultural life is a desirable result.

Certainly the value of the university becomes more questionable when we look at the kind of knowledge it produces and the relationship of this knowledge to an economy fueled by large-scale businesses and government — in other words, to the forces of modernization. In addition to asking what models exist for the cultivation of a Christian mind and what examples from the past evangelicals may recover for developing their own scholarship, an equally important question is where this scholarly activity is going to take place. Scholarship does not just happen in the lab, carrel, or office but also occurs at a particular place in the economy and at a particular point in time. Considerations about the location of scholarship in these senses of place, however, do not yield encouraging conclusions about the prospects for a Christian mind. Simply stated — though I hope not simplistically — the economy and purposes of academic life in late twentieth-century America are hostile to the development of a Christian mind. This proposition raises the question of whether evangelicals should be so enthusiastic about the modern university.[14]

13. On the relative health of intellectual life before the university, see, for instance, Thomas Bender, *New York Intellect: A History of Intellectual Life in New York City, from 1750 to the Beginnings of Our Time* (New York: Knopf, 1987; distributed by Random House); Richard D. Brown, *Knowledge Is Power: The Diffusion of Information in Early America, 1700-1865* (New York: Oxford University Press, 1991); and Alexandra Oleson and Sanborn C. Brown, eds., *The Pursuit of Knowledge in the Early American Republic: American Scientific and Learned Societies from Colonial Times to the Civil War* (Baltimore: Johns Hopkins University Press, 1976).

14. For other complaints, some of them injudicious, about the university's influence upon intellectual life, see Russell Jacoby, *The Last Intellectuals: American Culture in the Age of Academe* (New York: Noonday Press, 1987); Page Smith, *Killing the Spirit: Higher Education in America* (New York: Viking, 1990); and Mark R. Schwehn, *Exiles from Eden: Religion and Academic Vocation in America* (New York: Oxford University Press, 1993).

To his credit, Noll does acknowledge indirectly the problems inherent in the financing of modern intellectual life when he writes that some Christians are doing important scholarship at secular universities funded by none other than distillers, tobacco magnates, other megaindustrialists, and especially the federal government.[15] He also concedes that the costs of creating graduate schools for advanced research are high.[16] So, too, George Marsden has observed that "the growth of evangelical scholarship . . . reflects the growing suburbanization and affluence of our communities."[17] Yet, the economic dimensions of the modern academy appear to raise few doubts about the character of intellectual life under the aegis of the research university.

Part of the problem is that the evangelical assessment of the university misconstrues the nature of the institution's prestige and authority. Evangelicals have not examined thoughtfully what dependence upon gifts from corporate capitalists and support from large-scale nation-states has done to shape the nature and purpose of universities. For instance, Noll writes that the great universities "function as the *mind* of Western culture," defining "what is important," specifying "procedures to be respected," setting "agendas for analyzing the practical problems of the world," providing "the vocabulary for dealing with the perennial Great Issues," and producing "the books that get read and that over decades continue to influence thinking around the world."[18] So, too, Hatch argues for the unfettering of evangelical scholars in part because of the belief that Christian academics will help to solve "the thorny intellectual questions of the modern world."[19] Yet, when one considers the trivialization of learning that has occurred in the last decade during debates over political correctness and multiculturalism alone, the question immediately arises whether universities should be regarded as the arbiters of the life of the mind that many claim them to be. Is it possible

15. See his McManis Inaugural Lecture, "The Scandal of the Evangelical Mind," delivered at Wheaton College, 9 February 1993.

16. Noll, *Scandal,* 18-20.

17. Marsden, "State of Evangelical Scholarship," 353. For an extended critique of evangelical colleges which acknowledges the close relationship between the affluence and the scholarly credentials of American evangelicalism, see Douglas Frank, "Consumerism and the Christian College: A Call to Life in an Age of Death," in *Making Higher Education Christian,* 257-70.

18. Ibid., 51.

19. Hatch, "Our Shackled Scholars," 13.

145

to say, without sounding anti-intellectual and without losing the chance for tenure, that research and graduate institutions of higher learning have been detrimental to cultivating anything that can be properly called "a mind"?[20] The reason why twentieth-century evangelicals have not produced great scholars or interest in the life of the mind, then, may owe to the fact that twentieth-century Americans generally have not produced great scholars or interest in the life of the mind. And the reason why contemporary America has not produced great scholars or a vigorous intellectual culture may be that research universities have contributed directly to the sorry state of learning in the United States.[21]

The point here, however, is not merely that academics fed at the trough of universities overestimate the importance of advanced research and higher education. Rather, the argument is also that academics misperceive the current function of the university and the way this function has been shaped by the needs of corporate capitalism. Conceived in the abstract, most would agree that universities function as the mind of Western culture. But how important is the mind itself to Western society? Isn't it more likely that what really counts is the GNP or the Dow-Jones Industrial Average? Of course, the development of a global economy requires people with good minds not only to crunch numbers but also to produce the variety of goods exchanged on the market and to create machines that will crunch those numbers. But what modern society values finally has little to do with what is true, beautiful, and good, the perennial great issues. Instead, productivity, efficiency, and relevance are the criteria for determining the value of intellectual and cultural goods. Increasingly, the utilitarian pressures of

20. For critiques of the contemporary academy's inability to arrive at a meaningful set of intellectual standards, see The New Republic, "Special Issue: Race on Campus," 18 February 1991; Joseph Epstein, "The Academic Zoo: Theory — in Practice," Hudson Review 44 (Spring 1991): 9-30; Paul V. Mankowski, "What I Saw at the AAR," First Things (March 1992): 36-41; idem, "Academic Religion: Playground of the Vandals," First Things (May 1992): 31-37; and two reviews of Dinesh D'Souza's Illiberal Education: C. Vann Woodward, "Freedom and the Universities," New York Review of Books, 18 July 1991, 32-37; and Eugene D. Genovese, "Heresy, Yes — Sensitivity, No: An Argument for Counterterrorism in the Academy," The New Republic, 15 April 1991, 30-35.

21. For a bracing perspective on the collapse of intellectual life since the 1960s, see Daniel Bell, "The Culture Wars: American Intellectual Life, 1965-1992," Wilson Quarterly 16 (Summer 1992): 74-107.

the American economy set the agenda for the modern university. People pursue higher education not to think about great issues but to receive credentials for jobs that will yield a safe, middle-class existence. What is more, universities have functioned for so long as vocational institutions that people respect them not because of the books these institutions produce but rather because of the financial rewards they promise. Even in the training of academics — in their function as gatekeepers of the learned professions — universities function primarily as normal schools for teachers at colleges and universities. In sum, American higher education does not do a good job of cultivating the mind.[22]

The declining intellectual standards of the university can be attributed directly to its codependency upon corporate capitalism. Great industrialists funded America's first research universities (Johns Hopkins and University of Chicago), and similar financing transformed older liberal arts schools like Harvard and Yale into research and graduate institutions. The motives for founding these institutions was not to promote bookish culture, but rather to produce useful knowledge that would yield greater efficiency (both in material and human terms), greater human happiness, greater productivity, and also greater profits. To be sure, some of the industrialists like Hopkins and Rockefeller grew up in a culture of polite learning and so appreciated the life of the mind. But they founded institutions that became the principal means for certifying the authority and prestige of the natural and social sciences.[23] For this reason, it is ironic that critics of evangelical intellectual life take issue with the theology of fundamentalism. Though fundamentalist theology was often simplistic in its diagnosis of urban-industrial society

22. On middle-class careerism in the development of American higher education, see Burton J. Bledstein, *The Culture of Professionalism: The Middle Class and the Development of Higher Education in America* (New York: Norton, 1976); and more recently, Louis Menand, "What Are Universities For?" *Harper's* 283 (December 1991): 47-56.

23. See Hugh Hawkins, *Pioneer: A History of the Johns Hopkins University* (Baltimore: Johns Hopkins University Press, 1960); David F. Noble, *America by Design: Science, Technology and the Rise of Corporate Capitalism* (New York: Knopf, 1977); and Clyde W. Barrow, *Universities and the Capitalist State: Corporate Liberalism and the Reconstruction of American Higher Education, 1894-1928* (Madison: University of Wisconsin Press, 1990). Thorstein Veblen, in *The Higher Learning in America: A Memorandum on the Conduct of Universities by Business Men* (1918; reprint, Stanford: Academic Reprints, 1954), pointed out these problems at the University of Chicago.

and grew up in part in reaction to the forces which fueled the research university, fundamentalists perceived better than many academics the real threat that modernization posed to a Christian mind.

Of course, the industrialists who founded many of the research universities and their corporate descendants are not the only ones to blame. The federal government has also encouraged the utilitarian and vocational impulse within modern higher education by funding a variety of programs which have linked even more closely the university to the national economy. The Morrill Act of 1862 and the GI Bill of 1944, for instance, insured the dependence of a host of institutions and academic programs on the demand for specific vocations and commodities. Without elaborating the myriad of ways in which state and federal programs in higher education shape the utilitarian character of the university and facilitate the cooptation of the academy by big business, the point remains that economic interests, not intellectual merits, more often than not set the agenda for the modern university.[24]

By pointing out the capitalist origins of the modern university I do not intend to dismiss with a Marxist sneer contemporary higher education as merely the product of bourgeois society. Rather, my purpose is to point out the unwise if not unholy alliance that universities have made. For if universities are really concerned about cultivating the mind, then depending financially upon the benefices of corporate capitalism — both for the support and the end of higher education — is an error of enormous proportions. Even though more people go to college and university now than at any time in our history, university and college graduates do not come away from higher education with a high appreciation for ideas, books, artistic expression, and theoretical reasoning as good things in themselves. Rather, the overwhelming reason for going to college is to gain financial security. And the reason for this state of affairs has to be the modern university's dependence upon and, worse, failure to challenge the aims and aspirations rewarded by the modern political and economic order. Rather than defending and propagating the higher and transcendent aspects of human existence,

24. For the impact of federal funding on universities, see Roger L. Williams, *The Origins of Federal Support for Higher Education: George W. Atherton and the Land-Grant College Movement* (University Park: Pennsylvania State University Press, 1992); and Roger L. Geiger, *To Advance Knowledge: The Growth of American Research Universities, 1900-1940* (New York: Oxford University Press, 1986).

the university has accommodated itself to and in many instances sanctions a society which at best trivializes the good, the true, and the beautiful. Consequently, a lot of minds — not just evangelical ones — need to be changed about the purpose and nature of education if a genuinely Christian mind is ever to be cultivated.

If the aims of university education give pause, so should the knowledge they produce. Here it may be helpful to remember not just the socioeconomic but also the intellectual roots of the modern university. At the time that major American universities were founded, a profound debate — even more profound than the questions raised by Darwinism — was taking place about the nature and function of higher education. On the one side stood the new learning, which added natural and social sciences to the humanities and gave students the freedom to choose their course work. Pitted against the new learning was a curriculum dominated by the classics and moral philosophy. The new curriculum stood for academic specialization; the older instruction dominated by the humanities stood for antiquarian but nonetheless learned generalism. In many respects this struggle was political. The defenders of the classics feared that humanistic education would decline in importance if science were given equal footing in the academy.[25]

But the battle of the books also had a great deal to do with the nature and purpose of higher education. The old-time college may have produced terrible scholarship by the modern academy's standards, but it was truly interested in cultivating the mind, in asking questions about the nature and meaning of human life. To the older gentlemen and amateur scholars of the nineteenth century, science was too pragmatic and utilitarian. It was unconcerned with the higher ranges of human life; therefore it was unimportant and trivial. To younger scientists, aggres-

---

25. For the struggle between the old learning of the classics and the new learning of science (both natural and social), see Laurence Veysey, *The Emergence of the American University* (Chicago: University of Chicago Press, 1965); idem, "Plural Organized Worlds of the Humanities," in *The Organization of Knowledge in Modern America*, ed. Alexandra Oleson and John Voss (Baltimore: Johns Hopkins University Press, 1979), 51-106; John Chamberlain, "The End of the Old Education," *Modern Age* (Fall 1960); and Martin Green, *The Problem of Boston: Some Readings in Cultural History* (New York: Norton, 1966). For similar developments in England, see John J. Gross, *The Rise and Fall of the Man of Letters* (London: Weidenfeld and Nicolson, 1969); and T. W. Heyck, *The Transformation of Intellectual Life in Victorian England* (London: Croom Helm, 1982).

sive to secure a place in the academy and prestige in the wider society, the old learning was inferior because it was impractical. Latin and Greek did not make a lot of sense in the world of emerging cities, expanding industry, and cheap immigrant labor. Education, they believed, should make society better. But these scientists rarely asked questions about the good that serves as the basis for evaluating whether conditions are better. For humanists, education was about making individuals better and this project included not just moral behavior but also mental discipline. As we know, the new learning won, and it did so decisively, thanks to the creation and growth of research universities.[26]

In the process, the university transformed learning and called into question the older aims of higher education. Increasingly, humanistic scholars were forced to justify their activities in the new environment of scientific research and abandoned older humanistic ideals of integrated learning, of seeing things whole. Instead, insecure about their own status in the world of science, they embraced the research ethic that scientists promoted. This was a fatal move for the humanities. What had made the humanities valuable, no matter how dull and lifeless they may have been in the classroom, was their concern with larger and more general questions of value and meaning. By embracing the research ethic, humanists could say they were as scientific as biologists or sociologists, but they began to produce more and more obscure knowledge that was read less and less by people with a college education. So the modern university has not only promoted utilitarianism, but it has disemboweled intellectual culture by making it scientific, hence narrow and mechanistic.[27]

In fact, observing what passes for a college education in America, and examining the kind of esoterica that universities produce, the question immediately comes to mind: Do these institutions actually provide a legitimate model for developing the mind? Should evangelical academics really produce more books and more journal articles on obscure topics, even if they are by Christians? By producing such research, don't

26. Veysey, *Emergence of the American University*; and Dorothy Ross, "The Development of the Social Sciences," in *Organization of Knowledge*, 107-38.

27. See, for instance, the chapters on classical education in Veysey, *Emergence of the American University*; and Hawkins, *Pioneer*. Douglas Sloan, *Faith and Knowledge: Mainline Protestantism and American Higher Education* (Louisville: Westminster/John Knox, 1995), demonstrates well the effects of natural science's triumph on the teaching and study of religion.

Christian academics end up furthering the fragmentation of knowledge that has contributed to the secularization of academic life? According to David Martin, the key factor in secularization is differentiation. Once religion "becomes one specific sector, not the essence of the whole," thought ceases to be informed by theology, disciplines fragment, and society finds its purpose in meeting physical needs. Perhaps the goal of Christian scholarship should be to try to restore integration to a shattered intellectual landscape. But if the goal of Christian scholarship becomes the same as that of the research university — even if the divine emerges from esoteric research, just as Edwards saw God in the spider web — evangelical academics may be contributing further to the demise of intellectual culture while undermining the kind of culture necessary to produce minds, whether Christian or not.[28]

Differentiation — and the specialization of knowledge it encourages — ends up opposing any effort to sustain the kind of integrated and rooted culture — physically, intellectually, and emotionally — that is necessary for a healthy mind. Mental activity with a larger vision requires shared assumptions about what is important, the meaning of life, and the good. In other words, it requires homogeneity. This was what made *Christianity and Crisis* in the days of Reinhold Niebuhr and the *Reformed Journal* in the days of Richard Mouw so interesting. These periodicals, in their heyday, were produced by a fairly small, like-minded group of scholars working at a particular institution who shared a common vision and often shared a space where they could discuss ideas over lunch or coffee. These publications were not specialized, academically speaking, and did not present perspectives from all over the ideological map. This is what made them worth reading. Specialization, in contrast, undermines generalization. It is great for the production of goods and services in a consumer society. But it has never presented a cohesive view of the cosmos, another reason why modern universities and the political economy which sustains them comprise significant threats to meaningful intellectual life.[29]

If considerations about the purpose and products of the university

28. Quoted in Mark A. Noll, Nathan O. Hatch, and George M. Marsden, *The Search for Christian America* (Colorado Springs: Helmers and Howard, Publishers, 1989), 93.

29. This is largely Richard M. Weaver's argument in *Ideas Have Consequences* (Chicago: University of Chicago Press, 1948), chap. 3

were not enough to raise serious reservations about the possibility of developing a Christian mind, the track record of other Christians who have attempted to do so should also give evangelicals pause. Mainline Protestants, who were never marginalized in American higher education to the degree that evangelicals have been, made a valiant effort during the middle decades of the twentieth century to restore a Christian voice within the academy and to integrate their religious convictions with the world of learning. The chief manifestation of these efforts was the establishment of religious studies departments at both private and public institutions. Yet despite the considerable resources of the Protestant mainline, both theologically in the biblical theology movement and financially through the denominations and several foundations, the effort to make the university a place where Christian minds could flourish did little to redirect American higher education, let alone the study of religion, more narrowly.[30]

At roughly the same time that mainline Protestants tried to challenge the direction of higher education, Roman Catholics also attempted to harness the research university for Christian ends. But as Catholic scholars moved out of a parochial setting and into the academic mainstream, the commitment to Christian scholarship failed to withstand the acids of professionalization and academic specialization. As Philip Gleason argues, the upgrading of academic standards at Roman Catholic institutions improved the quality of learning, but it also "uncovered the deeper problem of whether there was any justification for a Catholic university, regardless of how good it might be."[31] The lesson from mainline Protestant and Roman Catholic experiences of this century might make evangelicals a tad more cautious, if not pessimistic, about the prospects for cultivating a Christian mind within the modern university.[32]

30. See Sloan, *Faith and Knowledge;* and D. G. Hart, "American Learning and the Problem of Religious Studies," in *The Secularization of the Academy,* ed. George M. Marsden and Bradley J. Longfield (New York: Oxford University Press, 1992), 195-233. For a different perspective on Protestant accomplishments, see Merrimon Cunninggim, *Uneasy Partners: The College and the Church* (Nashville, 1994).

31. Philip Gleason, "Immigrant Assimilation and the Crisis of Americanization," in *Keeping the Faith: American Catholicism Past and Present* (Notre Dame: University of Notre Dame Press, 1987), chap. 3, quotation on 77.

32. A related concern is what damage universities do to familial, regional,

Is the modern university, then, what Christian academics should try to emulate — something increasingly done through the processes of hiring and accreditation? If the contemporary practices and supporting economic structure of higher education promote the fragmentation of knowledge and culture, then shouldn't Christian scholars be thinking about alternative practices and structures for producing a Christian mind, ones that reinforce rather than undermine Christian thinking? In sum, what kinds of institutions and communities are necessary for the cultivation of a Christian mind?[33]

Yet, some may ask if there really is an alternative to the university. Isn't such lambasting of modern higher education really just another form of fundamentalist castigation of "the world"? Or more moderately, can't Christians selectively use specific features of the university without incorporating all of contemporary higher education's defects? To be sure, these criticisms of the university should not be read as an excuse for laziness or as a cover for anti-intellectualism. There are, however, alternative models to the modern university for the production of Christian scholarship, all of which come from the past. One such model is the medieval university, dominated by the scholarly tradition of monasticism. Other models come from the denominational seminaries of antebellum American society. These were the environments that produced the great Christian minds of Aquinas, Luther, Calvin, Charles Hodge, and John Williamson Nevin. Perhaps one of the most interesting models is the parish of Northampton, Massachusetts, that sustained the

---

civil, and especially religious loyalties. A large but unspoken aim of higher education is to make sure that undergraduates are weaned from the various parochial perspectives they bring to campus. Moreover, rather than enhancing local ties, universities are fully dependent upon and sustain artificial and rootless communities such as the professions. All sorts of studies show that higher education weakens the religious convictions of graduates. So why do evangelicals think the pursuit of higher learning will turn out to be a blessing for the community of faith? See Wendell Berry, "An Argument for Diversity," in *What Are People For?* (New York: Farrar, Straus & Giroux, 1990), 109-22; and Robert Wuthnow, *The Restructuring of American Religion: Society and Faith since Word War II* (Princeton: Princeton University Press, 1988).

33. On the tensions between producing scholarship and preserving the faith, see the interesting observations of Roger Finke and Rodney Starke in *The Churching of America, 1776-1990: Winners and Losers in Our Religious Economy* (New Brunswick, N.J.: Rutgers University Press, 1992), 173-98.

thought and work of Jonathan Edwards. What does it say about his Christian mind that he was freed from an academic setting and spent long hours producing sermons? Not only did his activities as an independent scholar/pastor sustain a brilliant mind, but what about the community in which Edwards worked, an agricultural, provincial, family-dominated town? How much was the rich local culture and political economy of the Connecticut River Valley responsible for the accomplishments of Edwards?[34]

In fact, what stands out about the environments that nurtured the minds of all the great Christian scholars of the past, from the medieval university cities of Paris and Oxford, to Northampton and the seminary towns of Princeton and Mercersberg, is that they were rooted in local cultures with some intellectual vitality and economic independence, where a variety of institutions contributed to the life of the mind, where intellectual life was not fragmented and specialized. In sum, many of the great Christian minds developed in settings that were not dominated by centralized nation-states and multinational corporations. This does not mean, as Wendell Berry might argue, that Edwards and Aquinas, who were closer to and more dependent on the land, thought more Christianly after milking the Jersey cows and scraping horse manure from their boots. But it does suggest that agrarian economies have been ones in which, to call to mind the title of a book by another agrarian, Richard Weaver, ideas had consequences. These were cultures and communities where theologians and men of letters were important because the transcendent truths with which such thinkers grappled had a tremendous bearing upon the destiny of souls and therefore on the lives of ordinary people. As Weaver argued,

> The spoiling of man seems always to begin when urban living predominates over rural. After man has left the country to shut himself up in vast piles of stone, . . . after he has come to depend on a complicated system of human exchange for his survival, he becomes forgetful of the overriding mystery of creation. Such is the normal condition of the *deracine*. An artificial environment causes him to lose sight of the great system not subject to man's control. Undoubtedly

34. On the importance of communities for intellectual life, see the essays in Thomas Bender, *Intellect and Public Life: Essays on the Social History of Academic Intellectuals in the United States* (Baltimore: Johns Hopkins University Press, 1993).

this circumstance is a chief component of bourgeois mentality, as even the etymology of "bourgeois" may remind us. It is the city-dweller, solaced by man-made comforts, who resents the very thought that there exist mighty forces beyond his understanding; it is he who wishes insulation and who berates and persecutes the philosophers, the prophets and mystics, the wild men out of the desert, who keep before him the theme of human frailty.[35]

Pre-modern societies were more conducive to the life of the mind simply because they didn't present as many distractions (or attractions) as modern society does. The life of the mind and spiritual truths mattered because the physical realities of this world were grim, "a vale of tears."[36] Conversely, consumer societies offer so many luxuries, comforts, and conveniences that the life of the scholar appears to be truly scandalous.

The dilemma for evangelical scholars concerned about the life of the mind, then, is doubly grave. Not only are evangelicals heirs to intellectual habits and spiritual exercises that undermine intellectual endeavor almost at every turn, but they also live in a society that makes intellectual work of the sort produced by Edwards, Luther, and Wesley a very cheap and therefore useless commodity. The question that needs to be addressed is this: To what extent can Christian higher education continue to depend upon the contemporary socioeconomic order for personal sustenance and institutional support when the very organization, products, and purposes of that social structure undermine the community and culture that is crucial to developing and sustaining a Christian mind? If, as Christopher Lasch has written, the religious right's advocacy of capitalism is naive because market forces undermine the institutions — family, church, and school — that the right defends, aren't Christian academics equally naive to think that evangelical higher education — or any meaningful education for that matter — can be sustained by a society whose only use for the life of the mind is as a path to higher earnings or as a means to make the corporate order run more efficiently?[37]

35. Weaver, *Ideas Have Consequences,* 115.
36. This point is supported by developments in American Methodism noted by Finke and Starke, *Churching of America,* 163-69.
37. Lasch, "Conservatism against Itself," *First Things* (April 1990): 17-23.

The real scandal of the evangelical mind may be to think, to hope against hope, that the transformation of American higher education and culture can occur without the accompanying recognition that modern society has fundamentally transformed the prevailing perceptions of and assumptions about the mind. Many will say that it is impossible (and, for that matter, undesirable) to turn back the clock, to go back to the rural communities that sustained the likes of an Edwards or a Hodge. But is it any more possible to produce Christian minds from the current structures of academic life? The Bible says that Christians can handle serpents and drink poison and not be hurt. To be sure, believers trust that God will sustain his people through all hardships, and this belief should be a comfort and source of strength to evangelicals in the academy. But if these believers are to think more carefully about the material conditions necessary for sustaining a genuinely Christian mind, they must wrestle with the question of whether they are able, as good stewards of God's creation, to live lives where playing with serpents is their only recreation and drinking poison is the whole of their diet. The analogy may be overdone. But the current predicament of intellectual life requires a candid and thorough assessment of what the structures of modern learning do to learning itself, and whether those structures are wholesome ones for Christian minds.

Advocacy in the Writing of Religious History

Understanding the Past, Using the Past: Reflections on Two Approaches to History

GRANT WACKER

THOMAS WOLSEY: You're a constant regret to me, Thomas. If you could just see facts flat on, without that horrible moral squint; with just a little common sense you could have been a statesman.

THOMAS MORE: Well . . . I believe, when statesmen forsake their own private conscience for the sake of their public duties . . . they lead their country by a short road to chaos.

Robert Bolt, A Man for All Seasons

I

Fresh from a twenty-year hitch in the Marine Corps, the young man grabbed my hand, crunched it warmly, and announced exactly what he was looking for in my history course: the straight stuff. "I don't pay ten grand a year to hear other students' opinions," he warned. "I can get that in the lounge anytime. What I want is the true story, the way it really was, straight from you." A day or two later another student

I wish to thank Stanley Hauerwas, William R. Hutchison, Peter Iver Kaufman, Russell Richey, and David Steinmetz for helpful critiques of this essay.

put me on notice, in the middle of a perfectly planned lecture, that she was expecting something quite different. "What does all this stuff about 'church' and 'sect' and 'denomination' have to do with the lives of real people?" she demanded. I mumbled something about useful organizing models. She responded doubtfully, I retorted dutifully, and the lecture fizzled in a mist of confusion. The student trailed me to my office. "I'm sick of all this Enlightenment crap," she exploded. "What I want to hear about are narratives, you know, the stories of the oppressed."

Welcome to Duke Divinity School. As far as that goes, welcome to the modern research university. Students typically phrase their concerns in the vocabulary of everyday life, for which we all might be grateful. But they think about the tension between disinterested scholarship and moral advocacy more than teachers usually give them credit for. What should we tell them? Indeed, what should we tell ourselves when we pause to reflect upon what we do and the rationale behind it? Should history writing be understood, as the first student did, primarily as detached inquiry pursued for its own sake, without any melioristic aims? Or should it be understood, as the second student did, primarily as a reformist enterprise that concerns itself only with topics that will make the world a better place?

Definitive answers to these matters remain elusive at best, so this essay's goal is considerably more modest. Rather than trying to come up with a grand theory about the moral obligations, or lack of them, that attend the historian's task, I wish to ask a more manageable question. Simply put, is it appropriate for the historian explicitly to evaluate the events of the past? (Shortly we shall see that the keyword here is not "evaluate," since everyone does that regardless, but "explicitly," by which I mean intentionally or self-consciously.) To move way ahead of myself, I shall argue that there is no one right answer to this question. Everything depends upon the aim of the moment, what the historian hopes to accomplish in any particular situation. In some cases it is fitting to give readers what the first student called for: the straight story, history without homiletic overlay. Understanding the past for its own sake, we might say. In others it is better to give them what the second student called for: an ethically accountable narrative, history with homiletic overlay. Using the past for present needs, we might say. The rule of thumb, in other words, is not to impose a rule of thumb. Or to adapt a line from poet James Russell Lowell, if new occasions teach new duties, then different occasions teach different duties.

II

Assuming that good history writing involves drawing distinctions between things that really differ, it may be helpful first to pinpoint some of the issues that I am not concerned with in this essay. In a word, I am not concerned with the structural realities that historians cannot change. Perhaps the central one is the value-laden nature of the data that they work with day by day. In one way or another all traces from the past reflect the assumptions of their time and place. And that is just the beginning. Which bits of data were preserved, and how they were preserved, reveal the moral hierarchies of countless intermediaries between past actors and the present-day historians who write about them. Moreover, the way historians organize those traces in works of history and then display them to others reflects their own values in numerous ways. All of these issues are important, but I am not concerned with them because they lie outside a scholar's power to change. If we wanted to wax theological about it, the sheer givenness of the past, and the pervasively moral nature of that givenness, might be labeled the original historical sin.

Nor am I concerned in this essay with the way that historians' own values force themselves, unbidden, upon their reconstructions of the past. Their personal perspectives impose themselves in all sorts of ways. The first and most dramatic, arguably, is the decision to play historian at all. That move ascribes a certain importance to the past, which many non-Western cultures, and many individuals within Western culture, would consider a waste of time to begin with. Moreover, scholars' values turn up in their choice of subject matter. A decision to scrutinize Baptists but not Catholics necessarily attaches a certain value to Baptists. One does not have to believe, with some postmodernists, that the subtext is more important than the text in order to appreciate that what gets left out of the story is part of the story too. Beyond all this, historians' values worm their way into the very pith of everything that they say about the past. They never just sit down and come up with "'true stories' that reproduce lives as they were lived," historian

Peter Kaufman notes. Rather they invariably "present lives as lived significantly, and significance is paradigm dependent." Another way of putting this is to say that students of the past construe the materials of other eras in ways that seem sensible to them, but the criteria for making those decisions are not printed in the stars. They grow from each historian's unique experiences of life. Yet once again none of these considerations affects the present inquiry because they, too, are given, just part of the territory.[1]

Moral advocacy even reaches down to matters of technique and style. Scholars betray their values by the scrupulousness with which they handle the data of the past. Although most like to think that they treat all evidence with equal care, the plain truth, of course, is that they do not. Timid facts crouching over in the corner (those that do not interest them very much) get overlooked, while brash facts (those that do interest them) push their way front and center into the narrative. But to repeat: in this essay I remain unconcerned with all influences of this sort, not because they are trivial, but because they are unavoidable. They stand as intrinsic parts of the process by which historians retrieve and interpret data from the past.[2]

This brings me then to the question — the sole question — that I do wish to address. Simply stated, should historians deliberately impose value judgments upon their narratives *above and beyond* the layers of evaluation that are already present in everything that they do? By "impose value judgments" I mean everything from inserting barely noticeable adjectives that suggest approval or disapproval to casting the narrative in terms of some grand pattern of cultural change that is deemed desirable or undesirable. Differently stated, whenever historians make a self-conscious decision to make the story appeal to or repel the reader, they impose value judgments above and beyond what is presented in the materials.

Many thoughtful critics would have us believe, of course, that any effort to separate the less normative from the more normative is bogus to begin with because everything is normative. It is turtles all the way

1. Peter Iver Kaufman, "Historians and Human Behavior: Biography As Therapy," *Clio* 18 (1989): 185.
2. The literally countless ways that values structure everything that historians touch are concisely and charmingly limned in Daniel J. Boorstin, "The Historian: 'A Wrestler with the Angel,' " *New York Times Book Review,* 20 September 1987, 1ff.

down, as the saying goes. And strictly speaking, they are right. All statements contain values of some sort. To say that it is 90 degrees outside with 100% humidity is not entirely different from saying that only a crazy damn fool would go outside on a scorcher of a day like this. The former assertion is not purely descriptive, for it reflects a positive evaluation of quantitative meteorological language, and the latter is not purely normative, for it involves an affirmation about the way things really are, independent of the observer's interests. Nonetheless, most readers readily sense that the first sentence is somehow different from the second. The former seems sober and straight up while the latter seems, well, a bit intoxicated. The former is, in a word, less moral, or perhaps we should say less moralistic, than the latter. And readers commonly name that difference by calling one sentence descriptive and the other normative, or one objective and the other subjective. Intellectuals can melt down the differences between those propositions as much as they like, but their efforts will not last. Sooner or later ordinary folk (which includes intellectuals when they have to do something useful like get their cars fixed) will find other ways to rearticulate their instinctive conviction that the first sentence somehow functions differently from the second.[3]

Historian Philip Gleason helps to clarify what is at stake here. He describes three levels of questions that students might raise about a past event. The first is the descriptive: what happened? The second is the explanatory: why did it happen? The third is the evaluative: was it a good thing that it happened? Gleason offers the story of John's and Mary's divorce as a case in point. The first question a historian of the divorce must face is the descriptive one: did John and Mary really get divorced or was it just a rumor? Given consensus about the meaning of the words involved — "John," "Mary," "divorce," and the like — and given sufficient data to make a judgment, determining whether John and Mary actually split up normally is a pretty straightforward task. Either they did or they did not. The second level of inquiry, the explanatory, is a good deal trickier. Historians who are remotely sensi-

---

3. Arthur Marwick unfolds a longer and more sophisticated version of this argument in "'A Fetishism of Documents'?: The Salience of Source-Based History," in *Developments in Modern Historiography*, ed. Henry Kozicki (New York: St. Martin's Press, 1993), chap. 7.

tive to the complexity of human relationships know that trying to explain why anyone's marriage broke up is fraught with danger. Their accounts are necessarily freighted with the baggage of their own marriages, their deepest presuppositions about human nature, and heaven knows what else. The third level of inquiry is by far the most complicated. Here the historian who dares to speculate on whether the divorce was a good or bad thing ventures out onto a human minefield. This is the evaluative level, and it is almost needless to say that countless considerations come into play. Even so, historians make judgments of that sort all the time in daily conversation, and they commonly assume, usually without too much angst, that it is in fact possible to offer reasonable answers even to such tangled matters as these in their professional work.[4]

Applying this model to what working historians actually do, only the most determined and unimaginative ones stop at the first level and limit themselves to a connect-the-dots description of what happened. Most go ahead and try their hand at explaining why the event took place as it did. Indeed, the ability to move from description to explanation stands out as one of the skills that distinguishes chroniclers from scholars. Yet few authors are content to stop even there. Most freely hazard a guess or two (or three or four) about whether the event was a good thing. They might do this subtly, by framing the narrative's underlying questions so that readers will respond in the desired way, or they might do it boldly, by coming right out and telling readers what they are supposed to think and feel. Either way, the sole issue before us in this essay is whether this third form of historical activity — namely, deliberate, self-conscious evaluation — is a good idea. Phrased as a question, is historians' always-powerful urge to appreciate or depreciate everything they see a regrettable feature of human nature and therefore one that they should try to minimize? Or is it a creative feature of human nature and therefore one that they should try to celebrate?

A judicious answer surely depends on one's purposes in crafting a work of history. Is the goal principally aesthetic, to understand the past in order to enrich the present? Or is it principally moral, to use the

4. Philip Gleason, *Keeping the Faith: American Catholicism Past and Present* (Notre Dame: University of Notre Dame Press, 1987), 216-20.

past in order to change the present? To be sure, these choices, as described, constitute the extreme poles of an abstract continuum. In real life, when historians actually sit down and start shuffling their proverbial notecards in order to see what patterns might emerge, the options rarely prove so clear-cut. But this way of posing the issue at least makes the alternatives clear, even if only analytically. The former goal of understanding the past suggests that historians would be well advised to confine themselves to levels one and two of Gleason's model — to questions of what happened and why. The latter goal of using the past suggests, in contrast, that they need to ascend to level three and forthrightly impose an ethical yardstick upon their materials.[5]

The key point is that differences in the overarching aim of a historical work entail quite distinct ways of handling the data. Generally speaking, understanding the past calls for, in Robert Berkhofer's words, an internal, actor-oriented approach, while using the past calls for an external, observer-oriented approach.[6] Let us think for a few moments about the nature of each approach. As I read Berkhofer, an internal, actor-oriented method seeks above all to collapse the investigator into the heart and soul of the one who is being investigated. It endeavors to enter into the actor's experience and then to gaze back out upon the world exactly as the actor did. This activity might be called "thin description": an intentionally wide-eyed re-creation of the actor's thoughts and feelings, exactly as he or she experienced them. Thus the aim of internal analysis is nothing more complicated — nor less stupendous — than to resurrect the dead and let them speak for themselves with all the force and beauty of their natal dialects. External, observer-oriented analysis, on the other hand, serves as a second order of inquiry. In this mode historians set aside actors' perceptions of themselves and seek to implicate them in larger frameworks of meaning. This endeavor might be as crude as insisting that a certain event was rotten to the core, or as sophisticated as saying that the event exemplified something like the splendor of the human saga itself. Either

5. Peter Novick, *That Noble Dream: The "Objectivity Question" and the American Historical Profession* (Cambridge: Cambridge University Press, 1988), ably discusses the implications of these options, especially in part 4.

6. Robert F. Berkhofer Jr., *A Behavioral Approach to Historical Analysis* (New York: The Free Press, 1969), chap. 1. I have borrowed Berkhofer's labels and models, but I do not assume that he would necessarily apply them as I have.

way, the scholar, now writing in the explicitly evaluative mode, strives to reconfigure the past in a pattern that seems morally responsive to the needs of the present. The aim is to speak back to the dead and, even more importantly, to give voice to the bystanders who were not permitted to utter a word at the time.

III

With this snapshot of the two approaches in mind, let us turn now to think about the virtues and vices of each. The internal, actor-oriented approach seems logically to come first, and its benefits are numerous. The sheer aesthetic pleasure of reconnoitering the past in its own terms — striving, however imperfectly, to see the past exactly as it saw itself — and for no other reason than that something interesting happened there, surely ranks high on the list. To be sure, not everyone finds it necessary to slam the car into reverse every time he passes a historical marker, and not everyone feels impelled to drive five miles down a country road to see the very spot where the Reverend James O'Kelley lies a'moldering in the grave. But many do, and for those specially afflicted souls, such moments offer one of life's little treats. More importantly, an ingenuous reading of the past helps to foster a sense of humor about humanity's foibles and pretensions, past and present. My students never cease to be amused when they hear about the German theologian who, when given a choice between going to heaven or hearing a lecture about going to heaven, predictably chose the latter. The point here is that Thomas Wolsey's "flat on" perspective (quoted in the first epigraph) highlights the disparity between advertised ideals and actual behavior. It enables readers to see the difference between somberness and seriousness, which is no small gain, for many of the funniest things in life are deadly serious, as anyone who has reared an infant or cared for an aging parent well knows.

Then, too, letting the dead speak for themselves may, ironically, help free the present from the shackles of the present. Knowing that most of today's crises have precedents, and that humans have somehow managed to muddle through all of them, is no small gain. When the past is allowed to speak for itself, to tell us what it has to say in its own language, it soon becomes apparent that the great bulk of human experience is not about "Great Awakenings" or "Social Watersheds" or "Cultural Earthquakes" at all but about the daily experiences of joy and loneliness and love and grief. There are limits, of course. Historian Bruce Lawrence has persuasively argued that nuclear weapons introduced a genuinely unprecedented set of variables into civilization's story. Yet the way that people have responded to such variables remains remarkably familiar, generation after generation. Beyond all this, when the past is permitted to speak to us it often provides answers that moderns do not expect — and some that they do not welcome — because it raises questions that moderns never thought to ask. The past exposes noble aspirations and pitiable failings where neither was imagined to exist. And hearing those distant voices clearly, moderns may be less prone to rush to judgment.[7]

The benefits of the internal, actor-oriented approach accumulate. Listening to the past without commentary dampens the temptation to universalize the parochial. Thoughtful men and women come to see that many of the ideas that they instinctively presume to be eternal and global are more transitory and local than not. Historian William R. Hutchison tells of a conference in Madras where one academic responded to another's admission that he was a career missionary by saying: "Don't apologize. All Americans are missionaries." The latter might well have said, "Don't apologize; all humans are missionaries, period." This is not to decry religious missions, which is an honorable enterprise, nor missionaries, who have served nobly. The point rather is that it is one thing to share the Good News (Christian or otherwise) after one has journeyed to the far shore and decided that things could be better, but quite another to proselytize because one cannot imagine how the world could be any different from one's own and still be legitimate.[8]

Finally, a rigorously internal approach helps solve some of the problems peculiar to the teaching and writing of religious history (which is where I, as a historian of American religion, necessarily begin). At the outset it is well to recognize that religious history stirs up more

---

7. Bruce B. Lawrence, *Defenders of God: The Fundamentalist Revolt against the Modern Age* (San Francisco: Harper & Row, 1989), esp. chap. 2.

8. William R. Hutchison, *Errand to the World: American Protestant Thought and Foreign Missions* (Chicago: University of Chicago Press, 1987), 1.

than its fair share of touchiness. To be sure, all humanistic inquiry involves deep commitments that begin far back in the nursery, the kitchen, and the bedroom, but religious history seems especially bedeviled by personal investments. It trades upon life's Big Questions, forever scrutinizing where the values that the culture holds most dear — and often most unself-critically — come from and whose interests they serve. And that is only the beginning of the problems religious history invokes. All but the most obtuse readers readily see that the discipline's natural tendency is to debunk. Readers quite reasonably begin to worry when they learn that all religious artifacts, including their own, can be substantially if not wholly explained without recourse to God. They desperately want to believe that their most cherished views about life and the after-life were discovered, not invented, and they shudder when historians suggest otherwise. Religious folk recoil when they find out that other men and women have fashioned intellectual and moral universes dramatically different from their own. It is important to note that the problem here is not pluralism per se, but the recognition that other men and women, holding other points of view, came to those positions intelligently and with moral integrity. As far as that goes, religious folk resist being studied at all, or treated as though their beliefs and rituals were a quantifiable part of the natural world. And for many the most upsetting part of all is to learn how shabby their own story — the story of their own tribe, their own sect — really is, for all too often it proves to be a tale of small-minded men and women inflicting large-minded cruelties upon anyone who got in their way.

So how does an internal approach to the past help believers cope? How does it de-fang the serpent of the historical study of religion, and especially of one's own religion? Not by telling lies, to be sure. Not even by telling little lies of prudent omission. Rather it serves them by letting the dead speak just as they were, eloquent and stammering, mellifluous and gasping. Thoughtful souls, newly burdened with an acute sense of humankind's "terrible predicaments," as Herbert Butterfield put it, may emerge from their encounter with the past feeling a "little sorry for everybody." If the price of such chastening is a sharpened vision of human pretension, the reward may be a heightened sense of divine faithfulness generation after generation. Yet such enrichment becomes an available resource only if believers take the fifth commandment, to honor their fathers and mothers — their forebears — with utter seriousness. And here it is worth remembering that the fifth commandment was the first commandment of the second table of the Law, the table that told folks how to get along with each other after they had taken care of the seemingly more manageable task of getting along with God.[9]

Altogether, then, there is much to be said for an internal, actor-oriented approach to history — and yet we have good reasons to remain wary. For one thing, internal, actor-oriented history easily degenerates into antiquarianism. The latter might be defined as a keen interest in certain events of the past, but without a systematic notion of how those events came to be and why they are worth knowing about in the first place. Antiquarianism is the everlasting trademark of those who know more than they understand. The type is easy to spot: the earnest soul who has mastered every detail of the Battle of Gettysburg but does not harbor the slightest notion why the *Gettysburg Address* may have been more than rhetorical bunting. Bluntly stated, the antiquarian fails to ask "so what?" — or more precisely, "why should anyone else want to know about this?" The plain truth is that no part of the human story is so large or sweeping that it cannot be ruined by being treated as if its importance were self-evident. By the same token, no patch of the human story is too small to warrant a historian's attention if he or she takes time to show how it illumines other times and places.

Another problem that harries internal, actor-oriented history is tribalism. This is scholarship that is fashioned with private, factional, parochial, or ethnic — in a word, non-public — criteria for what counts as good evidence, reliable warrants, and sound conclusions. Tribal history rarely suffers from factual inaccuracy in the strict sense of the term. More often the problem proves the opposite: an inordinate attention to details, yet all linked by explanatory frameworks that only insiders find credible. In the Christian tradition, for example, tribalist values often lead to what theologian Russell Spittler calls a "sacred meteor" theory of causation. In this framework the truly significant causes are not

---

9. H. Butterfield, *Christianity and History* (London: G. Bell and Sons, 1949), 92. For the main point of the paragraph I am indebted to David C. Steinmetz, *Memory and Mission: Theological Reflections on the Christian Past* (Nashville: Abingdon Press, 1988), esp. 25-33.

historical at all. They are extra-historical, tumbling directly from heaven or, if not from heaven, at least from some realm not open to the ken of outsiders. Beyond this, tribalism often entails what Sidney Mead called "historyless history," although "kangaroo history" might be more apt, for its practitioners try to jump over the immediate past in order to reclaim a distant past, a Garden of Eden, a Day of Pentecost, or a Council of Trent, that they regard as normative for all times and places. Again, the product is the same: a line of argument that makes perfect sense to insiders but leaves outsiders out, deleted from the narrative and wondering what happened.[10]

Both of these modes of history writing, antiquarian and tribalistic, pile up in a dead end, then, not because they are demonstrably wrong, but because they remain flat, dry, plain — in a word, uninspired. Internal, actor-oriented history need not fall into these traps, but often it does — and this is precisely where the external, observer-oriented approach comes to the rescue. If the first student described earlier, the one who wanted simply to understand the past, bespoke sober good sense, the second student, the one who wanted to use the past, rightly sensed that history can be made to speak a healing word to a broken world.

IV

An external, observer-oriented approach to history eagerly embraces evaluative frameworks. It takes actors' own understandings of their lives and recasts them in an idiom that is both chastened and enriched by the lessons of personal experience. We might pirate a line from Emerson to say that it trades upon thought passed through the fire of life. But there are protocols that must be observed. If an external, observer-oriented approach to history is to be responsibly executed, it must conform to at least two broad criteria: *intellectual plausibility* and *moral consistency*. The former is essentially a matter of credibility in the

---

10. Russell P. Spittler, "Scripture and the Theological Enterprise: View from a Big Canoe," in *The Use of the Bible in Theology: Evangelical Options*, ed. Robert K. Johnston (Atlanta: John Knox Press, 1985), 63. Sidney E. Mead, *The Lively Experiment* (New York: Harper & Row, 1963), 108-13.

modern academy, the latter essentially a matter of honesty in modern life. Each of these criteria deserves a few words of explanation.

Intellectual plausibility means, among other things, that any credible interpretation of the past must take historical context with utmost seriousness. That is to say that all events must be situated in the context of other events that took place in temporal, cultural, and usually geographical proximity.[11] Plausibility assumes that change is the normal state of affairs, that it is the absence of change that requires explanation, and that change takes place by natural rather than by providential means. Plausibility requires, furthermore, that the narrative must conform in some significant way to the readers' own experiences of life. If there are no threads of continuity between past events and present experiences, the former must remain mysterious at best, nonsensical at worst. And plausibility assumes that the textual evidence on which evaluations are based have been subjected to some hard-nosed tests of probability: Was the witness sober? Was the witness a known liar? and so forth. Beyond all this, intellectual plausibility demands, as science philosopher Stephen W. Hawking puts it, that historical affirmations must be open to disconfirmation. The line between critical history and imaginative literature is blurry at best, but the possibility that a proposition could be decisively disconfirmed comes as close as any to serving as a wedge by which properly historical texts can be separated from properly imaginative ones. Most biographies of Abraham Lincoln, for example, could be readily invalidated, at least at one level, by a single reliable sighting of John Wilkes Booth striding along the streets of Paris the morning of April 14, 1865. Conversely, it is difficult to imagine exactly what it would take to "invalidate" *The Scarlet Letter*.[12]

11. Occasionally a distant context may be more relevant than an immediate one. Arguably the Branch Davidian tragedy in Waco is better explained by ideas floating around sixteenth-century Europe than by anything going on in southern Texas in the 1990s. But the point remains: context is king. That is one of the key features that distinguishes plausible history from the "kangaroo" model that artificially hooks together contexts that cannot be shown to be organically connected.

12. Discussions of the criteria of intellectual plausibility, commonly simply called critical history, are legion. This particular paragraph draws especially upon Van A. Harvey, *The Historian and the Believer: The Morality of Historical Knowledge and Christian Belief* (Toronto: Macmillan, 1966), chap. 1, esp. 14-15; Morton White, *Social Thought in America: The Revolt against Formalism* (Boston: Beacon Press, 1957), chap.

Granted, the standards of intellectual plausibility are themselves increasingly contested these days by a number of interest groups. Since there is no universal, normative, General Public out there, what is plausible is tethered to a host of particularities such as region, class, gender, race, and religion. Ronald L. Numbers's acclaimed work *The Creationists* makes clear, for example, that intellectually coherent subcultures flourish when they do not march to the tune of the dominant university culture. In an academic world largely based upon evolutionary suppositions, Numbers shows, scientific creationists nonetheless get along quite nicely, reading and footnoting each others' books, schmoozing at each other's gatherings, worrying first and foremost about each other's opinions. To be sure, they would like to win the approval of the Stephen Jay Goulds of the world, but it is more important to gain the approval of others within their own subculture. What counts for good evidence, reliable warrants, and sound conclusions in their fixed social universe remains stubbornly distinct from what counts for good evidence, reliable warrants, and sound conclusions outside their subculture.[13]

Having said that, most of the history texts assigned in American colleges and universities are written by men and women who take their cues from another equally fixed and equally definable social universe. It is called the mainline academy. And the mainline academy insists upon such notions as contextualism, change, disconfirmation, and so forth. If the academy itself eludes an essentialist definition valid for all times and places, it is possible at least to describe the folk who inhabit its halls: they prefer the *New York Times* to *USA Today*, soft-soles to wingtips, Volvos to Cadillacs, worry more about tobacco use than alcohol abuse, and find jokes about Dan Quayle a lot funnier than jokes about Al Gore. Though academic mainliners know in their heart of hearts that they are not the only public that exists, the plain truth is that the mainline academy is the only public that is able to exert coercive sway over the "reality-defining institutions" of American life at large. Like it or not, the mainline academy rigorously polices the boundaries

---

2, esp. 12; John Van Seters, *Prologue to History: The Yahwist as Historian in Genesis* (Louisville: Westminster/John Knox Press, 1992), 24-34. The Stephen W. Hawking reference comes from *A Brief History of Time: From the Big Bang to Black Holes* (Toronto: Bantam Books, 1988), 10.

13. Ronald L. Numbers, *The Creationists* (New York: Knopf, 1992).

of what can or cannot pass muster as intellectually plausible in most sectors of society. Believing scholars might balk at the prospect that their cherished notions remain subject to their adjudications, but to deny it is to deny oneself a place at the discussion table.

Besides intellectual plausibility, the other large rubric that delimits external, observer-oriented history is moral consistency. When historians openly evaluate the data of the past they shoulder a responsibility to show that their renderings remain consistent with their own lives. When they say that the record is univocal — that is, that it bears only one meaning or a very small range of meanings — they invite the expectation that their private lives will in some sense correspond with their professional posture. At the same time, when they claim that the record is endlessly plastic, that it bears an unlimited range of meanings, they encumber themselves with certain real-life expectations. Thus it is not entirely clear why The Gospel of John or *Macbeth* should be regarded as hermeneutical black holes, open to infinite interpretive possibilities, while a paycheck or a tenure letter or a green card should be regarded as independent variables with fixed, nonnegotiable meanings. We do know why, of course. Ascribing endless porousness to the former range of documents carries few if any personal repercussions (except, perhaps, the happy possibility of getting another article published), while ascribing any porousness to the latter range of documents might result in considerable harm to one's self-interest. The point is simple. Adding layers of homiletic richness to the data requires a cold shower of moral consistency once in a while if it is to be taken seriously.

Since the mainline academy these days tends to emphasize the multiplicity of interpretive possibilities for all texts (except those that run close to the real-life quick), I shall linger for an additional moment upon the heightened accountability that historians of this persuasion take upon themselves. The events surrounding the 1876 death of the well-known gospel song writer P. P. Bliss illustrate the problem. As Bliss's biographer tells the story, Bliss and his wife were traveling from Buffalo, New York, to Ashtabula, Ohio, on an all-night train. Just outside of Ashtabula the train plunged off a trestle. Most riders, including Bliss, escaped unharmed. But when Bliss realized that his wife was missing, he climbed back into the flaming wreckage and ended up perishing with her. Now it is possible, of course, to interpret his motivations in several ways. Bliss might have gone back mainly to retrieve his wife's purse but, overcome by smoke, passed out and succumbed to the flames. Or he might have been disappointed with sales of his songs and decided to end it all right then and there in a glorious burst of defiance. And so forth. Yet none of those interpretations seems convincing. The almost certain truth of the matter is that Bliss loved his wife and hoped to save her. And it does not take an advanced degree in psychology or special skill in interpreting texts to figure that out. For all practical purposes, then, there are universals, or at least broad commonalities, of human experience, and late at night, when the phone rings with bad news, we all seem to know it.[14]

Morally consistent evaluation means more than congruence between the claims of historians and the way that they lead their daily lives. It also means fairness — fairness to the data and fairness to the reader. All too often historians use an external, observer-oriented approach as an excuse for one-sidedness. In this guise they focus upon a narrowly defined slice of the truth in order to serve a present-day cause, but in doing so end up telling less than the full truth. Precise truths easily lead to sprawling falsehoods because they fail to let the reader know that other viewpoints and other dimensions of the problem exist. Partisans of the Christian Right, for example, tell the exact truth but distort the full truth when they insist that founding fathers like Franklin and Jefferson faithfully attended their parish churches. At the same time, crusading secularists commit the same sin when they trumpet the news that Lincoln, who was a profoundly theological (if not explicitly Christian) thinker never affiliated with any church nor publicly espoused Christian doctrines.

And then there is, finally, what might be called the license to speak. Moral consistency requires that the historian hold certain credentials of attitude and temperament and life experience beyond the proverbial union card of the Ph.D. Something of what is involved here was captured a half-century ago in an unlikely source: "If Buddhists Came to Our Town," a brief but influential *Christian Century* article penned by Daniel Johnson Fleming, a world missions professor at New

---

14. D. W. Whittle, ed., *Memoirs of Phillip P. Bliss* (New York: A. J. Barnes, 1877), 295, 297. It is only fair to add that accounts of Bliss's death vary. See, for example, W. Thorburn Clark, *Hymns That Endure* (Nashville: Broadman Press, 1942), 37. My point is that given agreement upon the components of an event, some interpretations of it remain more plausible than others.

York's Union Theological Seminary. Fleming listed various virtues that Christian missionaries ought to manifest if they wanted to be credible. All of the virtues that Fleming outlined can be expected of historians too, for they also are missionaries of a sort. Like argonauts of old, historians trek back in time, retrieve the experiences of long dead actors, bring them forward, and implicate them in frameworks of value that the actors themselves might actually reject if given the chance. Yet historians proceed undaunted, for they, like missionaries, remain convinced that their schemes are somehow more true, or more useful, or more likely to produce further insight, than the actors' own.[15]

Let us consider Fleming's admonitions one by one. First of all, he urged, missionaries — we could just as well say historians — should acquire their message not by blind obedience to some outside authority, or by unthinking acceptance of their own cultural inheritance, but by an experience of life "extensive in range and time." They should not try to impose their values upon another culture unless they have excellent reasons to believe that their values afford better insight into life's great defining experiences than the ones already prevailing. Missionaries should preach their message with a "certain humility and teachableness of spirit," which means making every effort to appreciate the best that others have to offer. Missionaries should not make the hearing of their message compulsory. They should recognize the difference between a value system articulated in theory, that is, the way it might work in the best of all possible worlds, and the way that it normally works in real life. Missionaries should be disinterested, which means that they should not inordinately promote their personal interests or ease or power, nor even the special advancement of their own "tribe." Above all, missionaries should be, as far as possible, candid about what they are doing, laying their cards on the table, never employing covert methods in the interest of some higher cause. Though Fleming did not put it quite this way, his advice seemed finally to boil down to one powerful insight: missionaries — historians — have no right to evaluate and to change the Other until they earn it.

If the rigorous demands of intellectual plausibility and of moral

---

15. Daniel J. Fleming, "If Buddhists Came to Our Town," *The Christian Century*, 28 February 1929, 293-94. The article was a deadly serious spoof upon the pretensions of Christian missionaries in Asia.

consistency constrain the evaluative flights of the serious historian, we might well ask if the cost is worth the effort. The answer is decidedly yes, for an external, observer-oriented approach yields large dividends. Perhaps the most obvious is a richer, more copiously nuanced reading of the texts of their trade. Catholic convert Orestes Brownson made this point with memorable force 150 years ago when he assailed Protestant evangelicals for purporting to read the Bible just as it was, with eyes unclouded by preconceptions of any sort. What could be more absurd! Brownson exploded. The blank mind, the tabula rasa of Protestant mythology, was next to useless. Rather, it was the *cluttered* mind, the mind laden with strongly held values and sharply defined points of view, that was able to draw from the text of Scripture the extravagant wealth of divine revelation and apply it to contemporary life.[16]

External, observer-oriented history affords still another benefit especially apt for scholars who work primarily with religious materials. Unless they are writing high intellectual history (and sometimes even then), those materials often bristle with bizarre events. The more immediate are affirmations about supernatural interventions in human affairs — healings, apparitions, coincidences, and the like. Less obvious but arguably even more difficult to evaluate are persistent and pervasive manifestations of seemingly irrational behavior in the interests of a higher religious cause. How does the historian make sense, for example, of Nat Turner's bloody rampage against infants, or of Mary Baker Eddy's obsession with Malicious Animal Magnetism, or of Jim Elliot's virtual self-offering to Auca cannibals? A fair guess is that all of these persons would have scored high on any intelligence test, and all were manifestly functional in daily affairs. So how does the scholar explain a behavior pattern that, quite literally, makes no sense in the halls of the mainline academy?

Two options arise. One is to go back to the internal, actor-oriented approach and seek to describe what the subjects themselves thought that they were doing and, perhaps, how they were perceived by their contemporaries. The other option is to step up to the plate and take a

---

16. Orestes A. Brownson, "The Church and Its Mission," *The Christian World*, 18 February 1843, reprinted in *American Catholic Religious Thought: The Shaping of a Theological and Social Tradition*, ed. Patrick Carey (New York: Paulist Press, 1987), 115. At the time that Brownson wrote he was still technically a Unitarian, but converted the following year.

swing at some theory of what was really going on — fully embracing, in other words, a thoroughly external, observer-oriented approach. That does not mean that historians must go around puncturing their audiences' sensibilities. It is not always necessary, for example, to tell the local Women's Missionary Circle that the legendarily saintly Lottie Moon suffered from such abject melancholia that she may well have committed suicide by starvation. There is a time to speak up and a time to tame the tongue. But given an appropriate forum, the goal is to speak the full truth as the historian honestly sees it. This involves some theory of human motivation, some notion of what makes people tick. It involves assumptions about social process, whether it is driven by conflict or by consensus or by some combination of the two. It involves notions about the tempo of change itself, whether it comes in glacial increments or thunders down as an avalanche. Above all, it involves assumptions about metaphysics. Given what scholars know (and equally important, what they know that they do not know) about nature and culture, what is probable? What is possible but unlikely? What is impossible?[17]

Robert Mapes Anderson's magisterial *Vision of the Disinherited: The Making of American Pentecostalism,* published in 1979, illustrates the virtues of an explanatory scheme that frankly disavows the actors' point of view and proceeds from the standpoint of the observer. In that work Anderson forthrightly argues that the supernatural phenomena that were the stock-and-trade of turn-of-the-century pentecostalism are quite literally incredible because they were quite literally impossible. For him all miracle claims, however sincerely believed by the actors themselves, must be regarded as delusions. Here it is almost needless to say that none of the folk Anderson wrote about would have accepted his account as adequate, and many mainline academics would not either, precisely because his convictions about what is metaphysically impossible seem naive. But only the most determined partisan of the pentecostal cause could sweep aside Anderson's work as anything but a bold interpretation of religion's role in social and cultural process. External explanation is not for everyone, but then neither is professional hockey.[18]

---

17. Irwin T. Hyatt Jr., *Our Ordered Lives Confess: Three Nineteenth-Century American Missionaries in East Shantung* (Cambridge: Harvard University Press, 1976), 123.

18. Robert Mapes Anderson, *Vision of the Disinherited: The Making of American Pentecostalism* (New York: Oxford University Press, 1979).

V

Puritans commonly ended their sermons with an "Improvement," an application to daily life. This essay's "Improvement" is to suggest that historians, and especially religious ones, face analytically distinct tasks. The first is to believe everything that their subjects have said — the core of internal, actor-oriented scholarship. The second is to believe nothing that they have said — the core of external, observer-oriented scholarship. The third task is to figure out how the first two might be fitted together. That third task cannot be reduced to an air-tight formula any more than a successful marriage can, for it grows from the unique interaction of historians' personalities and the material they work with, day by day, even hour by hour. But there is no reason that a Thomist or a Mormon spin on the past should be any less acceptable in the academic marketplace than a Freudian or a Marxist one, so long as all of them are able to prove themselves both intellectually plausible and morally consistent in the ways that I have suggested. In the end, then, the liqueur of explicit evaluation sweetens any reading of the past, but only if it can be set out on the table and analyzed without expecting or receiving special privileges, either in Cambridge or in Wheaton.

In summary, the protocols of internal, actor-oriented analysis constrain historians to avoid both true/false and good/bad evaluations. At that level they are obliged not only to bracket judgments of that sort, but positively to appreciate both the factual accuracy of their subjects' claims and the ethical integrity of their behavior, however preposterous the former or repellent the latter. External, observer-oriented analysis is, however, an altogether different matter. It calls for multiple layers of evaluation. That does not mean that scholars are licensed to turn their craft into a soapbox, but it does mean that history writing loses a lot if it overlooks the wisdom of the present by focusing too intently upon the wisdom of the past. The historians who merit reading generation after generation — Bancroft, Parkman, Miller, Butterfield, Tuchman, Himmelfarb — are distinguished not only by their ability to write well and to illumine the contours of the past, but also by their ability to tell us how those contours might actually change our own lives and times. They give us, in other words, something to say when our students have the good sense to demand, "so what?"

A Transcendentalist's Aristotle: Nonevangelical Reflections on Conviction and the Writing of History

CATHERINE L. ALBANESE

HISTORICAL discourse enjoys no particularly high stature in the academy today. In an era in which postmodern cultural criticism has become a new *lingua franca* for the American university, history's nebulous style — somewhere betwixt and between the other disciplines — is not a cause for glee. As early as the 1960s, though, Hayden White was already complaining about historians' claim to "occupancy of an epistemologically neutral middle ground that supposedly exists between art and science." Criticized by social scientists for methodological softness, White declared, historians invoked intuition as a partner to objective analysis. They argued that "historical judgments should not therefore be evaluated by critical standards properly applied only in the mathematical and experimental disciplines." Criticized, on the other hand, by the literary for not plumbing the depths of human consciousness, historians championed the scientific side of history. They talked of data and evidence, which precluded " 'free' artistic manipulation," and they insisted that narratives must be driven by "the nature of historical materials themselves."[1]

History's ambiguous status did not keep White himself, in his book *Metahistory*, from a searching exploration of the historical imagi-

---

1. Hayden White, "The Burden of History" (1966), in *Tropics of Discourse: Essays in Cultural Criticism* (Baltimore: Johns Hopkins University Press, 1978), 27.

nation.[2] The burden of White's work in what by now has become a historiographical classic was that historians organize their narratives according to aesthetic canons that are variable but not unlimited. These arise out of foundational poetic acts that become tropes shaping a given historian's narrative. In other words, in White's view a historian *emplots* the production of a history, writing an account that like any work of literature rests on the basic visionary qualities carried by language.

Any historian's story, of course, employs figurative elements; this judgment is a truism with which all, or most, would agree. But White meant considerably more: the figures that he found in history went beyond simple embellishments and rhetorical devices used to enliven a tale and keep the interest of the reader. Rather, they were fundamental orientations to organize the controlling interpretive grid of the historian's work and to structure what was seen and reported. In White's examples, these primary figures were employed by major nineteenth-century European historians (his subject) in their narratives, and they could be identified, following familiar literary tropes, as metaphor, metonymy, synecdoche, and irony.

White went on to analyze the kind of narrative structure that resulted when one or another of the tropes worked to orient a given historian's work. Metaphor (analogy or simile), he found, was "essentially representational," and it resulted in a predictable type of historical account. Meanwhile, metonymy (the use of a part to stand for the whole) was "reductionist," and synecdoche (evocation of a part to stand for a *quality* thought to be inherent in the whole) was "integrative." Finally, irony (the denial figuratively of what was affirmed literally), in White's reading, was "negational."[3]

The point of this taxonomy of the "tropic" was that each of these figures shaped distinguishable forms of historical narrative. Gone was history as objective fact, the same in any rendition if all the data were in and had been duly considered. Present instead was history as complicated literary product, demanding scrutiny in aesthetic as well as evidential and scientific terms — aesthetic terms that were elaborated with elegance and sophistication in White's own theorization. It would,

2. Hayden White, *Metahistory: The Historical Imagination in Nineteenth-Century Europe* (Baltimore: Johns Hopkins University Press, 1973).

3. Ibid., 34.

of course, take us too far afield to follow White's rather complex argument further here. But the gist of his analysis is already suggested: each historian, however unaware, links cognitive argument to a particular linguistic figure. Hence, evidence is organized by controlling categories that lead to the multiplication and diversification of historical narratives. The result of each historian's poetic act is often profound difference in the representation of the past.[4]

All of this is, however, so much prologue for a series of reflections I want to introduce about the subject and theme of advocacy in historical representation. Let me try to summarize briefly. White's searching analysis of linguistic tropes in the writing of history needs to be read in light of his earlier remarks about the inexact nature of the discipline. And his analysis needs to be extended further to include another series of tropes by which historians organize their social and psychological relation to their work. What I have in mind are not aesthetic figures pure and simple but, instead, active and existential ones that engage the self with the stuff of history according to more properly moral modes.

White himself thought that the "ethical moment of a historical work" was reflected in the way that aesthetic "perceptions" (his "emplotment") and cognitive "operations" (his "argument") joined. For they could be linked, in his words, "so as to derive prescriptive statements from what may appear to be purely descriptive or analytical ones."[5] Here, though, I want to distinguish between an act of judgment of a given historical situation and its inhabitants, which — with White — I am happy to call ethical, and a *personal stance* toward historical material, which I set off from the former and identify as moral.

With these distinctions clearly in place, then, I want to propose that the moral imagination is, like the aesthetic, a primary mode for visioning the historical discipline and for organizing its material intellectually. The crux of my argument is that to speak of the *problem of advocacy* in American historical writing is to begin with a basic moral trope, an elemental way of perceiving and structuring a historian's relation to the work and a fundamental orientation, that is evangelical. As a taken-for-granted paradigm, the idea of advocacy defines the

4. For a synopsis of White's theorization, see ibid., 1-42.
5. Ibid., 27.

parameters of an imputed relationship between personal stance and historical writing. Presumably, the choice for the historian is to advocate openly, to advocate secretly, or to advocate not at all.

Such a construction of mental events represents a dominant mentality, a conceptual *habitus* — to borrow a term from Pierre Bourdieu — that comes bearing an ancient history.[6] For the model seems predicated, in the distant past, on an Old Testament God, "jealous" in demanding that people take sides for or against him and, even more, on a New Testament Great Commission to teach Christ to all the nations. It seems inescapably intertwined, too, with a Protestant history of Reformers who, in lands already Christian, were still impelled to correct, rebuke, and reannounce a gospel of grace. It hints further of being as strongly related, on New England's shores, with a Puritan religiosity in which the felt experience of conversion was privileged as the fountainhead of Christian commitment. And it suggests, finally, later evangelical elaborations of the mission mind throughout the nineteenth century and into the twentieth.

To move beyond its particular history — however broadly sketched here — and to help locate the advocacy model in a more general religious-studies perspective, we can turn to the set of classic distinctions introduced early in this century by Max Weber. The pioneering sociologist of religion distinguished between two kinds of prophets. There were those he called "ethical," like Zoroaster and Muhammad, who were emissaries of a high God preaching a religion of obedience and reform. And there were others he described as "exemplary," like the Buddha, who by personal example embodied and demonstrated a religious path.[7]

Beyond the prophets, of course, were the great religious traditions of the world that grew up in the presence of each prophetic ideal. Here the contrast is especially useful because it sharpens the ability to see the moral pattern at the core of the advocacy model. To follow the typology of an ethical prophet and emissary religion leads us to existing religious systems that are preeminently action systems. God

6. For the *habitus,* see Pierre Bourdieu, *Outline of a Theory of Practice,* trans. Richard Nice, Cambridge Studies in Social Anthropology (1977; reprint, Cambridge: Cambridge University Press, 1987), esp. 72-95.

7. See Max Weber, *The Sociology of Religion,* trans. Ephraim Fischoff (Boston: Beacon Press, 1964), 55-56.

and truth are transcendent — so that the distance from the ideal demands to be closed. Goals are located in the future, concern for history is prominent and primary, guidance for everyday action in the world is sharp and unambiguous, and the community takes precedence over self.

Standing in the shadow of this overarching model, the historian achieves stature as a kind of minor prophet. Bonds of memory tie him or her to the community, narratives by their structure exist as action accounts, and historical truth is ever beckoning as goal. In short, each historiographical act becomes a chance to try again to close the gap in human knowledge that keeps us from total truth. And in this context, the historian must serve as one who takes a stand — who is an *advocate*.

If all or any of this fairly describes the lineage of the notion of historical advocacy, the question, then — particularly if one does not come at life as an evangelical — is, does the trope of advocacy exhaust the active moral repertoire available to a historian? Should one assume that any historiographical act — anywhere, anytime — must of its nature be structured as minor prophecy of the emissary sort? Does once-found knowledge mean commitment to the mission mind?

Certainly, Hayden White's plural model of aesthetic or literary tropes in the emplotment of history teases us in the direction of multiplicity. And in this context the question becomes, can a negative theology of neither advocating nor not advocating find room? Can we consider advocacy, in a conceptual extension of White's model, as one moral trope among a series of basic ones available? Is it possible to think of advocacy as one among a number of personal stances — plural but not unlimited — that serve to orient different historians at a primary level?

To answer, I suggest a journey back to the Greco-Roman heritage that, beside the Hebraic, so influenced the early culture of the West. Specifically, I suggest that we turn to the *Physics* of Aristotle. Writing in the fourth century B.C.E., the Athenian philosopher was challenged by what challenges, in a different way, those of us who call ourselves professional historians — that is, the presence and process of change. And Aristotle articulated a masterful theory to identify explanatory factors, to capture in ordinary language the *why* of change. His words, in English translation, are worth quoting.

"An explanatory factor," then, means (1) from one point of view, the material constituent from which a thing comes; for example, the bronze of a statue, the silver of a cup, and their kinds. From another point of view, (2) the form or pattern of a thing, that is, the reason (and the kind of reason) which explains what it was to be that thing; for example, the factors in an octave are based on the ratio of two to one and, in general, on number. This kind of factor is found in the parts of a definition. Again, (3) the agent whereby a change or a state of rest is first produced; for example, an adviser is "responsible" for a plan, a father "causes" his child, and, in general, any maker "causes" what he makes, and any agent causes what it changes. Again, (4) the end or the where-for; so, when we take a walk for the sake of our health, and someone asks us why we are walking, we answer, "in order to be healthy," and thus we think we have explained our action.[8]

Aristotle, in his doctrine of the four causes, had formulated the classical Western statement about the world that can be seen and observed. The material cause was the substance out of which a given thing was made — the basic stuff of which it was formed. Its formal cause was the archetypal pattern that shaped its composition and the fundamental grid to which it conformed. Its efficient cause was the factor outside itself that was its maker; in other words, the active agent that shaped it. And its final cause was the reason or goal for its making, the intentionality that governed its structure and composition.

Aristotle was a biologist and a philosopher, and it seems clear that he did not have history in mind as he wrote. All the same, it can be instructive to apply his model to the realm of historical scholarship with a question about moral tropes hovering in the wings. It is easy, for example, to understand historiography's material cause as the substance of history — the content about which the historian writes. Its formal cause may be read as the pattern to which the material is shaped, the underlying plot structure that supports the narrative, and the interpretive canons according to which it is problematized. The efficient cause, of course, becomes the historical researcher who writes the ac-

---

8. Aristotle, *Physics*, bk. 1, chap. 3, in *Aristotle's Physics*, trans. Richard Hope (Lincoln: University of Nebraska Press, 1961), 28.

count. And the final cause may be seen as that historian's ends or goals — the reasons that the historian writes.

With the invocation of this Aristotelian scheme, the issue of the personal stance of the historical researcher assumes new complexity. Buttressed, especially, by the tropic explorations of White that I have already outlined, the historian's personal stance resists being read only in advocative (or nonadvocative) terms. In other words, using the Aristotelian distinctions, it is possible to find a place for the trope of advocacy as it figures and represents the evangelical habitus. But it is also possible to find a place for other figures and other tropes. For example, related to the material cause of the work, the historian's personal stance and consequent convictions raise questions about whether and how much the historian approves or disdains the constituent ingredients out of which the narrative gets constructed. Do the historical actors and what they do please or displease the historian? Do context and era excite or cause repugnance? Such responses by the historian are preliminary acts that may lead to further postures including advocacy, but quite simply they (the responses) may not do so at all.

Again, related to the second domain — that of formal causality — personal stance and convictions become silent shaping factors for the pattern the historian will discover in the material. Brought together by past intellectual, affective, and somatic development, these factors help constitute what Clifford Geertz identifies as a worldview and, more elaborately, what Annales historians understand as a mentality and what I have already called, in Pierre Bourdieu's term, a habitus.[9] These are the habits of mind and life, moral ones among them, that virtually guarantee that two historians working on the same material will never construct exactly the same tale. And these are basic ways of structuring that, wherever they may ultimately lead, need to be kept separate, at this juncture, from either acts of advocacy or their negation.

Next, related to the Aristotelian third and efficient cause, personal stance and convictions can become psychic "vital forces" to spur his-

9. For worldview, see Clifford Geertz, "Religion as a Cultural System," in *The Interpretation of Cultures: Selected Essays* (New York: Basic Books, 1973), 87-125; for the Annales school and mentalities, see Traian Stoianovich, *French Structural Method: The Annales Paradigm* (Ithaca, N.Y.: Cornell University Press, 1976). The Annales school was named for the French journal by that name established in 1929 by Lucien Febvre and Marc Bloch.

toriographical endeavor. They can supply the driving energy, the passion out of which the historian creates. They are the mysterious elixirs that can catalyze the worker out of whose mental equipment the form of the work arises. So the degree of the historian's involvement can be important here, and the resoluteness of the stance — the strength of convictions — can generate the resolve and determination that carry the historian through. But, once more, passion comes in many guises, and it is surely conceptually separable from advocacy per se.

And lastly, related to Aristotle's fourth and final cause, personal stance and convictions can, of course, influence the historian's goals. A historian might seek to corroborate or contradict a private way of seeing and to convince or persuade members of the scholarly community about that angle of vision through acts of historical revisionism. In so doing, a historian's motives might include correction of alleged error, complexification of a simpler account, enjoyment in the manipulation of materials, or — outside the work itself — the desire for ego enhancement through personal success and community acclaim. Other extra-scholarly goals might be unconscious or half-conscious combinatory and constructive efforts toward a personal philosophy of life or, according to the evangelical model, full and conscious acts of advocacy.

This Aristotelian reading of the relationship between the historian's personal convictions and the historical work must necessarily be brief and rough. It does, however, begin to suggest some alternatives to a construction of the relationship of personal conviction to historical writing purely according to an advocacy model. To pursue these hints toward a fuller and more nuanced statement, allow me to move past the objectivist constructions of Aristotle and on toward a more subjectivist gloss. Let me play moral poet here and bring a reconstructed tropic perspective to my Aristotle, using it to look more closely at the stance of the historiographical self.

In this context, the way that the scholar formulates historiographical questions becomes crucial. To ask, for example (in what seems an easy and obvious query), the place that personal convictions *should* have in academic work and higher learning is already to position the history-writing self according to American Protestant and evangelical ways of construing relationship. The "should" sounds a deontological conch shell proclaiming the path of duty. And it also proclaims a self that can be separated from the processes of creation, from the intricate intertwining of the Aristotelian causes (to bring back their ghosts). It tells of a self that becomes pilot and master in control even if, paradoxically, it is itself governed by its "oughts." In short, this is a self which, like a foot primed for action, is flexed and firmed.

What, we may well ask, are the historiographical alternatives to a self in flexion? What are the other moral tropes that might be available, and who is it that can function as a historian beside the advocative or nonadvocative self? What comes to mind first is an indulgent history-writing self at the opposite end of the spectrum. Here is, *pace* Hayden White and John Calvin both, the academic libertine and jack of hearts — the self expressing itself *un*selfconsciously, a self in relaxation happily pursuing the pleasure principle as its final cause. The historian who owns this self scorns the path of duty for the byroads of delight. So curiosity, gamesmanship, the exhilaration of intellectual sport, and play may provide the formal and efficient causes — the moral hedonism out of which this historian operates. Personal convictions are out to lunch; the historian is having fun.

This is not to say that the subject about which the historian writes is necessarily light or frivolous. Indeed, religious topics usually carry their own inborn seriousness and come with a certain weight. But it is to say something about the attitude with which the historian approaches the material: this is history done for personal gratification and grace and not for deontology. This is history in its first, naive rendition, history as Edenic encounter with the other.

Or, second and more complexly, the self of the history writer may be expressing itself self-consciously and aware. The historian is still having fun, but a self-reflexivity enters in. Here is the historian who knows the inner personal landscape and delights in doing the work outside it, who possesses, we might say, a self both flexed and relaxed to pursue the final cause of the work. Here is a yoga of materialization that involves watching the efficient and formal causes in the self and watching the material cause in the other (of the narrative) at once. And like the deontological self of the advocate, this historical self, which I shall call the *attentive* self, comes bearing hints of a moral ideal.

As unlikely as he may be as historian, it is the American transcendentalist Henry David Thoreau who perhaps best points to this attentive historiographical self that I have in mind. Writing in his memorable chapter on "Sounds" in *Walden*, Thoreau asked tellingly, "What is a course of history . . . compared with the discipline of looking always at what is to be seen?" He went on to explain that there were times when he did not read nor did he hoe his beans — when he "could not afford to sacrifice the bloom of the present moment to any work, whether of the head or hands." "Sometimes," he wrote, "in a summer morning, having taken my accustomed bath, I sat in my sunny doorway from sunrise till noon, rapt in a revery, amidst the pines and hickories and sumachs, in undisturbed solitude and stillness, while the birds sang around or flitted noiseless through the house, until by the sun falling in at my west window, or the noise of some traveller's wagon on the distant highway, I was reminded of the lapse of time."[10]

Thoreau was, as he said, rapt in revery, caught in the deep places of his own spirit. But his revery was also an exquisite attentiveness to the sounds of stillness around him. He was, he has told us, totally absorbed in the present, and the present his chapter announced was a present of sounds to be heard. It is, it seems to me, this sort of double consciousness that provides a third moral trope — after advocacy and hedonism — for the primary relationship of the historian to the narrative. The relationship is one of delight — Thoreau has refused to hoe his beans for the pleasure of sitting in the doorway. But the relationship is also conscious and intentional, and following one's pleasure, in an instructive way, becomes a disciplined pursuit.

The identification of this third moral trope — that of attentiveness — completes a provisional series and leads back to the historical ambiguities and aesthetic tropes with which, through Hayden White's observations, I began. With history neither purely art nor purely science, its third place to stand seems ineluctably moral. And given that condition, the personal stance of a historian is surely a moral wedge driving into historical material and — as surely — a serious element in narrative structuring and emplotment. It therefore needs to be set beside purely aesthetic acts of valuing in understanding how a historical narrative is shaped and constructed. But, as this account has emphasized, a personal stance may or may not be the same as choosing or refusing to advocate. My negative theology has invoked at least three

10. Henry David Thoreau, *Walden*, in *The Writings of Henry D. Thoreau*, ed. J. Lyndon Shanley (Princeton: Princeton University Press, 1971), 111.

personal stances — advocacy, hedonism, and attentiveness — toward historiographical work. And there may be more.

In my own case, certainly, historical work has been a process and an exercise — an intellectual yoga — that has helped, I hope, to school me in attentiveness. In that regard, historical work has been a fortunate vehicle for self-discovery and entrainment. The writing of history has encouraged an operation of intellectual self-fashioning: it has helped me to model myself according to a moral pattern that I find compelling.[11] Beyond that, though, the writing of history has brought my attention to bear ever more closely on the complex interaction of people and events that constitutes historical change. That, too, is according to a compelling moral pattern. For it seems to me that, like the chorus of sounds that Henry David Thoreau heard in the stillness, historical actions assume their own integrity and moral status even as I, as historian, attend to them.

Somewhere between an art and a science, as Hayden White and others, too, have noted, the historical discipline can rivet an advocative or hedonist or attentive self to the unfolding narrative of historical actors. For the attentive self, that means at once keeping to the mode of personal delight and being pulled into the chaos and confusion of historical deeds and times. Even for a transcendentalist, Aristotle always wins the historical day. Efficient cause, formal habitus, and final end all join in an insistent invitation to get lost in the moment and matter at hand.

11. My thinking here is influenced by some of the work of Stephen Greenblatt in *Renaissance Self-Fashioning: From More to Shakespeare* (Chicago: University of Chicago Press, 1980).

189

Seldon's Choice: Variations on a Theme by Asimov

PAUL A. CARTER

Roaming through culturally diverse communities on the planet Trantor at the heart of the galaxy thousands of years hence in Isaac Asimov's novel *Prelude to Foundation,* the author's alter ego, Hari Seldon, in his quest to discover the "Laws of Psychohistory," enters Mycogen, whose inhabitants grow luxury foods for the galactic aristocracy. Occasionally their high-tech food farm suffers crop failures, Seldon's local guide admits: "Even the most cleverly designed computer programs can't always predict what is essentially unpredictable."

Surely it's not all unpredictable, Seldon observes; "There are forces that guide and that care for us all."

His escort responds with anger: "You're accusing us of having *religion.*"

Trying to be diplomatic, the young historian only succeeds in digging himself in deeper. There is no disgrace in religious belief, he replies; many people on many planets believe in one form or another of religion: "We may disagree with them in one way or another, but we are as likely to be wrong in our disbelief as they in their belief." Anyhow, he didn't intend his question as an insult:

> But she was not reconciled. "Religion!" she said angrily. "We have no need of it."
>
> Seldon's spirits, having sunk steadily in the course of this ex-

190

change, reached bottom. . . . But she went on to say, "We have something far better. We have *history.*"

And Seldon's feelings rebounded at once and he smiled.[1]

Religion. History. Antithetical terms. If one thinks historically one
cannot profess religion, and vice versa. Sometimes even religiously
committed historians inadvertently give the impression that they have
made that choice, and come down on the side of history rather than
religion.

To take a practical example, from my own professional experience:
in 1991, not long before my retirement from the University of Arizona,
that university's press graciously brought out a retrospective collection
of fifteen of my previously published articles. In a small-scale imitation
of the promotion that goes on in more high-stakes realms of the book
business, two book-signing sessions took place; one at the annual convention of the state historical society, the other at a leading local sec-
ondhand bookstore. As a quid pro quo the bookstore proprietor, a wise
and erudite person as so many such booksellers are, asked me to give
a presentation about my new book to a regular Sunday evening meeting
of the local chapter of American Atheists.

I made the presentation — Daniel vs. Lions, as it were — and they
loved it. Since I had always thought of myself over the years as religiously committed, this episode among the friendly godless gave me,
as Hercule Poirot used to say, "furiously to think."[2]

My published work over the previous thirty-five years had been
in large measure favorably reviewed, both by historians who belonged
to communities of faith and by others who did not. Midway through
my college senior year before beginning graduate school I had experienced a personal religious reawakening; as John Wesley said of like
experience, "My heart was strangely warmed." But apparently in the
years following that experience there had been a substantial amount of
evasion, self-censorship, camouflage — whatever was sufficient to

---

1. Isaac Asimov, *Prelude to Foundation* (New York: Doubleday, 1988), 186, 187.
2. One disarming factor may have been a recognition, from observing the
formal business meeting of that group just prior to my presentation, that these
unbelievers were, like it or not, themselves functionally a congregation. G. K.
Chesterton's description of America as "a nation with the soul of a church" was
indeed far-reaching!

make the published work, despite its implicit faith commitment, pass muster for a significant number of historians, both churched and unchurched.

Evasion and self-censorship may have been in part a function of the times. I entered graduate study in the early 1950s, when in addition to any restrictions or inhibitions on religious profession there was restriction on *all* advocacies: dismissable as "present-minded" in contrast to the then-preferred "historical mindedness." A stern lecture on that very subject by the formidable Robert Livingston Schuyler, at the first session of the historiography course required of all graduate students at Columbia, was my initiation into the serious study of history. Not only must we eschew "present-mindedness," but also large generalizations; a vehement lecture in that same course, very much in a "Just Say No" mode, warned us specifically against the seductions of then-voguish Arnold Toynbee (that other great generalizer, Karl Marx, was not even mentioned). Narrow your topic, and write a monograph which ideally exhausts all the sources on that subject. Above all, don't generalize!

I did find a suitably narrow topic for a Master's thesis, but it was shot through and through with present-minded advocacy. Pedantically titled "The Debate over the Status of the Negro in the Unification of American Methodism," it described how black Northern Methodists, and other African Americans outside of Methodism, protested the reunion in the late 1930s of the Methodist Northern and Southern bodies that had split over the slavery issue before the Civil War, on the ground that in the supposedly greater interest of "church union" black Northern Methodists were, in effect, being railroaded into a Jim Crow church. The topic satisfied what were then the historical guild's requirements; it was an event in the past, albeit a rather recent past, about which no academic monograph had previously been written. But in 1951 any discussion of such a topic had obvious implicit reference to the then just emerging civil rights movement; and I was sufficiently "activist" to try to get an excerpt for the thesis published in time to influence the expected debate on racial segregation at the next (1952) Methodist General Conference.[3]

3. Under the far less pretentious title "The Negro and Methodist Union" the excerpt appeared in *Church History* 21 (March 1952): 55-70. A March publication date would have been in plenty of time for Methodism's quadrennial General Conference, in May, but the journal did not actually print until June.

After that initial exercise, I went on to write a dissertation on the Social Gospel in the years between the two world wars. Henry Steele Commager, quite typically, when I casually broached the idea, dealt off the top of his head an opinion that after the Rauschenbush era the Social Gospel had simply ceased to exist; an opinion which, judging from the surprise expressed in some early reviews of my work, was widely shared. The dissertation was intended to "set the record straight" on that point — but mine was not a dispassionate account of that Protestant phenomenon. On the "secular" side it reflected both a New Dealish political outlook, by that time commonplace among American historians, and a retroactive disquiet about 1930s isolationism. On the "religious" side it absorbed a good deal of the Niebuhrian neo-orthodoxy then in ascendance across the street from Columbia at Union Theological Seminary.

On the whole, despite some serious flaws which became apparent to me only later, the book version of that dissertation was well received. Its juxtapositions of liberal secular politics with neo-orthodox theology did not, then, put people off; indeed, sometimes it intrigued them. As Henry F. May (who has never had to exercise a Seldon's Choice of religion *or* history) summed up the book, its "text as well as his Preface indicate the influence of both Richard Hofstadter and Union Theological Seminary — a powerful and interesting combination, to say the least." [4]

Interesting, yes, Sidney Mead shot back in another review, but hardly powerful; the Reinhold Niebuhr influence which several readers had identified as one of the strengths of the book should have been singled out as one of its gravest weaknesses. It was a "historical error" on my part (Mead evidently believed, despite "postmodernism," that such errors could be committed, which implies a context of historical

---

4. Henry F. May in the *American Historical Review* (January 1957): 419, reviewing Carter, *The Decline and Revival of the Social Gospel: Social and Political Liberalism in American Protestant Churches, 1920-1940* (Ithaca: Cornell University Press, 1956). The fact that Columbia readily granted doctoral candidates the right to offer supporting minor fields at neighboring schools of theology suggests that Seldon's Choice at that time was not so clear-cut a disjunction as it has seemed more recently; William R. Hutchison, a historian whose career chronologically parallels my own, contends that "the idea that most of our secular colleagues are more dismissive of Christian presuppositions than of Marxist or other special commitments just doesn't seem to me to be the case." William R. Hutchison to Paul A. Carter, July 18, 1994.

truth) to have assumed that only via neo-orthodoxy could the erstwhile Social Gospel liberals have arrived at the "ethical paradox of an activist relativism." I had mistaken as innovative in my own time a religious perspective which in fact was as old as the republic. "Lincoln, for example, enunciated and exemplified a theologically oriented 'activist relativism,'" Mead pointed out; and something I had said of Niebuhr and the Niebuhrians might with equal appropriateness have been said of Abraham Lincoln: "The same religious scruples which enjoined one from equating the Kingdom of God with any given social order nevertheless required one to become involved in the struggle."[5]

Actually, an overemphasis on "Niebuhrianism" could be criticized from Niebuhr's own premises. In a book that coincidentally came out while my Social Gospel opus was making the passage from microfilmed dissertation into print, Reinhold Niebuhr acknowledged that the ghost of Carl Becker still walked: "Whenever we consider the historical drama, we confront . . . the fact that the observers of this drama are invariably themselves involved in the flux which they are trying to survey." I had been no more able than the rest of my generation of historians to step outside the flux; as Paul cautioned in Corinthians, "If any man think that he knoweth any thing, he knoweth nothing yet as he ought to know." "The problem of dubious character of all propositions about historical events is in fact insoluble," Niebuhr declared, sounding as assured as Becker or Charles Beard that objectivity in history is no more than a "noble dream." The theologian did hedge a little by allowing that "in the absence of omniscience we do fairly well in allowing various historians, reporting from their various temporal and ideological loci, to report and interpret the events of history."[6]

5. Sidney E. Mead in *Church History* 25 (December 1957): 397-99, reviewing Carter, *Decline and Revival*. In a personal letter, Mead amplified this: insofar as "a position of activist relativism" was "what Niebuhr represents, it has seemed to me that one explanation of his tremendous popularity in America is that in this respect he articulates one of the most deeply rooted strands of American thought. This is what I tried to suggest in the reference to Abraham Lincoln." Mead to Paul A. Carter, January 22, 1958.

6. Reinhold Niebuhr, *The Self and the Dramas of History* (New York: Scribner's, 1955), 53. Niebuhr's judgments on history, as on much else, shifted through time; three years earlier he had published *The Irony of American History* (New York: Scribner's, 1952), which loosely but comfortably can be fitted into the then-regnant "consensus school" of American historical writing.

Other historians involved in that flux, as well as a few politicians, adopted more or less "Niebuhrian" views. One of the most striking testimonies came from Arthur Link, a historian not usually associated with the history of religion, much less "church" history. In an essay on "The Historian's Vocation," published in 1962 in *Theology Today*, Link offered a further gloss on the Becker thesis of every man his own historian that could have come straight from the pages of Reinhold Niebuhr's *The Nature and Destiny of Man:*

> The ego in its unredeemed or natural state is not able to see history apart from itself. . . . Over and over I have found from my own experience that my own ego drives inexorably toward its own control, that is to say, it seeks to impose its own pattern upon events, selects its own evidence, and discards evidence when it is not useful, in short, writes its own history.[7]

A religiously premised confession of this shortcoming, Link argued, could be a recourse against the seductions of relativism.

But even if the converse to Link's confession should hold true — if the ego in its presumedly redeemed state is, or can become, "able to see history apart from itself" — that would still not definitively solve the problem of achieving objectivity in history. It would still leave the locus of historical judgment in the historian's mind rather than "out there," however one defines "there." A lingering (and, perhaps, too sweeping) rebellion against the philosophical idealisms of the nineteenth century prompts that this somehow won't do. "Ideas are not dangerous unless they find seeding place in some earth more profound than the mind," typically mused John Steinbeck in 1941. "Being so planted, growing in such earth, it ceases to be idea and becomes emotion and then religion."[8]

7. Arthur S. Link, "The Historian's Vocation," *Theology Today* 19 (April 1962): 74-88. Unlike many fellow travelers with neo-orthodoxy who wrenched Niebuhr's social and political ideas out of their theological context, Link made his *confessio fidei* avowedly Christian: the historian "enters into new life in which he can . . . be the kind of historian that God means him to be, when he is justified. . . . Standing under the shadow of the Cross, the historian finally sees the truth, the reality of history." Ibid., 80, 88.

8. John Steinbeck, *The Log from the Sea of Cortez* (1951; New York: Bantam, 1971) (the actual expedition log dates from 1941), 261. Steinbeck hardly rates as one

PAUL A. CARTER

But is religion, in whatever earth it is planted, a productively dangerous idea or only the opiate of the people? Suddenly in the sixties it again became proper to be "present minded"; people no longer had to dissemble their most ultimate beliefs; and in particular a Left perspective on history, after a decade or more of being smothered in Cold War scholarship, demanded the historical guild's attention and respect. In theory, Marxist historians exercising Seldon's Choice might have been expected to say: history, yes, religion, no; "the history of all hitherto existing society is the history of class struggles"; and although religion can at times be a sincere cry of the oppressed, it is at best an imaginary solution to the real problem. In practice, however, this was not always the way the categories of religion and history lined up.

Again, if I may offer my own professional experience as an example, I spent seven productive years, spanning the upheavals of the sixties, in the history department at Northern Illinois University, among colleagues who ranged in outlook from hard-bitten, *Chicago Tribune*–quoting Midwestern Republicanism to New Left and even Maoist views. As I researched, wrote, and tried out chapters of a book subsequently published by that university's press, these highly diverse colleagues were uniformly supportive, interested, and helpful. Furthermore, the history of religion seemed a sufficiently acceptable field to the other historians in that university to enable me to offer there a full-dress, two-semester course on the history of religion in America, a venture of a kind which other history departments in other state-supported universities were then rejecting as an unwarrantable intrusion. At Berkeley in 1963, for example, the history department adopted a forcefully written report that opposed the creation of a department of religion, manifestly on the ground that any need for such study could be nonredundantly met through existing departments and courses — medieval history, the sociology of religion, and the like.[9] On this policy

---

of America's more godly authors, and this work abounds in his characteristic bashing of "churchy" people, but at odd moments — such as an account of a Good Friday spent in a small fishing town down near the tip of Baja California — a moving, albeit left-handed piety breaks through.

9. I saw this internally circulated report during a year spent as a visiting lecturer at Berkeley. More pertinent than the expressed concern about possible redundancy, as was explained to me privately after a department meeting on the matter, was an anxiety lest the "religious right" in California use the existence of

issue, both Berkeley's and Northern Illinois's standpoints had, and still have, their staunch partisans and earnest belittlers. It is easy to miss the point that the decision to "do" the history of religion is not necessarily a decision to "do" religion per se.

Ironically, it was the *students* in NIU's admittedly (and proudly) radical history department in the 1960s, more than their mentors, who felt the urge to confront. One of my students reported that an attempt to use in a reading seminar Timothy L. Smith's up to then highly regarded monograph *Revivalism and Social Reform* was met with an anti-clerical barrage: organized religion has always been a tool of what in the sixties was called the "power structure"; revivalism has never been equatable with social reform. My own history of religion classes became so polarized over the next four years between would-be revolutionaries and missionary witnesses that teaching it became pedagogically impossible.

Of course we must not exaggerate the outspokenness of that era in academia. If some students in the 1960s were emboldened to call out in class "No, professor, you're wrong," others — many more, I'm afraid — learned that other 1960s gambit of "coming on" to what one perceives as the other person's bias, be it Marxism, religious belief, or whatever at the moment is "in." In NIU's history department in particular, some of them became coyly adept at asking the professor "What is your philosophy of history?", translatable as "Are you a Marxist?", and then shamelessly making fake radical noises if the answer was affirmative — or, following the model of the colleges' "silent generation" of the previous decade, taking care to say nothing at all.

Such a situation poses a rather acute ethical problem. Quite aside from the *writing* of history, there is in the *teaching* of history a problem of advocacy. Your students have a right to know where you stand, but also a right not to be compelled into the same stand by your ex officio status as an authority figure with the power to inflict an unsatisfactory grade. Early in the religion in America course I was asked in class, "And what is *your* religion?" Surmising that the question might cover a

---

such a program as an excuse to "proselytize." Such, as George Marsden ruefully notes, are the inhibitions laid upon persons who with naive good intentions pursue this kind of inquiry! On this point see Stephen L. Carter, *The Culture of Disbelief: How American Law and Politics Trivialize Religious Devotion* (New York: Basic Books, 1993).

willingness to adapt to or humor a professor's biases, I parried it with "I'm a Druid, and I practice human sacrifice." Colleagues at a conference on advocacy in the writing of American history in 1994 rightly took me to task for having thus ducked the issue; properly I ought, with Luther, to have said, "Here I stand." To the question whether taking such a stand could lead students — for the wrong reasons — to echo it, the only proper response from a religiously committed historian should have been, "God help me, I can do no other."[10]

In 1973, primarily for family reasons, I moved to Tucson and spent the next eighteen years, until retirement, at the University of Arizona. The books successively pushed through the typewriter during that time certainly reflected advocacy of some of my beliefs, religious and/or secular. Some of the commitment was political; for example, an interpretation of Antarctica as a testing ground for the demilitarizing and internationalizing of scientific endeavor — William James's "The Moral Equivalent of War" *manqué*. Some of the writing described (and, I must confess, lobbied for) twentieth-century American science fiction as an offbeat but at times highly effective mode of political and social criticism.[11] And some of it was religious, or at least expressive of what Henry May might call "religious sensibility": a chapter on religion in the 1920s titled "In God Some of Us Trusted"; two chapters in a book on the 1950s titled respectively "Under God, by Act of Congress" and "History, Mystery and the Modern World"; and finally, in a book published in 1989 which was intended to sum up a lifetime of teaching

10. These criticisms — I am indebted to that of Elizabeth Fox-Genovese in particular — were prompted by discussion of a question put by George Marsden in a paper entitled "Christian Advocacy and the Rules of the Academic Game," presented at the Consultation on Advocacy and the Writing of American History, Wheaton College, April 28, 1994: "Do not students have rights to know about the religious background of one's beliefs, just as they ought to know about Marxist, feminist, liberal, neo-conservative, gay advocacy, and other such viewpoints that openly influence scholarship? . . . Should a Christian scholar be forced to pose as something else?"

11. Science fiction in its own way often asks questions that go to the heart of the conflict between faith and unbelief. Contrast, for example, the bleak description by veteran science fiction writer Jack Williamson of the universe as "a terrible engine, running forever without control or goal or engineer, creating suns and consuming galaxies, unaware of anything alive," in *Beachhead* (New York: Tom Doherty Associates, 1992), 107, with the explicitly Christian argument in the "space trilogy" of C. S. Lewis.

history and writing about it, chapters on religion in antebellum America and on post–Civil War evangelical religion and politics. All this work, albeit researched and documented in the usual way, fell within the category of Charles Beard's "Written History as an Act of Faith."[12]

In the meantime, however, in the profession at large, the comparatively mild historical relativism of Charles Beard and Carl Becker had been succeeded by something far more virulent. Peter Novick in *That Noble Dream*, a massive and detailed survey of American historiography over the previous century, argued that by the time that work saw print in 1988 "as a broad community of discourse, as a community of scholars united by common aims, common standards, and common purposes, the discipline of history had ceased to exist."[13] This went far beyond the bare admission, commonplace since Becker's time, "that everybody looks at history from a point of view," Henry May pointed out in 1991. "Recently . . . it has been impressively argued that historical truth is not only unattainable but meaningless as a concept, that historians and other writers are always engaged in a struggle for class power whether they know it or not, even that works have no meaning or reference beyond themselves." Among "young historians . . . who feel most deeply threatened" by this state of affairs were some of "the most sensitive and intelligent," May contended, and they suffered from "no trivial malaise; it is a special form of the fear of meaninglessness, an ancient enemy that has long ravaged the days and nights of the young and gifted."[14]

According to the various deconstructionists, cognitive relativists, and other "postmodernists" cited by Peter Novick, any question as to what personal convictions, religious or otherwise, ought to have in historical scholarship can be answered quite simply: we have no choice in the matter. It is not a question of whether we *should* express such

---

12. Titles of these books, all published by Columbia University Press, are as follows: *Another Part of the Twenties* (1977), *The Creation of Tomorrow: Fifty Years of Magazine Science Fiction* (1977), *Little America: Town at the End of the World* (1979), *Another Part of the Fifties* (1983), and *Revolt against Destiny: An Intellectual History of the United States* (1989).

13. Peter Novick, *That Noble Dream: The "Objectivity Question" and the American Historical Profession* (Cambridge: Cambridge University Press, 1988), 628.

14. Henry F. May, *The Divided Heart: Essays on Protestantism and the Enlightenment in America* (New York: Oxford University Press, 1991), 154, 5, 6.

convictions: willy-nilly, we *do*. Nor are we able any longer to fall back on the judgment of our peers to discipline our biases, for that consensus of judgment — according to Novick — is now extinct.

Logically it would seem that for religiously committed historians it would be as acceptable to express such commitment as it would be for any other "particularists" (Novick's term) to profess theirs. If the historical profession in practice has now out-Beckered Becker, as intimated in a chapter title from *That Noble Dream*, "Every *Group* Its Own Historian," then religionists would be justified in claiming status as members of such a group, on the same principle that used to prevail in political broadcasting, of "equal time."[15] A committed religious believer understandably might shy away, however, from thus adopting the philosophy of "If you can't lick 'em, join 'em." To embrace fully the anti-objectivism so persuasively described in Novick's pages would be to make hash of any truth-claim undergirding the religious commitment, which the committed religious believer could hardly be expected to do.

A few have escaped from that existential dilemma by embracing radical skepticism, of a sort not discussed at all in Peter Novick's long book. Justification by faith is not historically conditioned: "Man's sin and God's saving purpose — they alone require and justify history as such, and historical time. Without original sin and final redemption, the historical interim would be unnecessary and unintelligible." So wrote Karl Löwith long before the onset of postmodernism in *Meaning in History* — a book whose paradoxical thesis is that there is really *no* meaning in history. Neither the "natural man" nor the Christian believer "pretends to discern on the canvas of human history the purpose of God"; therefore Everyman, in order not to fall into the ancient (and perennial) heresy of Gnosticism, *has* to be his own historian: "The skeptic and the believer have a common cause against the easy reading of history and its meaning."[16] The catch lies in that word "easy." Charles

---

15. It is noteworthy that Novick's index, apart from three passing references to Reinhold Niebuhr, omits any citation of persons classifiable as historians of religion or church historians — even though their kind of historical writing can be discussed in terms of Novick's categories, and is so discussed in, for example, Henry Warner Bowden, *Church History in an Age of Uncertainty: Historiographical Patterns in the United States, 1906-1990* (Carbondale: Southern Illinois University Press, 1991).

16. Karl Löwith, *Meaning in History* (Chicago: University of Chicago Press, 1949), v, vi.

Beard is said to have remarked toward the end of his life that writing history is like dragging a cat backward by the tail across a rug; it has never been easy.[17] The easy temptation is, rather, to retreat from the effort and say it's all subjective anyhow, as did Karl Löwith from a theological premise and as do the postmodernists from their nontheological premises.

Further, wrote Sidney Mead in a critique of Löwith's book, "It is arrogant to suppose that this is the only Christian view and hence that Christianity advances it as the only option." Against Löwith's insistence that "the profane events before and after Christ are not a solid chain of meaningful successions but spurious happenings whose significance or insignificance is to be judged in the perspective of their possible signification of judgment and salvation," Mead argued that, on the contrary, the paradox of the Incarnation gives the Christian "assurance that a clue to the meaning of history resides in the events of the history-that-happens. . . . For him there should be no 'profane events,' no 'spurious happenings.'"[18]

Conceding in 1992 that "recognition of subjectivity is inherent in Jefferson, Madison, et al. and in all of Christianity," and in agreement with Henry May that relativism can lead "to fear of valuelessness (one issue is as good as another, etc.)," Sidney Mead did not concede that such recognition is as far as one can go: "Beginning with the assumption of human finiteness . . . *including my own* I learn by comparing my opinion with yours, i.e., in engaging in conversation."[19] This had long been a concern of Mead's; in 1963 he had argued that out of such conversation may emerge a vocation of religious historical scholarship, "recognizable as valid by at least a significant number of general historians" — valid in the sense that colleagues in secular university departments of history may grant it to be "an acceptable view though it is not theirs." In that same 1963 essay Mead asserted that in one sense

17. Beard passed along this homely metaphor as a kind of apostolic blessing on a younger scholar, Eric F. Goldman. See Goldman, *Rendezvous with Destiny: A History of Modern American Reform* (New York: Knopf, 1952), xi.

18. Sidney E. Mead, "On the Meaning of History," *Christian Century* 78 (November 1961): 1361, 1364.

19. Sidney E. Mead, loose-leaf notes accompanying a photocopy (entire) of Bowden, *Church History in an Age of Uncertainty*. My thanks to Professor Mead for the loan of that copy of Bowden, with Sidney's own acute, enriching annotations.

"church history is a continuous meditation on the meaning of the incarnation" — a meditation he held forth to those unchurched colleagues as implicitly an acceptable way of understanding history.[20]

Two years after this friendly invitation, *Time* magazine on its front cover proclaimed the death of God. As usual with cultural movements which the mass media get hold of, that specific manifestation of unbelief proved short-lived. But it would surface again; it is after all a perennial human outcry, one that goes back to the "fool" — and others not so foolish, such as Lucretius — who according to the psalmist "hath said in his heart, there is no God." Given the historical persistence of that outcry, perhaps it was too much to expect of secularly oriented scholars in university history departments that they would grant the church historians' conception of history to be, on Sidney Mead's terms, "an acceptable view though it is not theirs."

The climate of opinion foreshadowed in the "death of God" controversy and more recently adumbrated as a "culture of disbelief" appeared to force one to face Seldon's Choice: history or religion; not both. Even in the kind of work done by members of the American Society of Church History, Albert C. Outler contended in his 1964 presidential address to that body, there had taken place "a radical secularization in ecclesiastical historiography."[21] One inference we may be able to draw from such pronouncements is that Seldon's Choice may not have been so much imposed upon religiously believing historians by their more worldly minded colleagues as *self*-imposed; a way of maintaining one's credibility among people less willing than Sidney Mead's hoped-for "general historians" to recognize the religious historians' bona fides. Nor need this have been done deliberately or consciously. Seldon's Choice may at times be a demonstration of that automatic "other-directed" adjustment classically described by David Riesman, an American trait from which not even the most contrarian in our contentious profession are entirely immune.[22]

20. Sidney E. Mead, "Church History Explained," *Church History* 32 (March 1963): 18, 19.

21. Albert C. Outler, "Theodosius's Horse: Reflections on the Predicament of the Church Historian," *Church History* 34 (September 1965): 259.

22. David Riesman et al., *The Lonely Crowd* (New Haven: Yale University Press, 1950). Riesman's now classic "inner-directed/other-directed" categories could, I suppose, be part of a *mentalité* specific to the 1950s and thus subject to the same

Historians of religion are of course not the only kind who some-times (wittingly or unwittingly) trade in personal commitment for pro-fessional credibility; often one interprets this trade as a suppression of one's own private biases in exchange for impartiality. "General" his-torians, as Peter Novick observes, went through two periods when they struck such bargains: the late Gilded Age, when they convinced them-selves that they were behaving "scientifically," and the 1950s, when (as previously noted in this essay) they instructed their graduate student apprentices to abjure "present-mindedness" and embrace "historical mindedness" — all unaware of the ideological cargoes which, accord-ing to Novick, the scientific and historical schools respectively carried. The social thinkers of the Gilded Age thought they were premising the questions they asked upon science, and many of them in pursuit of the argument were willing to let religious belief go by the board. But in the twentieth century, George Marsden observed in 1993, the problem for a believer has not been science but historicism.[23]

"It is really not possible to write excellent history about something one dismisses, however tacitly, as unimportant," Henry May sensibly comments. "To write excellent religious history, I believe, one must have something like religious sensibility or imagination." But: "Obviously, one does not have to be a believer." That word "obviously" contains a subtle semantic trap. Obviously, May is right; nonbelieving historians such as Perry Miller have written about religious belief. One can write about faith statements phenomenologically, or translate them (as Miller often did) into intellectual history, without compromising one's own belief or nonbelief. "It is possible to write well about something one totally disbelieves, fears or hates," Henry May asserts, provided that one defines reality broadly enough "to include the religious stream as well as the sociological banks between which it flows."[24]

The degree of empathy attainable by the historian of religion may, however, vary with the content of the belief being considered. A par-

---

destructive attention afforded by the anti-objectivists to 1950s historical writing. But so could the subsequent "death of God" and "culture of disbelief" vogues.

23. George Marsden, in discussion at one of the sessions of the Wingspread Conference on "New Directions in American Religious History." Racine, Wisconsin, October 21-23, 1993.

24. Henry F. May, "Religion and American Intellectual History, 1945-85," in *The Divided Heart*, 31f.

ticularly poignant example may be afforded by that civilized eighteenth-century skeptic Edward Gibbon, whose chapters on the beginnings of Christianity have been behind-the-barn reading for budding
young freethinkers for two centuries. And yet, Geno Geanokoplos has
argued, when Gibbon wrote about historically held beliefs which took
the form of logical discourse and therefore were accessible to his own
rationalist bias, such as controversies within Byzantine theology, he
could set forth the issues between the contending parties meticulously
and fairly. But when he turned his attention to such matters as the
visions of the monks on Mount Athos in the ninth century, that same
bias made it impossible for him to think or empathize his way into their
situation; poor dears, they were probably suffering from malnutrition![25]

Whether one writes of such matters sympathetically or otherwise,
however, to write about religious beliefs *historically* is inevitably to
distance the writer from the beliefs — even when, as in Judaism and
Christianity, the beliefs are founded upon claims of the reality of certain
historical events. Much as the cultural anthropologist, however much
admiring the values expressed in a tribal rain dance, cannot escape
being caught up in his/her own culture's systems of belief and disbelief
— the investigator in the field probably does not expect that the dance
is actually going to make it rain — the historian of religion, caught up
in the same cultural systems, remains at a distance from his/her subject
matter, which remains safely in the past. The statement "This is important," however necessary in order to do "excellent history" à la Henry
May (and I think he is right on this), is still a long, wrenching existential
jump from the statement "This I believe."

Biblical scholars have experienced the same kind of distancing.
They have also, perhaps more than some of them have been aware,
fallen into the trap of culture-bound present-mindedness. German biblical criticism in particular, Dyson Hague argued in 1909 when such
scholarship was near its apogee, "deals with the writers and readers of
the ancient Orient as if they were modern German professors."[26] The
same projection of current concerns, including political agendas, into

25. Geno Geanakoplos, "Edward Gibbon and Byzantine Ecclesiastical History," *Church History* 35 (June 1966): 170-85.
26. Dyson Hague, "The History of the Higher Criticism," *The Fundamentals*
(Chicago and Los Angeles, 1909-10), 1:90.

the biblical past has been charged by critics of the currently media-hyped Jesus Seminar; as one young scholar recently put it, the historical Jesus is currently being portrayed as "a wandering Jewish sage with pithy maxims and oddball humor" in whom one now discerns "more of David Letterman than Pat Robertson."[27]

What Albert Schweitzer wrote in his classic account of the state of New Testament scholarship at the turn of last century evidently continues to apply: scholars look down a well that is two thousand years deep and see at the bottom only the reflection of their own faces. Schweitzer himself, at the last minute, broke free from that kind of historical boundedness in the closing paragraph of *The Quest of the Historical Jesus*, with its call to followers in that quest to "learn in their own experience Who He is."[28] Not *was*; not safely distant two thousand years away, but present tense, *is*.

If a confession of faith testifying to such an experience seems not credible to a conscientious nonbeliever who has not undergone it also, the more extreme kinds of relativism proclaimed by some of the advocates described in the closing pages of *That Noble Dream* would seem to allow no standard of credibility at all. To insist that *all* one can carry away from a lifetime of historical scholarship is a narcissistic reflection from a pool — a narcissism only slightly modified by projecting it upon the faction or special interest to which one adheres (as Novick puts it, "every group its," not "everyman his," own historian) — is to deny, in effect, that real things happened in real time to real people. Moreover, it is to deny that real value can be placed on such things: what Dr. King stood for was good; what Hitler stood for was evil. It would take a peculiarly heartless kind of relativism to accommodate, as just one more of the groups playing in the game, those twisted souls who argue that historically there was no Holocaust![29] The "self-styled postmodernism"

27. Scott Manetsch, "Black-Balling the Bible: Martin Luther Critiques the 'Jesus Seminar,'" a lecture sponsored by the University of Arizona's Division for Late Medieval and Early Reformation History, Tucson, Arizona, June 20, 1994.

28. Albert Schweitzer, *The Quest of the Historical Jesus* (New York: Macmillan, 1948), closing paragraph. I heartily agree with what Paul Tillich once told an audience of seminarians: "There are only about a dozen books that theological students really *have* to read — but this is one of them."

29. Revulsion at the horrors of Nazism was "one of the principal anchors of the twentieth-century mind," Thomas Haskell reminds us, and "we know that we

depicted comprehensively in Novick's book "quickly passes into nihilism," Eugene Genovese points out; enlisted in the service of an ideology it perforce adopts the cynical, self-serving agenda of Pontius Pilate: "What is truth?"[30]

"The fact that moral values or principles may clash does not invalidate them," the philosopher and occasional historian Karl Popper writes. The relative relevance of such principles to differing situations; their relative accessibility to different persons; even the question whether they be "discovered" or "invented" — "all this is quite distinct from relativism; that is, from the doctrine that any set of values can be defended."[31] Moreover, and aside from the moral issue, to deny that in the fullness of time real things happen to real people is ultimately self-destructive. "One could not be sceptical about history without being sceptical about everything else," comments Arthur Danto, "and this, finally, destroys whatever specific force relativism might be thought to have with regard to history. . . . History is no more and no less subject to the relativistic factors than science is."[32]

So much the worse (or better!) for science, some of the more thoroughgoing relativists reply; and indeed the scientific community, thanks to fundamental misinterpretation in some quarters of Thomas Kuhn's postulate of successive "paradigms" of scientific worldviews, has of late suffered its own erosions of relativism. Stephen Jay Gould, paleontologist and occasional philosopher of history, has some wise words to say on this head:

---

cannot permit that anchor to break loose." Quoted in Novick, *That Noble Dream*, 627. See on this point Pierre Vidal-Naquet, *Assassins of Memory: Essays on the Denial of the Holocaust* (New York: Columbia University Press, 1993).

30. Eugene D. Genovese, "Marxism, Christianity, and Bias in the Study of Southern Slave Society," esp. 5-6, a paper presented to the Consultation on Advocacy and the Writing of American History, April 30, 1994. Genovese went even further in the group discussion of this and other papers: postmodernism, as it asks Pilate's question, "is a totalitarian ideology."

31. Karl Popper, *Unended Quest: An Intellectual Autobiography* (London: Routledge, 1992), 116. See the addendum titled "Facts, Standards, and Truth: A Further Criticism of Relativism," in the 4th and later editions of Popper's *The Open Society and Its Enemies* (London: Routledge, 1962), 369-96.

32. Arthur C. Danto, *Analytical Philosophy of History* (Cambridge: Cambridge University Press, 1965), 110, as quoted in Bowden, *Church History in an Age of Uncertainty*, 244.

Most of us are not naive enough to believe the old myth that scientists are paragons of unprejudiced objectivity, equally open to all possibilities, and reaching conclusions only by the weight of evidence and the logic of argument. We understand that biases, preferences, social values, and psychological attitudes all play a strong role in the process of discovery. However, we should not be driven to the opposite extreme . . . — the view that objective evidence plays no role, that perceptions of truth are entirely relative, and that scientific conclusions are just another form of aesthetic preference. Science, as actually practiced, is a complex dialogue between data and preconceptions.[33]

For "science" and "scientists" in the foregoing passage, substitute "history" and "historians." Here, scientists and historians, whether religiously motivated or not, can make common cause; both can acknowledge, with Professor Mead, that they are finite creatures engaged in conversations, and comparing notes, with other such creatures.

Some of my own history students have found the following metaphor helpful in coping with the new relativisms: "The umpire calls 'em as he sees 'em, but there are other umpires on that playing field, and each sees the way the ball was played from a different angle. But the ball did, in fact, land fair or foul."[34] Inevitably when we make that judgment call somebody is going to cry "Kill the umpire!" but in this ball game there is no instant replay. All of us are caught, like Gould's scientists, in a complex dialogue between our preconceptions and the data. We must, as Bruce Catton so eloquently has said, "look for the truth with the eyes that never saw . . . comb through the chaos of trash and falsehood, the disjointed reports and the uncertain traditions and tales, and try to make something meaningful out of it all" — which is to say, we must work out our salvation in fear and trembling. "If our work has any final value," Catton goes on, "that value must depend very largely on our ability to see the essential truth beyond the darkness and the error, and to create a faithful picture out of something that

33. Steven Jay Gould, *Wonderful Life: The Burgess Shale and the Nature of History* (New York: W. W. Norton, 1989), 244.

34. This quotation is from the introduction to Paul A. Carter, *Politics, Religion, and Rockets: Essays in Twentieth-Century American History* (Tucson: University of Arizona Press, 1991), xxxi.

never makes itself explicit."[35] For now we see through a glass, darkly; but then face to face. Both religion and history, as we experience them, are reflected in that glass, and Seldon's Choice need not be either/or.

---

35. Bruce Catton, *Prefaces to History* (Garden City, N.Y.: Doubleday, 1970), 93, as quoted in the preface to Bowden, *Church History in an Age of Uncertainty*, xiii.

One Historian's Sundays

LESLIE WOODCOCK TENTLER

Most Sunday mornings find me at St. Cecilia's Catholic Church in Detroit. The parish, which dates from the early 1920s, is a product of the decade's automotive boom. The church itself, a handsome neo-Gothic affair, bears witness to the prosperity of those happy years (happy, at least, for Detroit), as do the bungalows and duplexes that line the surrounding streets. Built by and for an upwardly-mobile working class, these modest houses look tired and increasingly dilapidated now. In the not-so-distant past, however, they embodied hope and a measure of security, both for the white ethnics who initially inhabited them and for the newly prosperous African Americans who inherited those same houses in the late 1960s and early 1970s.

Unlike most inner-city parishes, St. Cecilia's has weathered the transition of its neighborhood from white to black, thanks in good part to innovative pastors and an excellent school. The congregation today, which numbers roughly seven hundred families, is mostly African American. The surrounding neighborhood, however, is deep in the course of a second transition, having to do this time around with class rather than race. St. Cecilia's parishioners are on the whole a prosperous lot, and as they have moved in growing numbers to the city's fringes and into its suburbs, their "old neighborhood" has become increasingly poor, drug-plagued, and violent. This second transition may ultimately prove the more difficult for the parish to negotiate.

Many of St. Cecilia's parishioners today are converts to Catholicism, and nearly all were raised in a world where Catholicism bore the stamp of alien things. So the Sunday liturgy is marked by a greater attention to ritual detail than is the case in most of today's Catholic churches. Having embraced "otherness," the parishioners are anxious to maintain a distinction between their own ranks and those of the Baptists, or so the affinity for incense, genuflection, and holy water would suggest. But many of these same parishioners have been loathe to surrender completely the warmth and spontaneity of evangelical worship. The 11 o'clock mass at St. Cecilia's features a gospel choir, and the ritual kiss of peace is a time not for hurried handshakes but for embracing. Alphonsus Liguori and Thomas Dorsey rub liturgical elbows at St. Cecilia's, and if the effect is sometimes incongruous, the result nonetheless is a curiously vital worship.

Still, one should not romanticize St. Cecilia's. Although this parish is very nearly familial in the care it affords those in need, it is also "like family" when it comes to rivalry and bickering. Class tension simmers just below the harmonious surface of parish life, and echoes of the gender wars are everywhere. So St. Cecilia's does not exactly provide an escape from the workaday world — parish politics, indeed, have quite a lot in common with the academic variety. (In both cases, emotion tends to be expended in direct proportion to the triviality of the issue ostensibly at hand, and in both cases the "real" issue has almost invariably to do with status and *bella figura*.) But for all this, St. Cecilia's is the place that knits me up and makes me whole. It is here, amidst incongruity and contradiction, that I know, however ephemerally, "a self that touches all edges" — to borrow from Wallace Stevens.

To say this is both to reveal and conceal. On the one hand, I acknowledge — as I seldom do in academic settings — that my self-understanding and worldview are shaped in important ways by Catholic ritual practice. I also betray, albeit indirectly, my uneasiness with Catholic legalism, especially in the realm of sexuality. For largely historical reasons, the legalist tradition in Catholic moral theology has almost no resonance in the contemporary black parish. What I have not addressed is the question of belief, which can to some extent be separable from that of religious observance. What theological convictions underlie my presence at St. Cecilia's? What meaning do these convictions have for my other-than-Sunday-morning existence, most especially as a historian?

Neither question is easy to answer. I am a skeptic by virtue of upbringing and professional training and perhaps by virtue of temperament. At the same time, I have a strong sense of responsibility to what I would call the essence of Catholic tradition. What this means in practice is a willed adherence to a set of quite conservative theological propositions (more or less summed up by the Nicene Creed), coupled with an endless battle against a historicist's doubts. This does not mean that I regard or experience belief as unreasonable. (The world is bound to have a farfetched explanation, to paraphrase Wilfred Sheed.) But supernaturalism of any variety is suspect in a scientific age, and nowhere more so than in the secular university. Like most believers today, I do a lot of compartmentalizing: theological concepts rest in one mental box, secular notions about causality and motivation in another. In certain moods, I am almost persuaded that my work as a historian proceeds independently of my "religious self."

This impulse is strengthened when I consider my inheritance as a Catholic historian — a term that I rarely apply to myself, preferring to be regarded as a social historian who happens to be interested in religion. In its most stridently apologetic mode, Catholic historiography is arguably not history at all, but more properly classified as theology of history — and not very good theology at that. These days, church history is seldom written in this vein. For contemporary Catholic historians, a more serious danger is probably posed by an excessive alienation from their tradition and a consequent myopia with regard to its strengths. Still, the bad examples of the not-so-distant past warn against an easy meshing of theological and secular preoccupations and modes of thought. Better to keep one's theology firmly in its separate mental box than to produce histories like these.

Things are not quite so simple, however. A Christian must of necessity grapple with the question of meaning in history. And this grappling will presumably have some effect — though not necessarily a predictable one — on the history she teaches and writes. It is true that the search for meaning proceeds for most of us in the realm of shadows; at best, we see through a glass darkly. That God acts in history is a fundamental Christian tenet. But the Christian God is a hidden God, concealing as well as revealing himself in the historical order. "The divine concealment is of such a character that no Christian may think that the judgment or meaning or significance [to be found in history] is unambiguously clear to him as a human being," as E. Harris Harbi-

211

son has said.[1] Nonetheless, to assert that history has a meaning beyond what we as ephemeral beings might generate is to place oneself, intellectually and emotionally, in a distinctive camp. Our own lives look different from this vantage point. Should not the record of our collective life look different too?

And yet it is notoriously difficult to make the leap. I can speak with far greater confidence about the effects of belief in my private life than on my "public" work as a historian. I can at least sometimes think in terms of the providential with regard to my individual existence, but am virtually incapable of doing so with regard to the historical order. Indeed, save for my interest in matters religious, I can see no obvious ways in which my written work betrays a Christian author — though it probably betrays an author who regularly votes Democratic. It almost seems that we have come back to the compartmentalized mind, with the "theological box" reserved for use in the evenings and on Sunday.

The problem, of course, is that the compartmentalized mind is for practical purposes a fiction. Historians should know this intuitively: the writing of history, after all, is ultimately an informed act of the imagination. Certainly we must be attentive to the canons that govern the process of informing; the extent and quality of our research does matter. But the act of imagining is inevitably conditioned by who we are — by the experiences, assumptions, values, and biases that constitute what we like to regard as the totality of our selves. When it comes to the act of historical imagining, in other words, the mind's putative "boxes" are remarkably permeable, and their contents get jumbled together in sometimes unanticipated ways. Our encounter with the mystery of the past is in part an encounter with the mystery of ourselves.

A certain tentativeness is thus in order when it comes to any discussion of the ways in which religious convictions affect historical writing. But there can be no doubt that such convictions, no matter how ostensibly "private," do in fact affect a believer's reconstruction of the past. The extent to which and the ways in which this happens will necessarily vary from one historian to the next, and the marks of belief

---

1. E. Harris Harbison, "The Marks of a Christian Historian," in *God, History and Historians: An Anthology of Modern Christian Views of History,* ed. C. T. McIntire (New York: Oxford University Press, 1977), 331-56, quote from 339.

in a given historian's work may not be readily apparent to most readers
— even, in some cases, to the historian herself. With regard to my own
work, I have upon reflection identified three ways in which religious
belief has fundamentally shaped my historical sensibilities. But I suspect that the effects of belief on my work are in fact more far-reaching,
simply because belief is so integral to my self-definition and experience.
This is most emphatically not the same as saying that I am a good
Christian, although I will argue that Christian belief has made me a
better historian.

One simple but significant "advantage" afforded by belief has
been the broadening of my social horizons. St. Cecilia's ensures that I
am regularly removed from the academic world, and immersed in a
world of nurses, schoolteachers, police officers, seamstresses, bus
drivers, and auto workers. (Yes, there are some left in Detroit.) It also
ensures that I regularly have the experience of being in the racial minority, but that is admittedly not usual for American churchgoers. I don't
want to exaggerate the extent to which St. Cecilia's has enlarged my
experience. Like most local religious institutions, it draws its members
from a relatively limited social class spectrum. Nor would I argue that
religion is the only means by which academics can expand the boundaries of their personal worlds. Political activism might do the trick, as
might various forms of local voluntarism or even involvement in sports.
Religious institutions, however, are especially adept at creating communities of meaning. By their very nature they address the most basic
questions of human existence; their rituals, symbols, and vocabularies
generate strong feelings of identification and loyalty. I have an "other-
than-Sunday" connection to only a handful of my fellow parishioners
at St. Cecilia's, but I am nonetheless bound to them all by powerful
shared experiences and assumptions. There is an ease and intimacy to
our relations that I have never seen replicated in my stints as political
activist or community volunteer.

The effect of this has been to put a certain distance between me
and the academic world. It's not simply that I am reminded that life is
larger than the university. That I am so reminded is a salutary thing,
but I know full well that life is also larger than St. Cecilia's. It is, rather,
that St. Cecilia's as a purely social experience provides what might
almost be called a critique of academic habits and priorities. Those
parishioners I have come to know are thoughtful and intelligent, but

few of them place much value on the intellectuality that is so fundamental to the academic enterprise. Most work in occupations that put
a far higher premium on teamwork than historians do. And while few
of them are indifferent to status or material rewards, they have almost
no knowledge of or interest in the particular status-preoccupations of
academics. (Theirs is, moreover, mostly a world without tenure, and so
we give thanks every Sunday for the mere fact of employment — any
employment.) St. Cecilia's is in these respects probably a lot like most
congregations that gather for Sunday or Saturday or indeed for Friday
worship. The view from the parish hall has its own limitations, but it
is seldom the same as the view from the Ann Arbor dinner party.

Does a view from the parish hall make me a different historian
than I would otherwise be? I think it does. Academic subcultures are
necessary things, but they have an unfortunate tendency to reward and
thus enforce particular orthodoxies. To make matters worse, the nature
of life in universities and university towns is such that the academic
subculture can easily seem to define the whole of meaningful existence.
All of us, in short, need distance from and perspective on the world in
which we normally live and move and have our being. I have been
ruminating recently (and in this regard) on the debacle of Sovietology
in the West. How could so many talented and well-trained academics
have been so wrong about the nature and durability of the Soviet
system? Ideology was clearly a factor in some cases, as was restricted
access to documents and other data. But there is obviously more to the
story, and I suspect it has a lot to do with the peculiar limitations of
life within the academic bubble, where we are too comfortable, intellectually and otherwise. Whatever else it does, my time at St. Cecilia's
disturbs that comfort and makes me aware of its seductions. I like to
think that not simply different but better historical thinking is the result.

The power of St. Cecilia's to disturb my comfort is most profoundly rooted in the sacred stories — the myths, if you will — through
which this community defines itself. These turn on the paradoxical
nature of God's relations with humanity; they speak — to borrow from
Simone Weil — simultaneously of gravity and of grace. Our Sunday
liturgy reenacts a narrative which centers on unconditional love and
resurrection, but which also features betrayal, cruelty, injustice, suffering, and death, from none of which are we promised immunity. In-
dividually and collectively, we appropriate these stories, reimagining

214

ourselves and our world in terms of their basic assumptions. (Our revelation interacts with our experience, in other words, and as this happens we become part of a living tradition.) In the process we are all of us capable of self-deception, even of bad faith. But I have witnessed the power of these stories in the lives of the most imperfect hearers. These are stories that call into radical question much of what we normally regard as "true," even of what we normally regard as good. "Like Judaism, Christianity is unimaginable except as a critique of the existing order, any existing order," as Bernard Reilly has said.[2]

The presence in my life of this alternative mythic structure has clearly had an effect on my "secular" thinking. It provides an essential corrective to the naive assumptions — for so they increasingly seem to me — that undergird contemporary liberalism. At the same time, it pronounces against cynicism and despair, not just on the grounds of the dangers these pose to the soul but on the grounds of their absolute wrongness. Equipped on the one hand with a sober appreciation of humanity's deeply flawed nature and on the other with a profound hopefulness concerning the worth and destiny of the human race, I think in all modesty that I am remarkably well situated for the purpose of "doing history." One could presumably achieve a similar perspective by other-than-religious means. But in my own case, the religious dimension has been essential.

The importance of Christian myth in my life has had the additional effect of reinforcing — perhaps even giving rise to — my propensity as a historian to see human beings preeminently as generators of meaning. Nothing, in my view, is more central to the historical enterprise than the means by which individuals and groups endow their existence with coherence and significance. That they are profoundly affected as they do so by such variables as ethnicity, gender, and class is obvious. But these factors need not, and generally do not, wholly determine the various strategies by which human beings make sense of their situation. This is not quite the same as asserting a spiritual dimension to existence. It is, however, to argue that human beings normally behave as though such a dimension existed.

Given these assumptions, it is inevitable that I should regard

---

2. Bernard F. Reilly, "Christianity and Context," *Catholic Historical Review* 75, no. 2 (April 1989): 205-10, quote from 209.

religion as an essential subject for the historian. Human beings do indeed have other-than-religious ways of ordering life and endowing it with meaning. But religion is clearly a principal and remarkably durable means of doing so. I would not argue that religious history should be the preserve only of believers. We can all think of distinguished contributors to the field who would not so identify themselves, and think even more readily of devout contributors whose contributions we could do without. It is nonetheless true that the field of religious history is disproportionately peopled by the religiously committed. This has in the past cast the field in something of a suspect light for many historians, and even today may make some of us believer-practitioners hesitant to assert the significance of our work and our perspective for the profession as a whole. If we fail in this regard, however, we do a disservice not only to ourselves but to the profession of which I believe we are so important a part.

If religious commitment can contribute in significant ways to good historical thinking — facilitating a critical stance with regard to academic mores, a sober realism with regard to the merely human prospect, an appreciative attentiveness to culture in the fullest sense of the term — it can also restrict the historian's field of vision. For example, I suspect that the persistence of the denominational mode in American religious history stems in good part from the extent to which even sophisticated academic historians are often committed to, and engaged by, particular theological traditions. We are all aware of the shortcomings of the denominational mode. It fosters an excessive institutional bias in our work, and limits our ability to speak to such "macro-issues" as the general contours of religious development in North America and the meaning of religion for that vague but lively entity we call American culture. The denominational mode is especially inadequate for recent religious history, given the permeability since 1945 of denominational and even confessional walls. And yet the denominational mode is alive and well, despite its arguably being a principal cause of the oddly ambiguous status of American religious history. Honored for its achievements, the field still bears something of a stepchild's relation to the larger historical profession.

Religious commitment may also incline the historian to a tidier vision of belief than the evidence might warrant. Creedally oriented and concerned with intellectual coherence as many of us are, we may

216

One Historian's Sundays

find it hard to credit the varieties of belief and experience that can characterize even highly literate religious groups.[3] I detect in myself, for example, an impulse to assimilate the excesses of Catholic devotionalism to more orthodox categories of belief, and to assume that any connection, no matter how tenuous, to the church's sacramental life implies adherence to its central theological tenets. This may not be a wholly bad thing; certainly it is preferable to that counter-impulse which finds superstition and magical practice around every church-going corner. But it constitutes bias all the same, and of a particularly insidious kind, given the lacunae in the evidence that is normally available to us. It's a bias that can easily inhibit fruitful speculation and subtly obscure the multivalent character of religion, which, as David Hall has rightly noted, "comprehends a range of actions and beliefs far greater than those described in a catechism or occurring within sacred space."[4]

But if one's field of vision is likely to be in some way restricted by religious commitment — or by any other set of commitments or indeed by the absence of such — the generally high quality of recent work in religious history suggests that the religiously engaged historian occupies a position of potential strength. Some of the best recent work in the field has been done by religiously committed scholars. The phenomenon is hardly peculiar to religious history. Labor history, women's history, African American history — each of these lively fields is the province of scholars who are open and often passionate about their political allegiances. Commitment does not of course protect against the production of what I will dare to call objectively bad history. Examples of such can readily be found in each of the aforementioned fields. But we need not be prisoners of our commitments, or their unwitting servants. Whatever else our professional training has done, it has provided us with crude but usable tools for evaluating the biases inherent in our sources and ourselves. Liberated from naive assump-

3. The vision of the politically committed can be similarly skewed. Many of my own assumptions about politics have been undermined by conversations with my fellow parishioners, few of whom fit the political categories I learned as an activist. Nor do they generally fit the categories that tend to define politics in today's university.

4. David D. Hall, *Worlds of Wonder, Days of Judgment: Popular Religious Belief in Early New England* (New York: Knopf, 1989), 18.

217

tions about objectivity, historians have not thereby been freed from high standards with regard to research — from obligations to thoroughness and honesty. Indeed, given their stance on the objectivity question, historians today are under a particular obligation to be honest with regard to themselves — to be aware of, and open about, the assumptions, values, and perspectives they bring to their work.

What this requires of religiously committed historians, I think, is a greater willingness to speak frankly and to the profession at large about the meaning of faith for their understanding of the world, by which I mean everything from contemporary politics (including the academic variety) to human nature and history. This will not be easy. Our profession, for all its new openness to minority perspectives, is still deeply suspicious of perspectives explicitly rooted in religion. And especially for those of us from non-evangelical backgrounds, public discussions of faith are likely to be awkward. For most Catholics even today, religious commitment is most naturally expressed through ritual gesture rather than personal testimony. But the task before us is sufficiently important to warrant our suffering bouts of self-consciousness and even the disapproval of our colleagues. If the historical profession has been enriched by the alternative visions of feminists, ethnic minorities, and champions of the working class, should not the legitimization of our own alternative vision — or visions — have a similarly happy effect?

Indeed, a religious perspective on history can arguably address certain problems that have come in the wake of the discipline's new diversity. The religious perspective must ultimately speak in universal terms. It cannot be concerned exclusively with particular subpopulations of the human species, nor can religion as a historical phenomenon be regarded as the exclusive property of particular groups or classes. So although religiously committed historians often produce narrowly focused scholarship, contributing as they do so to the fragmentation of the profession, they are nonetheless obliged at least occasionally to think in grander terms. The content of their speculations will probably not be acceptable to most of their colleagues, but perhaps their example will encourage a greater interest in "wholes" as opposed to "parts."

Finally, I would urge those of us for whom religion is a primary area of research to redouble our efforts to connect that research to the larger American story. This is especially important for historians who work mainly in the late nineteenth and twentieth centuries. The United States may have evolved into the most secular of nations, but religion has not ceased to be a factor in its politics and culture. One might be deceived in this latter regard, however, by the many works of historical scholarship that ignore, or largely ignore, the role of religion in modern American life. It is up to us to redress the balance, simply because no one else is likely to do so.

Let me close by drawing attention to a wonderfully pregnant drama that is unfolding in part on my own geographical doorstep — a drama that confirms the continued significance of religion for American life and indeed for America's international relations. I refer to the growing Islamic population of the United States, a substantial portion of which has settled in certain of Detroit's older suburbs. The group's experience in this country exhibits striking parallels to that of both Jewish and Christian immigrants. The move to America often means for Muslims a more intense consciousness with regard to religious identity, and sometimes a greater devoutness. Mosques are typically social and educational centers as well as houses of worship; they play an important integrative role in the lives of many recent immigrants, who are frequently more active in mosque-based activities than they were at home. Communal identity for the multinational Muslim population in this country is more and more confessionally based. The longer a Muslim is resident in the United States, the more likely he is to identify himself in religious as opposed to national terms, religion becoming in the process a form of ethnicity.

What this has meant in essence is the evolution of a distinctively American Islam, albeit an Islam with a fair degree of internal variety. "In a sense America has become a kind of laboratory for creative Islamic institutions," as a recent study has pointed out.[5] The changing status of women in the American Muslim community has been an especially important impetus to religious reform. Like Jewish women before them, Muslim women in this country have claimed for themselves a role in public worship, and they are frequently among the most active members of the local mosque. Young women look forward to higher education, careers, and reasonably egalitarian marriages. (My Muslim female

5. Yvonne Yazbek and Adair T. Lummis, *Islamic Values in the United States: A Comparative Study* (New York: Oxford University Press, 1987), 23.

students, even those who persevere in traditional dress, are among my most disciplined and ambitious.) Muslims in the United States, in short, are living out a profound religious reformation, and their experiences seem to be echoed in significant ways by those of their counterparts in western Europe. Who can tell what the ultimate effects of this reformation will be for Islam in other parts of the world?

The future of Islam in the United States, however, is not unambiguously rosy. The rate of religious intermarriage is already high, especially in those many communities where Muslims are a small minority. Large numbers of Muslims, moreover, have at best a tenuous link to the local mosque, although they normally identify strongly with Islam. But the history of Jews in this country suggests that an ethno-religious identity is not easily perpetuated in the absence of regular religious practice. Indeed, Jews and Muslims may eventually find an ironic common ground in the United States, for they are more and more likely to possess here an odd form of shared history.

One could go on. Nothing has yet been said, for example, about the possible effects of the Islamic presence on American Christianity. But I think the point has been made: a remarkable religious drama is being played out in the present-day United States, and remarkably little attention is being paid to it. That so few American scholars are fluent in Arabic or Urdu is obviously part of the problem. (An adequate study of American religious history requires far better language training than our graduate programs typically afford.) I suspect, however, that the problem is more fundamentally rooted in the resolute secularism of the American academy, especially those parts of the academy that study advanced industrial societies. Let us resolve to do what we can to assist our colleagues to a more genuine multiculturalism.

Afterword: Cultural Shouting Matches and the Academic Study of American Religious History

LEO P. RIBUFFO

FOR THE PAST six years, countless pundits and political activists, as well as a growing number of scholars (including some contributors to this volume), have declared that our country is racked by a "culture war," and many of them have agreed that the religious front ranks in significance with the battles over race and gender. The propensity for exaggeration in general and use of the metaphor of war in particular suggest that our most prominent cultural combatants share more characteristic American traits than they think they share. Despite their pervasive hyperbole, there has been no religious warfare in this country since the years before the (real) Civil War, when federal troops marched against Mormons, and Catholics and Protestants sometimes killed each other during election day riots. On all fronts, our so-called cultural war is more accurately described as a cultural shouting match. And it is merely the latest shouting match in a long line of arguments to define a normative American way of life.[1]

Academics usually make metaphors, not war, and even their visceral urge to shout is usually repressed. Thus the Consultation on Advocacy and the Writing of American History sponsored by the Whea-

---

1. For the most intellectually respectable rendition of the "culture wars" position, see James Davison Hunter, *Culture Wars: The Struggle to Define America* (New York: Basic Books, 1991).

221

ton College Institute for the Study of Evangelicalism — the source of most of the essays in this volume — was friendly and fun. Undoubtedly there would have been more shouting if the conferees had been more representative of the historical profession or of American religiosity. Rather, the roster of scholars present reflected Wheaton's reputation as the "evangelical Harvard." A critical mass of participants were evangelical Protestants who sometimes identify themselves as "Christian scholars." There was a smattering of practicing or cultural Catholics, a few Protestant theological liberals, and a Mormon. Despite abundant references to the ways in which African Americans, militant feminists, and gays had legitimated advocacy within the historical profession, no African Americans, militant feminists, or gays were recruited to comment on that presumption. Nor were there any Moslems, Hindus, Christian Scientists, Seventh-Day Adventists, Protestant fundamentalists, New Age channelers, or — remarkably for an academic meeting — Jews. Thus the conference — and resulting book — was grandiosely misnamed. The focus of discussion was advocacy and the writing of "mainline" religious history (a category that now certainly includes works by evangelicals).

Four issues were jumbled together at the Wheaton sessions, and they still have not been sorted out in this book. These are, first, that historians of the United States pay insufficient attention to religion; second, that scholars of religious history are insufficiently respected by their colleagues; third, that these first two problems derive primarily from a bias against religious faith by secular faculty; and fourth, that advocacy from a religious perspective — actually, from an evangelical or moderate Catholic perspective — is not only as legitimate as other biases now esteemed in higher educations but also provides educational advantages.

The complaint that religious history is marginal to American historiography elicited no debate — and, at the simplest level, needs none. It is obviously true. In Chapter 7, Paul Boyer shows that textbooks generally adopt a "secularization paradigm" and discuss religious issues only when these are connected to social change. Moreover, most conference participants could illustrate the situation with anecdotes from their own careers. Political and diplomatic historians, my own professional cohort for the past decade, almost never know the work of such important scholars as George M. Marsden and Mark Noll.

Historiographical questions small, medium, and large would profit from a profession-wide discussion of their religious dimension (or lack thereof). In Chapter 5, Eugene D. Genovese shows how attention to matters of faith, including the intricacies of theology, can illuminate the history of slavery. In Chapter 6, Elizabeth Fox-Genovese, a self-described "skeptical feminist," shows how attention to questions of faith, including politically conservative uses of Scripture, can illuminate the history of women in the nineteenth century. Moving into this century, a partial answer to the perennial question, "Why is there no socialism in the United States?" would be "Because there have been so many theologically conservative Protestants and Catholics in the United States." Anyone seriously interested in the ways in which the United States differs from other countries — a problem usually subsumed under the fighting words "American exceptionalism" — should pay attention to the persistence of popular piety, the shape of religious pluralism, and the frequent invocations of God's blessing by national leaders. In many cases, religious factors per se will turn out to have been less significant than others, yet historians cannot know that until religious factors have been weighed in the discussion.

Since everybody at the Wheaton consultancy had written about religion at some point in his or her career, and since most of us are not as famous as we want to be, there was also virtual unanimity on the second point, that historians of religion are insufficiently esteemed by their colleagues. There was no consensus, however, on the third issue, the reasons *why* the historical profession remains so distressingly oblivious to our importance.

Most of the evangelical scholars at the Wheaton meeting agreed on an answer: the academy harbors a hostility to religion, and anyone openly professing religious faith risks ridicule. In Chapter 7, Methodist Paul Carter recalls that he excluded from his books any reference to his "personal religious awakening" and now doubts that they would have been received so well if he had lapsed from a neutral tone. In Chapter 12, Leslie Tentler Woodcock, a kind of Niebuhrian Catholic, recalls comparable misgivings about revealing her own faith to colleagues. According to evangelical D. G. Hart in Chapter 8, the modern research university smothers faith and wisdom beneath a "disemboweled intellectual culture."

No American historian has sounded this complaint more fervently

— or more frequently — than George Marsden. Although the indictment presented in Chapter 1 is less strident than the version in his book *The Soul of the American University,* Marsden still sees a "deep-rooted prejudice against substantive religious views." Indeed, prejudice borders on persecution. According to Marsden, Christian scholars are "virtually required to keep their religious views hidden" by the incongruously absolutist Deweyite pragmatists who control these institutions.[2]

The charge of rampant bias against religion by college and university faculty is unsubstantiated in this volume and, to my mind, vastly overstated in general. In the fashion of the current cultural shouting match, the complaining evangelicals confuse the whole university with its history and literature departments. Professors of accounting, chemistry, or mechanical engineering seem immune to the epistemological crisis allegedly sweeping our campuses, and thus they seem quite content to confine their religion, in the familiar American fashion, to a few hours on weekends. These men and women may not fit the Institute for the Study of Evangelicalism's definition of "Christian scholars," but they probably consider themselves both sufficiently scholarly and sufficiently Christian (or Jewish or Moslem). Even social science and humanities professors at elite universities, the focus of conservative denunciations in the cultural shouting match, join their families in baptisms, confirmations, and religious weddings more often than their critics suppose.

Nor are academics — including historians — immune to moral exhortations tinged with religion. In 1994, for example, the most famous evangelical layman in the world, former President Jimmy Carter, addressed a crowded session at the Organization of American Historians convention. After an effusive introduction by OAH President Eric Foner, a Marxist, Carter gave one of his standard speeches, a call for personal activism to help the poor and oppressed. No one listening could have missed that Carter's rendition of the social gospel was rooted in his Baptist faith. Judging from the standing ovation Carter received, no one seemed upset either.

In short, "Christian scholars" too quickly attribute their pro-

2. George H. Marsden, *The Soul of the American University: From Establishment to Established Nonbelief* (New York: Oxford University Press, 1994), 429-44.

fessional marginalization to prejudice when they should see instead the influence of intellectual fads and the routine machinations of academic politics. For two decades, the historical profession has been dominated by a *version* of the left that specializes in compensatory accounts of the oppressed at the expense of other interesting topics (including study of the oppressors, whose actions fascinated earlier generations of liberal and radical scholars). Junior faculty and graduate students typically go along to get along. In this environment, historians who write about presidents, diplomats, and soldiers also complain that their work receives insufficient attention — and they, too, are right.

Despite comparable exclusion from the historiographical fast lane, the evangelical scholars' main arguments for the "mainstreaming" of religion differ significantly from those made by political, diplomatic, and military historians. The latter groups argue, for example, that presidents are worth studying because they can blow up the world, and cite the Cuban Missile Crisis as a case in point. Similarly, Christian scholars *could* insist that white Protestants merit historical study because they dominated American culture for two centuries and still comprise a majority of the population (including a substantial number of the economically oppressed).

Instead of building an old-fashioned intellectual case for the importance of their subject matter, Marsden and Noll tailor their arguments to fit the reigning fads and buzzwords. At least as a tactic, they begin with two related premises. Invoking the now obligatory references to Thomas Kuhn, Michel Foucault, Clifford Geertz, and Richard Rorty, Noll writes an obituary for "objectivity." With objectivity interred, Marsden elaborates that "all scholarship is to some degree political and . . . interpretive traditions reflect the interests of competing communities." In these circumstances, inclusion of religious scholars in the first string lineup at the "academic game" is made to sound like elementary fair play. It would enhance "diversity." In Chapter 9, an irenic Grant Wacker sees no reason why a "Thomist or a Mormon spin on the past should be any less acceptable in the academic marketplace than a Freudian or a Marxist one, so long as all of them are able to prove themselves critical, that is, both plausible and responsible."

Even as a means of securing professional recognition this strategy is flawed. There is scant evidence that the marketplace, academic or otherwise, is governed by elementary fair play, let alone by Christian charity. Merit aside, academic advancement typically requires the mobilization of constituencies as well as buzzwords and the making of deals as well as metaphors. Since the evangelical scholars did not invite prominent authorities on race, gender, and sexuality to their party at Wheaton College, they should not expect invitations to the worldly galas sponsored by the American Historical Association, Organization of American Historians, and American Studies Association.

But the problems run deeper. As politely as possible, D. G. Hart wonders why his fellow Christian scholars care so much about the baubles hawked in the academic marketplace. An "evangelical mind may be too much to ask," Hart writes in a reference to Noll's noted book, *The Scandal of the Evangelical Mind*, but if one can be created, the corrupt academy is not the place to do it. Rather, Christian scholarship can best flourish in small, organic communities. Much as Marsden resembles Cotton Mather in his later years, trying to carve out a niche for godly learning in a secularizing society, Hart stands ready to join Roger Williams in the wilderness.[3]

Meanwhile, the Enlightenment shades of Voltaire and David Hume hover over Murray Murphey and Bruce Kuklick. Everyone may be biased, Murphey and Kuklick say, but some biases are worse than others. As Kuklick puts it, the "supernatural" beliefs held by Christians are "different from the rational biases of everyone else." Thus Mormons and Thomists should not be in the same intellectual league, let alone the same line up, as Freudians or Marxists (however badly the latter might play the academic game). Universities exist to create and disseminate knowledge — "ideas that are true, or at least can be true with high probability on the basis of evidence," Murphey writes. Acceptance of any lower standard would produce "bedlam."

As is often the case in our cultural shouting match, adversaries yell past each other without meeting each other's arguments. Viewing the academic ascendancy of biases which seem less grounded than their own — and which command a much smaller following in the country at large — the evangelical scholars seek recognition as a legitimate interest group. Aside from their pro forma funeral service for objectivity, they are not — in the context of this volume — concerned with

3. Mark Noll, *The Scandal of the Evangelical Mind* (Grand Rapids: Eerdmans, 1994).

epistemological issues, let alone ultimate truth and falsity. Nowhere do they claim that Christianity belongs in higher education because Jesus is the Son of God whose life and death are the central events of human history. On the other hand, Murphey and Kuklick see *only* an epistemological issue. Pointedly rejecting the "reduction of the intellectual to the social," Kuklick would bar even bland Christian teaching for reasons of "empirical inadequacy." Moreover, Kuklick accuses the evangelical scholars of writing in "bad faith" because they do not say in their monographs what they believe in their hearts and minds, that Christianity belongs in the classroom because Jesus Christ is the Son of God.

The inference of bad faith in too harsh. Since the evangelical scholars represented here believe, along with their puritan intellectual forebears, that God typically operates through more-or-less comprehensible natural processes, they can legitimately focus on those "means," especially when addressing unregenerate academics. In doing so, they are no more guilty of bad faith than Cotton Mather or Roger Williams.

Nonetheless, two important issues are left murky by the evangelical interest group and their allies. How do religious scholars in general and "Christian scholars" in particular differ *in their scholarship* from other historians — or sociologists, anthropologists, literary critics, and political scientists? And what would religious "advocacy" look like in journal articles and classrooms at nondenominational schools? In Chapter 10, Catherine L. Albanese finds reason to worry about the focus on "advocacy," a concept she associates with Old Testament prophets and puritan preachers that seems to preclude a more accepting — even laid-back — approach to the past.

Only Noll attempts to define a minimum Christian doctrine, and he does so very briefly. As an evangelical Christian, he believes that the supernatural is real, that miracles occurred in the past, and that the greatest miracle, the return of Jesus, will occur at same unspecified point in the future. As a scholar, however, he recommends to the academy only those Christian ideas with valid secular cognates. For instance, because of our alien state, humanity must settle for relative rather than absolute truth; in a sense Adam and Eve prefigure Richard Rorty. Whether or not the analogy between original sin and the limits of rationality is valid, it was popularized before Noll was born by Reinhold Niebuhr, who had no trouble making his way in American intellectual life.

Marsden says almost nothing about his own faith, stressing instead that he and other Christian scholars abide by the rules of the academic game and would continue to do so. They would not cite private revelations or offer supernatural explanations (a view seconded by Wacker). Indeed, Marsden considers religious beliefs irrelevant to most routine historical "detective work." In the final analysis, Christian historians differ from other historians mainly in their greater openness to religious topics and a deeper understanding of those topics derived from what Marsden calls "background beliefs." Intuitively familiar with the territory, they are better guides than secularists, much as African Americans, militant feminists, and gays bring heightened awareness to other specialties.

This is standard "identity politics" — or, more precisely, identity history — with an evangelical twist. It should prompt the same qualms as other forms of identity history. For instance, the Christian scholars think that their personal religious background provides a better knowledge of the territory than it does. And especially because they hold that belief, other historians should beware of deferring to what might be called their claims of emotional expertise — except perhaps out of courtesy in some settings. Marsden's assertion at the Wheaton conference that evangelicals typically wrote the best books about evangelicalism required several participants to repress an urge to shout.

Despite their frequent claims of heightened critical abilities, practitioners of all sorts of identity historiography exude more positive thinking about *some* aspects of American history than the past warrants. Insofar as religious studies has thus far reached the historiographical mainstream, it has done so through the study of (usually non-Protestant) ethnic minorities. Indeed, immigration history is the (usually unacknowledged) precursor of identity historiography. At least since the publication of Oscar Handlin's book *The Uprooted* in 1951, its practitioners have been relentlessly upbeat. Although the list of favored minorities has grown longer since Handlin's heyday, the basic story remains the same: Jews and Catholic ethnic groups struggle upward along parallel paths — and sometimes in tandem — while facing harassment from white Protestant nativists. The frequent conflicts *among* ethnic minorities are usually ignored or attributed to a few "extremists."[4]

4. Oscar Handlin, *The Uprooted: The Epic Story of the Great Migration That Made the American People* (Boston: Little, Brown, 1951).

Would religious history follow the same route to positive thinking after entering the historiographical fast lane? Perhaps not, but there are reasons for wariness. On the one hand, the Christian scholars interest group consists of men and women whose high intellectual standards clearly differ from those of William Bennett, Lynne Cheney, and other conservative ideologists who promote a relentlessly upbeat history of "religion-in-general." On the other hand, both their scholarship and the scholarship of their non-evangelical allies reveals little interest in the dark side of American religious history — including the pervasiveness of intrareligious conflict — that stretches from Massachusetts Bay to Waco. After all, Catholics and Protestants *did* kill each other during election day riots before the Civil War; they also trod parallel paths in denigrating Jews and cheering military expeditions against Mormons. And while courting sympathy for themselves as an embattled minority in the early 1990s, fundamentalists and evangelicals nonetheless heaped abuse on the Branch Davidians and other "cults."

My qualms are not meant to disqualify anyone from the academic game or, more importantly, from a fair chance to have his or her ideas evaluated seriously. Even when combined with puffery or defensiveness, religious background beliefs have enriched our historical understanding. There is no doubt that scholarship on theologically conservative Americans — especially fundamentalists and evangelicals — would have drifted even deeper into the doldrums if Marsden, Noll, Wacker, Hart, and their fellow Christian scholars had not written on the subject. On a very personal level, Woodcock shows how participation in her local Roman Catholic Church has served to counteract academic insularity and naive optimism. In many respects, the Christian scholars and their Catholic allies represented in this volume resemble those historians who drew on their experiences as New Left activists when rescuing the history of American radicalism from comparable historiographical doldrums.

In short, although intellectual questions must not be *reduced* to social issues (to recall Kuklick's derisive phrase), the problem of religious advocacy does have a social dimension that deserves attention. For Kuklick and Murphey, the university is a place where learned adults struggle to discover and disseminate truth; for most Americans, it is a place they send their teenagers with some trepidation. Significantly, while Boyer, Carter, Wacker, and Woodcock explicitly discuss teaching in their essays, Kuklick and Murphey say nothing about the matter.

Similarly, these two secularists give little sense of the ways in which faculty actually decide to hire, fire, or promote colleagues, or, for that matter, how students and professors actually read books. Indeed, Kuklick and Murphey's rendition of intellectual life on campus is so stylized that readers might be amazed to learn that both have chaired departments at a major university, or that Kuklick has written insightfully on the politics of professionalization in several academic disciplines and one nonacademic game (baseball).[5]

Both this utopian view of academic life and the exaggerated fears of intellectual chaos if religious advocacy encroaches on campus derive at least partly from the *Zeitgeist* of our cultural shouting match. On sober reflection, there is no need to fear that one drop of supernaturalism will ruin a good mind, or that every forthright theist in a history department represents a falling domino in the centuries-old "war" between science and religion.

Despite their absolutist rhetoric, militant secularists in humanities and social science departments already live in peaceful coexistence at our colleges with what Kuklick calls the "common religious heritage of Judeo-Christianity." Given the balance of forces influencing these places people send their teenagers with trepidation, a secularist first strike would be ill advised. Certainly, Kuklick and Murphey are unlikely to agitate for the abolition of chaplaincies, picket a lecture by Niebuhrian diplomat George Kennan, or protest an honorary degree for Jimmy Carter. Nor are they likely to urge the dismissal of Hegelian philosophers, Jungian psychologists, or Straussian political scientists whose worldviews teeter on the verge of supernaturalism. They are even less likely to risk litigation by asking job candidates in history or American studies for their opinions of transubstantiation or the great chain of being. And they are least likely to call for the removal of a colleague who, after a distinguished career as an avowed atheist, embraces a supernatural faith but continues to write fine history (a transition made by one of the essayists represented here).

Such consistent secularism would not only be imprudent, it would

5. Bruce Kuklick, *The Rise of American Philosophy: Cambridge, Massachusetts, 1860-1930* (New Haven: Yale University Press, 1977), *Puritans in Babylon: The Ancient Near East and American Intellectual Life, 1880-1930* (Princeton: Princeton University Press, 1996), and *To Every Thing a Season: Shibe Park and Urban Philadelphia 1909-1976* (Princeton: Princeton University Press, 1991).

also be foolish. No one reading a book or listening to a lecture buys the argument whole hog. Rather, we typically buy the intellectual wheat and discard what we consider chaff. For example. Kuklick, like most thoughtful students of international relations, has been influenced by the great diplomatic historian William Appleman Williams, a Marxist Episcopalian vestryman, even though Williams's critique of American foreign policy is rooted in his quirky version of the social gospel. This is also the selective way in which secularists address the work of long-dead theists — whose religion is routinely accepted as a natural result of their historical contexts. No thoughtful scholar would dismiss George Bancroft's account of the Constitutional Convention because he thought that God ultimately guided the proceedings, or ignore William Prescott's investigation of the Spanish conquest of Mexico and Peru because it bore the marks of New England Brahmin anti-Catholicism, or discard William Albright's studies of ancient Mesopotamia because he promoted the veracity of Scripture.

Although it would be "pernicious" to force Kuklick to teach supernatural beliefs he rejects, he should be willing to tolerate — and even appreciate — others who embrace those beliefs if their intellectual merits compensate for this defect. The issue is not whether supernatural beliefs belong in primarily secular universities — they are already there — but whether or not faculty exponents of those beliefs, evaluated on a case-by-case basis, advance the cause of teaching and learning. An evangelical sociologist is not the same thing as a scientific creationist in the biology department.

Even so, those case-by-case evaluations will be more difficult than the proponents of religious advocacy think. While Murphey and Kuklick exaggerate the steepness of the slippery slope into intellectual bedlam, Marsden, Noll, and their allies have not thought through the implications of their own position.

Suppose that a candidate for a professorship in European diplomatic history volunteers that he is a "fairly traditional Protestant of the Reformed theological heritage," as Marsden describes himself. That phrase is sufficiently vague to cover not only Marsden but also the Niebuhrian Baptist Jimmy Carter, the separate fundamentalist Jerry Falwell, and the Pentecostal Pat Robertson. Could prospective employers probe further without violating federal law? Questions of litigation aside, *should* they probe further? If so, they might want to know whether "traditional" Protestantism in this instance includes the theory of pre-millennial dispensationalism, and, specifically, whether the job applicant agrees with many other dispensationalists that the Common Market was predicted in the Bible and signaled the imminent return of Jesus Christ. Do affirmative answers automatically bar the candidate from further consideration?[6]

This is not a rhetorical question. The premillennialist job seeker might also be the foremost expert in the economics of the Common Market and a great teacher happy to entertain secular perspectives in the classroom. Moreover, the answers from contributors to this book might be surprising. Noll, who in *The Scandal of the Evangelical Mind* advocates a dialogue between evangelicals and fundamentalists, would probably evaluate the job seeker on his general intellectual and pedagogical merits. But judging from his book *The Soul of the American University*, Marsden has a vested interest in the *right kind* of theological conservatism and clearly regards exponents of Bible prophecy as the wrong kind. Hart considers some form of supernaturalism (e.g., the virgin birth) more grounded than others (e.g., dispensationalist claims that current events were predicted in the Bible).

When push came to shove, Kuklick's amiability and curiosity might transcend the rigid secularism embedded in his worldview. After all, if he is willing to edit a book — this one — with a smart evangelical, why not sit in a department meeting with one? For my own part, I would gladly hire a thoughtful and tolerant dispensationalist if he were otherwise the strongest job applicant. Indeed, I might have less difficulty coexisting with him in the university than with economists who reduce human motives to rational expectations, public policy pundits who formulate grand theories of the presidency without examining the private papers of any president, and postmodern literary critics who think that Jean Baudrillard understands the United States better than C. Wright Mills.

Both the intellectual and social aspects of religious advocacy — and other sorts of advocacy — on campus are more complicated than

---

6. Marsden, *Soul of the American University*, 7. I posed an earlier version of the question of a dispensationalist job seeker in my review of this book. See Leo P. Ribuffo, "God and Man at Harvard, Yale, Princeton, Berkeley, Etc.," *Reviews in American History* 23 (March 1995), 170-75.

the loudest voices in our cultural shouting match suggest. Indeed, the broad questions at hand will probably outlive the shouters. This book, at least, opens a way to discussing them honestly and thoughtfully.

The foundations of this ancient abode are sure . . . . they are
being strengthened and will probably . . . . until the time when . . . . [and]
are . . . . waves . . . . become the foundations . . . . of the . . . .